BILINGUAL EDUCATION

Teachers' Narratives

BILINGUAL EDUCATION

Teachers' Narratives

Nancy Lemberger
Long Island University

LEA LAWRENCE ERLBAUM ASSOCIATES, PUBLISHERS
1997   Mahwah, New Jersey   London

Lawrence Erlbaum Associates, Inc., Publishers
10 Industrial Avenue
Mahwah, New Jersey 07430

Library of Congress Cataloging-in-Publication Data

Lemberger, Nancy.
    Bilingual education : teachers' narratives / Nancy Lem-
berger.
        p. cm.
    Includes bibliographical references and index.
    ISBN 0-8058-2258-5 (pbk.)
    1. Education, Bilingual—United States—Case studies.
2. Linguistic minorities—Education—United
States—Case studies. 3. Language experience approach
in education—United States—Case studies. 4. Teachers—United States—Case studies. I. Title.
LC3731.L46 1997   97-6296
370.117'5'0973—dc21   CIP

Books published by Lawrence Erlbaum Associates are printed
on acid-free paper, and their bindings are chosen for strength
and durability.

Printed in the United States of America

10 9 8 7 6 5 4 3 2 1

Contents

Preface   **vii**

PART I: INTRODUCTION

1   Evolution: From Teacher to Researcher, From   **1**
Dissertation to Book

2   A Context for Understanding the Bilingual   **8**
Teachers' Narratives

3   How to Use This Book   **21**

PART II: EIGHT TEACHERS' NARRATIVES, DISCUSSION, AND EPILOGUE

4   Sofya   **33**

5   Manouchka   **43**

6   Diana   **54**

7   Heather   **68**

8   Sandra   **82**

9   Mariana   **96**

10   Jean   **106**

11   Luz   **121**

12   Themes and Issues Emerging From the Narratives   **137**

13   Epilogue: The Stories Continue...   **150**

PART III: BILINGUAL EDUCATION RESOURCES

14   Theoretical, Background, and Practical Information   **157**

     Appendix A: Glossary of Terms   **171**

     Appendix B: Sample Interview Questions   **181**

     Appendix C: Diana's Literature Study Circle Questions   **183**

     Appendix D: Poem for Heather's First Grade Class   **185**

     References   **187**

     Author Index   **193**

     Subject Index   **197**

Preface

This book grows out of the joys and challenges I experienced as a Spanish–English bilingual teacher of culturally and linguistically diverse students. In the mid-1980s, as a bilingual education graduate student, I wanted to find out what other teachers had experienced and how they made sense of bilingual teaching. I found little research on bilingual teachers' experiences. Bilingual teachers and their stories have been my major area of interest since I started graduate school. My goals in writing this book are to tell what it is like to be a bilingual teacher, to help other (and prospective) teachers understand the complex nature of bilingual teaching, to share some successful teaching strategies that other teachers have used, and to encourage teachers to find their own solutions despite limited support.

What is special about this book are the different stories told by eight teachers. I hope others will be able to relate to the experiences of these teachers; experiences that will help them reflect on their own situations. Because no other book focuses on bilingual teachers in this manner, it serves to inform preservice and veteran teachers about the field of bilingual education on a very personal level.

The book is structured in three parts. Part I, the Introduction, contains (a) an explanation of how the book evolved and its relation to other qualitative research, (b) a very brief context about bilingual education, and (c) suggestions for how to use the book. Part II begins with eight bilingual teachers' stories, giving a glimpse of them as people and presenting their schools and programs, their successes and struggles, and their solutions and coping mechanisms within those contexts. Part II concludes with a discussion chapter that looks at the teachers' collective strengths and challenges comparatively, connecting these to broader issues. The teachers' stories are also revisited in an epilogue (chapter 13). Part III, "Bilingual Education Resources," consists of useful information for the practitioner, including foundation texts on the theories and practices of bilingual education; demographic information; listings of curricula, tests, and literature mentioned by the teachers; and professional network sources.

ACKNOWLEDGMENTS

The process of writing this book has been a long one, which I could not have done alone. First, I am deeply grateful to the eight teachers who opened up their hearts and classrooms to share the intimate details of their lives and careers with me. Their continued patience, support, and willingness to work with me and their belief in the project were invaluable. Without them there would be no book.

Second, I thank my editor, Naomi Silverman, whose "tough love approach," patience, and understanding helped support my creative process in giving birth to this book. Her belief in the power of sharing the teachers' stories in this book never wavered. We have been through a lot together along the way! Additionally, I thank the reviewers at various stages of the book's development, Catherine Walsh, Judith Lessow-Hurley, Irma J. O'Neill, Teresa Pica, Sonia Nieto, María Torres-Guzman, and several anonymous readers, for their time and meticulous suggestions that helped shape and improve the book.

Third, I thank Long Island University (LIU) and those associated with it. Release time from courses granted from the Faculty Development and Research Release Time Committees allowed me to develop the initial stories and to write the book. My LIU colleagues from our research support group, Mina Berkowitz, Susan Zinar-Grundberg, Christine Casey, Veronica Shipp, and Laurie Lehman, as well as Associate Dean Isabel Pascale, gave me helpful feedback from a perspective outside the field of bilingual education. I am also indebted to my many bilingual education students for their reflections and reactions to early versions of the stories.

I warmly thank my many dear friends and colleagues, Yvonne Martínez Thorne, Lucía Rodríguez, Lillian Ortiz, Maria Guida, Maureen Coghlin, Genevieve La Riva, Keith McGiver, Olga Rubio, Carmen Mercado, Andrés Pérez y Mena, and Carol Murayama for their assistance, careful reading and feedback of drafts, and moral support. I would also like to thank my colleagues from the former New York Multifunctional Resource Center (MRC): José A. Vázquez, Michelle Haddad, John F. Hilliard, Grace Fung, and Don Braswell for their direct and indirect techincal support of this project. I am particularly indebted to my friend, Iwan Notowidigdo, from the MRC and the New York Technical Assistance Center (NYTAC), for his help in re-conceptualizing the chapter 2 context figures. Janet Lu, from the former Northern California MRC, also helped me identify the Asian teachers. In addition, Alex Stein, a noted bilingual education historian and Team Leader for Two-Way Programs for the Office of Bilingual Education Minority Language Affairs (OBEMLA), greatly helped me with the flow and details of the historical and programmatic information in chapter 2. Other thanks go to Judy Lambert, Bilingual/Bicultural Consultant from the California State Department of Education and to Kris Anstrom, Information Analyst from the National Clearinghouse for Bilingual Education (NCBE) for their last-minute resource and reference information. Special thanks also go to Judith Burke and Sue Batkin for their careful transcriptions of the interview tapes. I want to express gratitude to my other support network of friends for their care and concern through the ups and downs of my life of which this book has been part.

Finally, I express my heartfelt thanks to my parents who have always been there for me throughout my life. I give special thanks to my father, Melvin Lemberger, for his generosity in buying me a computer and printer and for paying the bicoastal phone bills which enabled my mother and me to edit this book. My mother, Dorothy Lemberger, has been an inspiration to me in many ways as an intellectual, a mentor, and a friend. I couldn't have written this book without her encouragement and word-for-word review of the many drafts. I am deeply grateful to you all!

—*Nancy Lemberger*

I

INTRODUCTION

1

Evolution: From Teacher to Researcher, From Dissertation to Book

BACKGROUND

I started studying French in elementary school and continued through my sophomore year in college. In my junior year of college, I switched to Spanish when I realized I would use it more often because of the number of Spanish-speaking people in California. After 2½ years of immersing myself in Spanish through study and travel to Mexico and Guatemala, I graduated with a minor in Spanish. Spanish came very easily to me because of all the French I had taken and my strong desire to learn the language. After college, I traveled for a year in South America, where I both reinforced my Spanish and also picked up Portuguese while visiting Brazil. When I returned from South America I was unsure what I wanted to do, so I enrolled in a bilingual teacher education program sponsored by Title VII. A year of student teaching and bilingual methods courses certified me as a bilingual teacher. I became a bilingual teacher out of my love for Spanish. I see the process of becoming bilingual as a lifelong journey, one in which I am still involved.

When I started teaching, I had no idea that bilingual teaching was so controversial, stigmatized, and complex. For 6 years, I struggled as a Spanish–English bilingual elementary school teacher in Oakland, California. Part of this struggle was caused by lack of support from my principal and colleagues, who did not understand the purposes of what is needed to develop bilingualism. During that time, I obtained a master's degree in curriculum and bilingual education.

At the classroom level, despite my teacher training and master's degree, I still faced daily dilemmas such as, "What should I do with 30 kids whose language dominance varies from Spanish to English and all the shades in between?" "What kind of curriculum should I use for Omar, who has just come from Mexico to my fourth-grade class and doesn't know how to hold a pencil because he has never gone to school before?" "How do I work with Guillermo, who is very bright, fully bilingual, finishes his work in 2 minutes, and starts to read the encyclopedia because he's bored?" "How do I teach my class with inferior and inappropriate Spanish materials and books?" Somehow, I learned to survive by creating my own materials and developing meaningful learning opportunities for students; by individualizing instruction; by having students help one another; and by taking students out into the community and bringing the community into the class through trips, projects, and guests. The effort to do this in an unsupportive environment was at great psychic expense that caused me to burn out. I found myself becoming impatient with the children. I needed a change. When the chance came to move to New York to pursue a doctorate in curriculum and bilingual education at Teachers College Columbia University, I looked at it as an opportunity to begin to find answers to these teaching questions.

As a doctoral student, I took with me the inquiries I had about bilingual teaching. I wanted to find answers in the research that would have helped me and would be helpful to other teachers. As I started reviewing the literature on bilingual education, I found little information from teachers in their own voices or about their own experiences. For my dissertation study, I decided to ask bilingual teachers about their careers, to see if they had encountered similar situations to mine, and to find out what they had learned and what others could learn from them. In my study, *Bilingual Education: Teachers' Voices* (Lemberger, 1990), I interviewed four New York City veteran Latina, Spanish–English bilingual teachers about their experiences teaching mainly Spanish-speaking Caribbean K–2 children.

I wanted to show teachers' work and struggles over time from both historical and practical perspectives. As I observed them, listened to them, and documented their experiences, I realized the power of their stories in describing some of the realities bilingual teachers face daily. What I learned from them is that bilingual teaching is both challenging and rewarding. They, like me, had experienced a similar lack of support in their schools, but were quite resourceful in creating rich learning contexts for students. These four teachers, indeed, were heroines in the lives of many of the children and families with whom they came in contact. Their contributions were so great that I wanted to find a way to share the impact of their stories with as many teachers as possible and to answer the call made by Ada (1986), a bilingual teacher educator, to hear the unheard voices of bilingual teachers. A book on bilingual teachers' stories seemed a valid means of accomplishing those goals. This book grows out of that study and my commitment to helping teachers understand and deal with the complexities of teaching culturally and linguistically diverse students.

THE RESEARCH PROCESS:
SELECTION, DATA COLLECTION, AND
NARRATIVE CASE CONSTRUCTION

I thought my dissertation could be easily converted into a book without much modification. To my surprise, as I began to focus my study for a different audience than my dissertation committee, the data and form had to be completely discarded. What remained was my conviction about the importance of bilingual teachers' stories and the method of researching them. For several reasons, the compelling stories of the four New York City teachers, although important, could not be used in this book. First, the data were collected in the late 1980s. By the time I was ready to put this book together, their experiences, the policies, and the contexts were dated and had changed considerably. In the process of redesigning my study, the reviewers suggested that the bilingual teachers' stories, reflecting a broader range of languages, regions, grade levels, and program models should be included. So, I decided to collect new data from the eight selected teachers (see the "Overview of Teachers" chart on pp. 28–29 for teachers' backgrounds, ages, languages, number of years teaching, grades, teacher education, program models, and regions). All the teachers coincidentally were women, as are the majority of elementary teachers.

I gained access to these eight teachers through personal contact and recommendation. In 1992, while in Madrid for the Spanish Children's Literature Institute, I met two (Sandra & Jean) interesting and caring bilingual teachers, who I invited to work with me on this project. I was then working at the **New York Multifunctional Resource Center (MRC)**[1], a **Title VII** bilingual technical assistance and training center. Through my contacts (district bilingual coordinators, other **MRC** associates, and bilingual teachers), I received recommendations for dedicated, committed, and excellent bilingual teachers from which I selected the remaining six teachers.

As a bicoastal person with roots in California, I had access to teachers in the New York and California areas. For that reason, all but one teacher (Sandra, whom I met in Spain) is from either New York or California.

---

[1]Bold-face terms are defined in the glossary in Appendix A.

Because California has the largest population of **limited English proficient (LEP)** youth in the country (estimated 1.2 million; Dolson, 1994), it seemed an important place to gather information. I secured permission from district personnel and principals to interview and observe the teachers for this study. The teachers gave their consent, agreeing to be interviewed and observed, and to participate in writing their narratives.

The data collection consisted of interviews and observations. Together for 3 to 4 hours of tape-recorded interviews and discussions, each teacher and I discussed their lives, schools, and teaching experiences (see Appendix B–Sample Interview Questions). What I was trying to get at was the inside story of those personal experiences of what each teacher brought to her teaching context (see Figs. 2.1 and 2.2 and Table 2.1). The discussions were informal and semi-structured, much like what qualitative research methods specialists Mishler (1986) and Dobbert (1982) advocate. The purpose of these discussions is to capture an authenticity of the practitioner's experiences. Discussions took place in school, classroom, or home settings. I promised to respect each teacher's anonymity, which enabled her to speak freely without fear of repercussions from administrators and/or colleagues. Initially, I gave each teacher a pseudonym that started with the same letter as her first name. However, several teachers didn't like the names I chose, so they chose others. Luz chose her grandmother's name. Diana wanted the English name her father picked for her. Manouchka selected the name of a wonderful student of hers. Sofya insisted that I use her real name because she felt she had nothing to hide.

The interview questions were just a starting point from which we often deviated. I tried to be a good listener, encouraging each teacher to share her personal and professional experiences. My experiences as a classroom teacher, a staff developer, researcher, and teacher educator contributed to the richness of our discussions. These discussions were co-constructed by both of us, grounded in our particular strengths and experiences. I observed each teacher in her classroom for 1 or 2 days. Rather than just being a passive observer, I interacted with and helped the children when I could. Participating in the classrooms with the teachers helped me build rapport. These observations added to the discussions about teaching approaches and particular children.

After the interview tapes were transcribed, I began the long process of writing the narratives. I reviewed each transcript for content that was most interesting and best showed the teachers' lives, programs, and efforts. Because the interviews were not uniform, the narratives also focused on different areas. Dealing with so much data and transforming the spoken word to written text was a labor-intensive task. My goal in writing the narratives was to maintain the words and essence of each teacher's own story. Rather than writing "about" the teacher, each narrative was written in the first person, so the teacher's message could speak directly to the reader.

When I completed the first drafts, each teacher received a copy of her narrative to verify its accuracy. I wanted to make sure that what I had heard and written was consistent with what each teacher had said and was how she wanted to be portrayed. The teachers, for the most part, made minor changes in wording and clarifications. A common response to reading the cases was: "It's so me!" This indicated that I had represented the teacher accurately. With their feedback, I then reworked the narratives, further cutting, clarifying, and taking into consideration how each narrative fit with the others. I asked the teachers to also review the second drafts in a similar manner.

In the process of writing and rewriting the narratives, my voice merged with the teachers, demonstrating what Connolly and Clandinin (1990) called the "Multiple I's," where it's not just the teacher's voice that is heard but the researcher's as well. My story is told implicitly in what I focused on in the interviews, how I selected and interpreted what to tell. But these are not the only "I"s involved in the telling/hearing of this story. Our collective stories invite you, the reader, to see your work as part of the story. These stories represent many unheard voices telling what really goes on in schools. In essence, I have become the teachers' mouthpiece to amplify and convey their words and stories. Because teachers are busy responding to the complex daily realities and demands of teaching (Jackson, 1968), it is often difficult for them to get their message out. Through our collaboration, the teachers felt honored and were willing to have me share their stories.

WHY IS IT IMPORTANT TO LISTEN TO TEACHERS? RATIONALE AND CONCEPTUALIZATION FROM THE LITERATURE

No study can represent all bilingual teachers serving the many language groups throughout this country. Admittedly, many groups, regions, and levels (beyond elementary) could not be included, not because they are not relevant, but because this book's purpose is to use a few teachers' stories as a starting point for understanding and reflecting on the complex nature of bilingual teaching.

My purpose in writing this book is to offer a useful resource for teachers and prospective teachers who work with non-native speakers of English by giving them a glimpse of what some bilingual teachers have experienced. This book does not aim to generalize and prescribe about bilingual teaching; rather it specifies and describes what it means to these eight teachers to be a bilingual teacher. Please view each teacher's story as an individual from a particular ethnic/language group. Generalizations about particular groups should not be made based on any individual teacher's experiences and perspectives.

All too often, literature written for teachers tells them what they should do without asking them about their own experiences. Rarely have teachers been asked what they really do and need, or about the realities of their work with their students and the effects of policies and curricula they are asked to implement by federal, state, district, and school mandates.

This book springs from the growing movement of qualitative participatory research that values teachers' experiences and sees them as contributing to a knowledge base on practice (Shulman, 1986). The theoretical underpinnings are derived from three interrelated research areas: teacher research, teachers' narratives, and teachers' voices. This book responds to the call for teachers' voices (Hargreaves, 1996) and addresses the "general lack of information on classroom life. What is missing . . . are the voices of the teachers themselves" (Corchran-Smith & Lytle, 1990, p. 2). Teacher research is conducted by teachers, researchers, or, as in this study, collaboratively among the two. This study falls within the area of what Shulman (1986) termed "classroom ecology" where teaching is "presumed to be highly complex, context-specific, in which differences across classrooms, schools are critically important" (Corchran-Smith & Lytle, 1990, p. 3). Through telling teachers' stories "insights into the particulars of how and why something works and for whom, within in the contexts of particular classrooms" (Zumwalt, 1982, p. 235, cited in Corchran-Smith & Lytle, 1990) and schools are shared and can be analyzed.

Connolly and Clandinin (1990) referred to narrative as both a phenomenon and a method of inquiry. As a phenomenon, narratives are the stories themselves, which characterize human experience. As a method of inquiry, "narrative names the structured quality of experience [and] . . . its patterns" (p. 2) which can be studied. Story/narrative has become a central focus of conducting research in the field of teacher education because of its potential to speak to practitioners and accurately represent the demands of teaching (Carter, 1993). These "first and secondhand accounts of individuals, teachers, students, classrooms, written by teachers and others" (Connolly & Clandinin, 1990, p. 4) can capture the richness and variety of teachers' experiences and actions and describe the complexity of teaching (Carter, 1993). As such, "stories have the power to direct and change our lives" (Noddings, 1991, cited in Carter, 1993). Narrative can allow the reader to vicariously walk in another's shoes and to entertain other ideas and positions. Nevertheless, teachers characterized in narratives by researchers are often "stick figures" depicted to show the researcher's view of effective practice (Carter, 1993). This book, in describing each teacher personally, professionally, and contextually, attempts to avoid collapsing and romanticizing the view of the teacher (Hargreaves, 1996) in that way.

Hargreaves called for voices to be heard and studied across different contexts. "What matters is that teachers' voices are heard comparatively and contextually" to strengthen the construct of voice as a valid means of contributing to wider dialogue about educational transformation (Hargreaves, 1996, p. 17). He also recommended that a broader range of voices be included, where the voices of marginalized and disaffected teachers are heard. This study attempts to do that by highlighting the voices of bilingual teachers, who by association with language minority children, have been marginalized within both school and society (Ada, 1986; Goldstein, 1987; Montero-Sieburth & Perez, 1987). The eight teachers' stories make visible their efforts to counteract their own and their students' marginalization and their struggles to teach effectively and gain acceptance within the contexts of their particular schools.

2

A Context for Understanding the Bilingual Teachers' Narratives

What is a bilingual teacher's life like? In Part II you will read about the complexities faced by eight bilingual teachers. To better understand their stories, they must be seen within a broader context of bilingual education. The complex nature of bilingual education has been extensively written about by others (see resources in Part III for an annotated listing), so, for this reason it is only briefly addressed here.

In Fig. 2.1, the teacher is situated at the center of the four contexts of the classroom, school, community, and society. These four contexts are constantly changing and consist of people (their individual and collective histories and realities), institutions, policies, and resources within each. Although teachers' work is mainly focused in the classroom and the school, factors from the community and societal contexts also affect their work. In the figure, the context boundaries are delineated by solid lines; however, these are often blurred within and across contexts. Looking at this figure one might ask, "How is the work of a bilingual teacher different from that of any teacher?" Other teachers interact across the same contexts, but the political, cultural, historical, social class, demographic, and economic influences have made bilingual education and teaching controversial. These influences overtly and often covertly affect the interactions in the four contexts. Table 2.1 illustrates many of the "contextual factors" with which the teacher may deal within and across each of the four contexts. This is by no means a complete list of all the complexities that might affect what goes on in bilingual teachers' classrooms and schools.

As unique individuals, teachers bring their personal qualities, histories, and experiences as members of society, communities, schools and classrooms to their teaching. Figure 2.2 shows the individual factors from childhood, language learning, schooling and pedagogical experiences, and attitudes that profoundly shape each teacher and the interactions in the various contexts. Although two-dimensional figures cannot accurately account for the intricacies of lived experiences, Figs. 2.1 and 2.2 and Table 2.1 show the many influences, factors, and contexts that make bilingual teaching complex.

The personal experiences, classroom, school, and community contexts are richly described in the eight teachers' stories. To provide a broader understanding of the controversial nature of bilingual education, background information on the societal context is briefly described here.

THE SOCIETAL CONTEXT OF BILINGUAL EDUCATION

Contrary to popular opinion, the United States is not (nor has it ever been) a monolingual English-speaking nation. This country has a long tradition of multilingualism. Even prior to European contact, there were 500 to 1,000 indigenous languages or dialects spoken in the United States (Grosjean, 1982). The new country opened its door to diverse peoples (some voluntary immigrants and others involuntary) to settle and build it. From colonial times to the early 1900s, education in languages other than English was accepted and flourished in some ethnic communities.

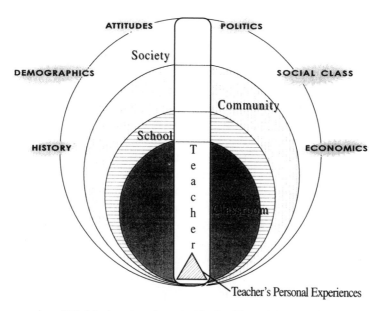

FIG. 2.1. A context of complexities faced by a bilingual teacher.

TABLE 2.1

Contextual Factors Affecting the Work of a Bilingual Teacher

Society	Community	School	Classroom
• Policies–local, state, federal • Legal mandates, decisions • Bilingual program models • Funding • Research • Teacher certification	• Parents • Businesses • Health and social services • Other institutions	• Administration (principal, school board, superintendent) • Teachers (bilingual/monolingual) • Other support staff • Students • Physical plant • Curriculum	• Students (bilingual/monolingual) • Curriculum • Curriculum materials • Teaching practices • Assessment practices • General content • Language and cultural content

Historically, bilingualism has both been tolerated in the United States as well as restricted. Democratic values espouse freedom supposedly for all. Even though citizens have freedom of speech, the Constitution dictates no official language. The societal hegemonic forces have been very successful in promoting English without any official language policy (Crawford, 1995). There has been a double standard in terms of bilingualism. For the rich, learning a second or foreign language has always been valued and expected, whereas for the poor, speaking a language other than English has been seen as a deficit to be remediated, replaced, or eradicated. Since the early 1900s, the attitude has prevailed that it is un-American to speak a language other than English. The schools have historically promoted the interests of those in power (i.e., White Americans). The interests of people of color and speakers of other languages were mostly overlooked until the 1960s, which resulted in massive school failure among ethnolinguistic minorities (Crawford, 1995). Prior to the 1960s, most students who spoke languages other than English were placed into English-only classes (also referred to as *submersion* or *sink-or-swim*). A small portion of those students succeeded, but many failed. This kind of tracking held many students back and restricted their employment opportunities. During that time, it was possible to secure well-paying, blue-collar jobs in agriculture and manufacturing without finishing high school. However, in recent decades, as these well paying jobs have declined, high school, technical school, or some college education is often required to advance beyond a minimum wage job.

The schools have been the main vehicle to promote U.S. values and to assimilate immigrants and speakers of other languages. Stein (1986) differentiated assimilation into two styles: military and missionary. Military style assimilation occurred in this country's early history through conquest and land acquisition when speakers of other languages were forced to assimilate at gunpoint (e.g., Native Americans in the boarding schools, Spanish speakers in the Southwest).

In more recent history, missionary-style assimilation started during the cultural deprivation era (Crawford, 1995). In the 1950s, cultural deprivation theorists posited that home and community environmental factors were to blame for minority students' underachievement. "To make it America, culturally inferior children needed to master the language and values of the dominant society" (Thomas, cited in Crawford, 1995, p. 34). As a result, federally supported intervention educational programs emerged with the mission to correct the differences caused by race, class, language, and culture. This assimilationist stance has prevailed in society and has shaped compensatory educational programs since the 1960s. Many citizens, including immigrant parents and school personnel, ascribe to this assimilationist attitude.

Not all schooling of immigrant children was of this assimilationist nature. During the early 1960s with the influx of privileged Cuban refugees, bilingual education was "reborn" with the experimental implementation of a "two-way" program at the Coral Way Elementary School in Dade County,

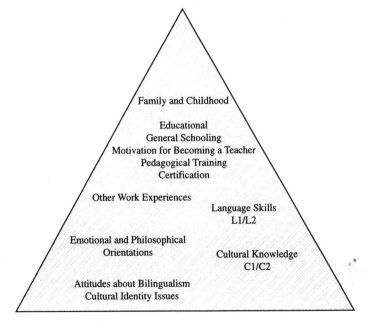

FIG. 2.2. The teacher's personal experiences.

Florida (Crawford, 1995). The goal of this privately funded program was full bilingualism for its Spanish-speaking Cuban and mainstream English-speaking children. Program success was due to its well-trained teachers, its private funding from the Ford Foundation, and its enriching additive bilingual focus. Additive bilingualism aims to add (rather than subtract) a second language to a child's first language resources (Lambert, 1984 cited in Ovando & Collier, 1985). That successful **two-way** model set the stage for other bilingual education programs to be considered. However, for the most part, bilingual programs have been more remedial focused than enrichment-oriented.

Since the 1960s, as growing numbers of language minorities, particularly Hispanics, began to gain economic and political power, they started using the judicial and legislative governmental branches to make schooling more equitable and to address the massive school failure of culturally and linguistically diverse students. As a result of the Civil Rights Act of 1964, and Supreme Court cases such as *Lau v. Nichols* (1974), attention was finally paid to language minority students' learning needs through federal and local policies. Under Title VI of the Civil Rights Act, children could no longer be discriminated against or excluded from programs receiving federal assistance on the basis of race, creed, sex, or national origin. School districts receiving federal assistance were required to ensure access of national-origin minority children to public education" (Ambert & Meléndez, 1985). The act was a first step in eliminating the barrier to equal educational opportunity.

FEDERAL LEGISLATION AND FUNDING

Federal monies were at last available for programs such as the Elementary and Secondary Education Act (ESEA) of 1965. Through Title I of the ESEA of 1965, some funding was allocated on a formula basis to children of below a certain income level. The first programs for language minority children were mostly **English as a second language (ESL) pull-out** programs, which had limited effectiveness because of their decontextualized approaches. Hispanic American interest groups pressured Congress to amend the ESEA. In 1968, under ESEA, Congress passed the Federal Bilingual Education Act (BEA) also known as **Title VII. Title VII** was originally created to recognize the learning needs of poor, limited-English-speaking children. The poverty criteria was later dropped. **Title VII** provided "financial assistance to local educational agencies to develop and carry out new and imaginative elementary and secondary programs designed to meet these special educational needs" (P.L. 90-247 cited in Castellanos, 1983, p. 8).

Bilingual education under **Title VII** means: "The use of two languages, one of which is English, as mediums of instruction" (BEA of 1967, Statutes-at-Large 81, cited in Santiago Santiago, 1978, p. 34). No specific program models were recommended, because schools were supposed to design their own models through experimentation. Title VII's three-fold purposes were: "(1) to provide English language skills, (2) maintain the native language skills, (3) support the cultural heritage of the students" (Castellanos, 1983, p. 83). Federal intervention focused on designing compensatory programs that would help children overcome the "language handicap" (Crawford, 1995). These remedial programs aimed to compensate for the deficit associated with speaking the native language (Castellanos, 1983).

Originally the intent of BEA/Title VII was to design innovative program models, so that states and local school districts could eventually become responsible for continuing the implementation of these programs. This rarely became the case. Since the beginning, the federal government has remained a mainstay of the bilingual programs, significantly influencing their funding, design, and implementation.

The passage of **Title VII** did not ensure that local school districts implemented bilingual programs: "Funding was critical if local authorities were to be lured into adopting policy" (Santiago Santiago, 1978, p. 34). Title VII was a voluntary grants program for projects that chose to apply. Title VII programs were funded through "seed monies" for limited time periods (usually about five years). Guidelines for the use of these funds in creating innovative programs were unclear because the decision making was left up to the discretion of local educational agencies. **Title VII** funds are competitively granted to schools or districts to supplement, rather than supplant, the regular education program. Problems in initiating bilingual programs included a lack of certified teachers, identification and assessment tools, curricula, materials, and research. The programs, according to Stein (1986) had to be created "out of thin air" (p. 33). Subsequent reauthorizations of **Title VII** supported the training of teachers and funded research studies to show the efficacy of instruction in two languages.

Title VII has long been a "political football," with policies affecting language minority children going back and forth, monies being continually stretched to serve more students with less resources. From U.S. Department of Education data sources, it is estimated that there are 3 million **language minority** elementary and secondary children, and the numbers are projected to keep increasing (C. B. Stein, personal communication, July 19, 1996). Other sources from 1990 census data estimate **LEP** students from 5 to 7.5 million (Waggoner, 1993). Because **Title VII** grants are competitive, not all eligible students receive services. **Title VII** serves only about 10% of the **LEP** students nationally. This leaves other students to be served by state or local programs or many not at all. About 20% to 25% of LEP students receive no services at all (C. B. Stein, personal communication, July 19, 1996).

Title VII has been reauthorized and refunded by Congress in 1974, 1978, 1984, 1988, and 1994. According to the political climate, funding priorities have shifted with each reauthorization. After 1974, reauthorizations to support the native language have consistently been weakened (Fitzgerald, 1993). The federal government wanted to encourage support to programs that allowed districts so-called "flexibility of instructional approaches." Starting in 1984, monies were allowed to fund "Special Alternative Instructional Programs" that use structured immersion (an all-English model). The move toward funding immersion programs reflected the negative stance of the Reagan administration toward bilingual education.

In 1968, **Title VII** funding initially allocated $7.5 million (Crawford, 1995). According to Stein, (personal communication, July 19, 1996) from 1969 to 1981, Title VII monies increased incrementally to $180 million, but during the Reagan years (1982–1986), monies dipped to $120 million (about 25%). Then from 1986 to 1995, funding increased again to reach $206.7 million (López, 1995). Although $206.7 million sounds like a lot of money, it represents less than 1% of the total education budget (Stein, personal communication, July 19, 1996). Bilingual education funding is only a minuscule part of the $9.3 billion ESEA budget (López, 1995).

The present situation of Title VII funding and priorities is still highly politicized. With the 1994 reauthorization of **Title VII,** the budget was stalled and severely cut by the Republican Congress and Senate. On almost a weekly basis, the National Association of Bilingual Education (NABE), through its facsimile and e-mail networks appealed to its members through "Action Alerts" to protest the cuts to Title VII, Title IX–Indian Education, and Immigrant Education. The 1996 fiscal year budget was enacted on April 24, 1996 at $178 million (a cut of $22.6 million from the preceding year). These funds are for instructional programs and immigrant education only. No funds were allocated for professional development of bilingual teachers or support services (which includes dissemination of information). These cuts may be very damaging and may eventually undermine the long-range continuance of bilingual education (for current federal legislation and funding information on the Internet, point your browser to: http://www.ed.gov.updates).

Political conservatism and xenophobic attitudes underlie the funding issue. This conservatism is again rearing its head in recent anti-immigrant legislation, such as Proposition 187 in California, official English legislation in 23 states (Torres, 1996) and an official English bill passed in Congress (Schmitt, 1996). Many of these initiatives are generously supported by privately funded lobbying organizations such as U.S. ENGLISH, INC.

The general public often opposes using taxpayers' money for programs to support the development and maintenance of a language other than English. Passing on a non-English language was acceptable as an individual choice, but should not be a governmental responsibility. Government funding of native languages would lead to "ethnic attachments" (Epstein, cited in Crawford, 1992) and "ghettoization" of linguistic miniorities, encouraging "greater separation" rather than "greater intergration" (Crawford, 1992, p. 87).

The term "bilingual education" is a misnomer that the general public may not understand completely. Bilingual implies an equal use and development (or maintenance) of two languages and cultures. Crawford (1995) stated that the language maintenance issue was the Achilles heel of bilingual education, because some mainstream citizens did not want to support long-term instruction in a language other than English. Programs supporting language maintenance are rare and often seen as segregationist.

In actuality, the prevailing model has been the **Transitional Bilingual Education (TBE)** model, a program where the native language is temporarily used (for 1 to 3 years) to develop literacy and content area skills with increasing doses of English that eventually replace the native language. Cummins' (1994) work posits that second language development in academic subjects takes from 5 to 7 years as opposed to 1 to 2 years to develop conversational second language proficiency. Early exit **transitional bilingual education** has been less effective in promoting English academic development because of its limited time to develop cognitive skills in the first and second languages. Researchers have found more additive models, such as late exit maintenance (Ramírez et al., 1991) and "**two-way**" or developmental programs (Thomas & Collier, 1996) more effective to develop first and second language academic achievement. **Two-way** programs are characterized by an integration of language and content where both native speakers of English and speakers of another language reinforce their native language as they learn a second language. Although 75% of **two-way** programs have been in Spanish–English, other **two-way** programs have been conducted in Russian, Arabic, French, Hmong, Korean, Chinese, and Portuguese (C. B. Stein, personal communication, July 19, 1996). Some successful **two-way** programs have been fashioned after the Coral Way model in the cities of Washington DC, Boston, New York, and Chicago. These programs were based on models and research adapted from the "one-way" Canadian immersion programs, where English-speaking children were taught functional and academic competence in French (Lambert & Tucker, 1972). For language majority children, this model promotes additive bilingualism, whereas for **language minority** children it promotes subtractive bilingualism.

The issue of the amount of time being used to develop the native language can be deceptive. Legarreta-Marcaida (1981) observed languages in transitional bilingual education elementary classrooms and found that the bilingual teachers themselves perceived that they used more native language than they actually did. In actuality, implementation of any one model in the strict sense often does not occur. Teachers interpret and implement a program model based on their own beliefs about bilingual education and the dominant language they speak (Lemberger, 1990). When the classroom door is closed, they may or may not follow the designated model.

With the latest **Title VII** reauthorization in 1994, the program model categories, such as **transitional bilingual education,** have been dropped in favor of more comprehensive services aimed to develop and enhance programs in individual schools or school systems. The goal in changing the policy language and foci of the programs is to move away from the stigma associated with bilingual education programs.

Court Cases and State and Local Policies

Federal policies and funding are only one piece of the intricate bilingual education puzzle. Court cases, state, and local initiatives have also shaped the creation and implementation of bilingual education programs. Both Title VI of the Civil Rights Act and **Title VII** set precedents for important legal cases that had tremendous impact on bilingual education. One of the most important cases, *Lau v. Nichols* (1974), was a class action suit filed on behalf of 1,800 Chinese-American students, who attended San Francisco public schools where subjects were taught in English, a language students could not understand. In 1974, the Supreme Court unanimously ruled that the students were being discriminated against and not being provided an equal educational opportunity. Judge William O. Douglas (1974, cited in Ovando & Collier, 1985) stated that "There is no equality of treatment merely by providing students with the same facilities, teachers, and curriculum; for students who do not understand English are effectively foreclosed from any meaningful education" (p. 34).

Related to the Lau decision, a memorandum called the Pottinger Memo, issued in 1970 by the Department of Health, Education, and Welfare, specified that school districts take affirmative steps to correct program deficiencies that neglected the needs of **LEP** students. Providing the same teacher and books to all students was deemed unacceptable. Although the Lau decision specifically endorsed no program model, it gave a strong push for equal educational opportunity for limited English-speaking students. According to Teitelbaum and Hiller (1979), "Lau raised the nation's consciousness of the need for bilingual education, encouraged additional federal legislation, energized federal enforcement efforts, . . . aided the passage of laws mandating bilingual education, and spawned more lawsuits" (p. 21).

Following the Lau decision, Congress passed the Equal Educational Opportunity Act of 1974, which extended Lau to all public school districts, not just to those receiving federal financial assistance (Teitelbaum & Hiller, 1979). Lau was important in fostering the creation of bilingual programs. However, much resistance resulted from programs implemented as a result of court order or mandate. "Antipathy of school personnel to bilingual education may intensify with judicial involvement" (Teitelbaum & Hiller, 1979, pp. 21–22).

At the state level, prior to the 1960s, no state-mandated bilingual programs existed. In fact, many states had laws mandating English-only instruction. According to Ambert and Meléndez (1985), "In seven states teachers could face criminal penalties or revocation of teaching licenses if they conducted bilingual classes" (p. 38).

With limited Title VII funds, pressure grew at the state level to enact local bilingual education legislation to meet the needs of **LEP** children (Ambert & Meléndez, 1985). However, Santiago Santiago (1983) stated that support for implementation of bilingual education at the state level was even more limited than at the federal level and mostly transitional in nature.

States have had particular influence on licensing and certifying bilingual teachers, but have been slow to respond to the training needs of bilingual teachers. Most states did not respond until the 1970s, following the start of federal funding for **Title VII** teacher education programs (Santiago Santiago, 1983).

Each state has developed its own legislation and policies to serve language minority children. For example, some states such as Texas and Massachusetts have mandates for transitional bilingual education programs (Crawford, 1995). State policies have also wavered according to political climate. For example, since 1976, California, with the **Assembly Bill (AB) 1329** (the Chacon–Mascone Bill) and later **AB 507**, had more prescriptive and supportive bilingual education legislation and policies, but in 1987, Governor Deukmejian allowed that legislation to expire (Powell, 1995). Attempts were made to reinstate the legislation, but the governor vetoed them. Nonetheless, the California State Department of Education has tried to uphold the principles of the bill.

Education is political, particularly bilingual education. Bilingual education policies have hardly been a matter of what is educationally sound for children, rather they have been a matter of who is in power and whose votes are being courted. For example, some prominent Republicans, such as Ronald Reagan (as governor), appealed to Hispanic-American voters by supporting bilingual education in California, only to reverse this support during his presidency (Crawford, 1995).

Another example of the political nature of bilingual education policies can be seen with the New York City's Aspira Consent Decree that resulted from *Aspira v. The Board of Education* of 1974 (Santiago Santiago, 1986). Aspira, a Hispanic advocacy group, brought a class-action suit on behalf of 180,000 Puerto Rican students whose language and learning needs were being neglected the Board of Education. The Aspira Consent Decree, which is still in effect, mandates transitional bilingual programs for the city's Spanish-speaking students. The decree established guidelines for identification of students, curriculum, and assessment, provisions for qualified teachers, and parent notification procedures. The original decree stated that students could exit the program upon reaching the 21st percentile on the *Language Assessment Battery* (LAB; 1982),[2] an English language proficiency test. This cut-off point was not decided on by psychometricians or language specialists; rather, it was a compromise made in court between Judge Frankel and the New York City Board of Education (Santiago Santiago, 1978). In 1989, that cut-off score was raised to the 41st percentile after much struggle by bilingual educators and advocates who knew that such a low cut-off point (the 21st percentile) allowed youngsters to exit the program without a firm enough native language or second foundation.

NATIONAL DEMOGRAPHIC TRENDS

Also important to understanding the context of bilingual teachers are the national demographic trends. Barringer (1993) citing 1990 census data, showed 32 million U.S. residents (and citizens) over the age of 5 speak languages other than English in the home. Also, 14% of all residents (or one in seven) speak a foreign language, showing an increase of almost 38%

---

[2]Italicized tests and curricula are annotated in chapter 14.

since the 1980 census (Barringer, 1993). Immigration from Asia, Latin America, the Middle East, and Eastern Europe is projected to continue. (See the demographic chart in Part III for the top 25 languages spoken from 1980 to 1990.) What is not visible in a chart are the reasons behind immigration. Some of these reasons for immigration surface in the teachers' stories, in their personal experiences and those of their students. The flux of different immigrant groups is often related to world politics and economic situations. A basic tenet underlying U.S. immigration, since colonial times, is the search for a better life (Molesky, 1988).

There are 3 million **LEP** students out of a school population of 44 million. The **LEP** population is increasing at 6% to 7% per year (C. B. Stein, personal communication, July 19, 1996). This diversity has and will have significant impact on the U.S. schools. The numbers of **language minority** youth, both English-speaking (from English-speaking Caribbean and other countries) and non-English-speaking are clearly on the rise (see Table 14.2). Hispanic Americans and Asian Americans are the fastest growing segments of the student population, especially in the gateway cities of Los Angeles, New York, and Miami (U.S. Department of Education, "A Back to School Report," 1996). Schools need to be better equipped to handle this diversity through recruiting and training of teachers. The need for qualified bilingual education teachers is a high priority (Council of the Great City Schools, 1996).

Current estimates for needed bilingual teachers are as high as 170,000 nationally (Headden, 1995). To meet these shortages, different states and districts have allowed bilingual teachers to enter the profession through emergency credentials or waivers as in California. For example, in 1990, half of the California bilingual teaching staff were on such waivers (U.S. Department of Education, 1990). These shortages of trained personnel are often felt greatly at the school level. The California State Department of Education has responded to the increasingly diverse student population by establishing new teacher preparation and examination requirements for new and already certified teachers as Cross-cultural Language and Academic Development (CLAD) and Bilingual Cross-cultural Language and Academic Development (BCLAD) specialists. These new credential programs unify the fields, philosophies, and strategies of bilingual education and ESL (Walton, 1992) and have potential to better prepare a corps of teachers to deal with the dramatic demographic changes that California is experiencing.

This brief discussion of the societal context of bilingual education may seem far from what occurs in the classroom. It, nevertheless, provides a backdrop showing the history, policies, tensions and attitudes that may underlie what goes on within the classrooms, schools and communities of the eight teachers whose stories are told in this book.

3

How to Use This Book

I asked a former student (a bilingual teacher of 5 years) to read the eight first-draft narratives. Her response to them was, "This is what's missing in teacher education courses, hearing the teachers' voices!" The teachers' stories got her "adrenalin going" as she compared her setting with those of the teachers. She became inspired, wanting to write a proposal to create a dual language program in her school.

These teachers' stories are meant for you, the reader, to get ideas and information about how others have made sense of their work. The narratives, presented in Part II of this book, are intended to help you see yourself in relation to other teachers, and to break the endemic isolation that teachers face, especially bilingual teachers. They aim to provoke your reactions and to engage you in asking questions such as: "How does my situation compare with those described?" "What would I do in a similar case?" "How can I adapt what the teacher did to my particular situation?" "What can I take from them that will help me?" Ultimately, the teachers' stories should inspire you to take action to make your situation better for yourself, your students, and their families. As you read, note your impressions, reactions, and questions. Try to think about the underlying issues and/or theories that are represented in and across their stories.

The "Overview of Teachers" chart (see pages 28–29) keeps the stories and details about each teacher straight. As you read, the teachers mention certain terms, curricula, tests, and literature that they use. These are listed and explained in Part III "Bilingual Education Resources." Curricula, tests, and literature are italicized in the text and referred to in chapter 14. These are provided so you may learn more about them and/or obtain them if you are interested. The terms and programs in boldface throughout the text are defined in the glossary (Appendix A).

QUESTIONS FOR REFLECTION

The following questions, organized around specific themes, are provided as a starting point to reflect on, discuss, think, and write about the issues, theories, and practices that emerge from the narratives.

1. Background experiences: How do the teachers' (and your own) schooling and personal experiences as students and/or second language learners affect their teaching approaches? How did their personal experiences shape their practices and influence the connections they made to students and parents?

2. Teaching styles: Are there inconsistencies in the teachers' philosophies? How are these inconsistencies reflected in their practice? What did you find most interesting about the teachers' practices? How do their classroom practices (in reading, language development, culture, and content areas) compare with yours? What would you do in a similar situation? What theories are reflected in the practices?

3. Program policies and their impact on teachers and students: What are the different program models? How are they similar and different? How do they compare with what is going on in your school? How do the programs compare with models described in bilingual education literature? How have the programs been shaped by particular school and community contexts? How have program and testing policies enabled or inhibited teachers to foster dual language development and academic achievement?

4. Curricula and materials: What are the biggest problems that the teachers encountered with bilingual curricula and materials? Why are these problems consistent across language, grade, region, and program model? What have been the teachers' responses to limited curricula and materials? How does their experience compare to your own?

5. School culture support and obstacles: What is the nature of the school climate? What support did the teachers receive from administrators and colleagues? How has that support impacted on the bilingual teachers' work? What coping mechanisms did they use? How does the school culture affect the work of teachers?

6. Parent–teacher relations: What efforts did the teachers make to orient parents in their adjustment to this new society and school system? What did teachers do to reach out to parents? What mutually beneficial effects did their efforts have on the children and families?

7. Teacher education: What were the varied formal and informal bilingual teacher education training and experiences that the teachers received? What were some of the different paths to certification? What is the value of on-the-job training?

WORKSHEET GRIDS

The following worksheet grids are provided as organizational tools that will help you highlight themes/issues from each case (Grid 1) and across cases (Grid 2). Copy them and fill them in as you read each case.

GRID 1

Theme Chart for Individual Teachers

Teacher_____

Themes	Background Experiences	Teacher Education	Bilingual Program Model	Teaching Styles or Approaches
Highlights				
How does it compare with you?				

Curricula and Materials	Administrative Support	Parent–Teacher Relations	Collegial Relations	Unique Features

GRID 2
Cross Case Theme Chart

(Compare and Contrast Themes Across the Different Teachers)

Teacher	Background Experiences	Teacher Education	Bilingual Program Model	Teaching Styles or Approaches
Sofya				
Manouchka				
Diana				
Heather				
Sandra				
Mariana				
Jean				
Luz				

Curricula and Materials	Administrative Support	Parent–Teacher Relations	Collegial Relations	Unique Features

		Overview of Teachers		
Teacher	Age	Origin/Ethnicity	Languages	Years Teaching and School Settings
Sofya	57	Russian, born in Ukraine of former USSR, immigrated at age 45	Russian/English	20 in Ukraine, 5 in U.S. public school
Manouchka	32	Haitian, born in Haiti, immigrated at age 10	Haitian-Creole/ English	5 in private school, 6 in public school
Diana	42	Chinese, born in Hong Kong, immigrated at age 16	Cantonese, Mandarin/ English	2 in private child care, 6 in public child care, 6 in public school
Heather	38	Vietnamese, born in Vietnam, immigrated at age 25	Vietnamese/ English	4 in New Comer Center in NE, 7 in N. CA
Sandra	31	European-American, born in IL	Spanish/English	3 in public school in S. CA, 4 in public school
Mariana	42	Puerto Rican/ Italian-American, born in NJ	Spanish/English	2 in GED program, 3 in Head Start, 8 in private school, 4 in public school
Jean	50	European-American, born in CA	English/Spanish	11 in public school
Luz	42	Chicana, born in ID	Spanish/English	16 in public school

Grade Levels Taught	Present Grade Level	Higher Education, Major, and Teacher Preparation	Bilingual Program Model	Location and Region
1 and 2	1/2	Pedagogical College in Ukraine (equivalent to BA), in U.S. liberal arts and educations courses, MA-Some coursework	Transitional	Queens, NY/ Urban
2 and 4/5	2	BA-Special Education, MA-Bilingual Education	Transitional	Brooklyn, NY/ Urban
Pre-K-1	1	BA-Elementary Education, Bilingual Certificate of Competence, MA-Some coursework	Transitional	N. CA/Urban
K-6	1	BA-Education with a Bilingual/Bicultural Emphasis MA-Some coursework	Transitional	N. CA/Suburban
2 and 3	2	BA-Spanish, Bilingual Certificate of Competence, MA-Some coursework	Transitional	S. IL/Suburban
Pre-K-GED	4/5	BA-English Literature, MA-Teacher Education & Curriculum	Dual Language	New York City/ Urban
K-2	1	BA-French, MA-Bilingual/ Cross Cultural Education	Spanish Immersion	N. CA/Suburban and Rural
K-6	4	BA-Sociology and Psychology, 5th year bilingual credential, MA-Some coursework	Maintenance, Enrichment, and Sheltered English	N. CA/Urban

II

EIGHT TEACHERS' NARRATIVES, DISCUSSION, AND EPILOGUE

In chapters 4 through 11, the eight teachers' narratives are ordered according to program model so that their stories may be compared across different programs. The first five teachers work in transitional programs. The remaining three teachers work in more additive type programs (e.g., maintenance/enrichment, immersion, and two-way dual language programs). The narratives are also clustered by language, starting with teachers who work in languages other than Spanish. Following the eight teachers' stories (chapters 4–11), chapter 12 discusses themes and issues that emerged from the teachers' narratives, and implications of their stories for bilingual education. Chapter 13 is an epilogue updating the teachers' stories.

4

Sofya

BACKGROUND

Let me introduce myself. My name is Sofya. I am a Russian bilingual teacher at a Queens public school in New York City. When I came to America in 1982 from Russia, I never spoke English before. When you read what I say, try to see beyond the language of how I speak and understand that how I teach my children comes from my heart. I became a teacher because I love children. Becoming a teacher in Russia was not easy for me, especially since I am Jewish. My passport had a special stamp showing that I am a Jew. I finished (secondary) school with a red diploma, which meant everything was excellent. When I started college and passed the entrance tests, they cut me because they looked at my passport and saw I was a Jew. So the next year my father paid 1,000 rubles (about $1,000) to the college principal to let me in. As Jews, we weren't treated equally or fairly.

After finishing college, I taught for 20 years at a school in Kharkov, a Ukranian city. I was the only Jewish lady in the town who was a master teacher. One of the best compliments paid to me in my school was when someone said, "Sofya, you are not Jew. You are our kind of people. You are Russian." I worked very hard to be accepted. Things were different then. There was no fighting between different groups like what's happening now. Armenians are killing Ajerbaijians. Ajerbaijians are killing Georgians.

For all those years, I taught Russian language, literature, and music in the same school. In Russia, we have a different system where children attend one school from first to tenth grades. I had one class of students for 10 years and another class for 10 years. After such long-term contact with the children, I was like part of their family. I'd be invited to their weddings.

Originally, I came to this country because I couldn't look into the 60 eyes of my 30 children and lie anymore. For years, I had lied telling them that everything was alright, that everything was for everybody. It was a lie, because everything wasn't for everybody. They were poor and didn't have hardly any food to eat. We had to say that the Communist Party is the best party in the whole world, that the party works for the people! The party told us, "You can buy anything that you want in the store! You can go anywhere you want! You can say what ever you want! All people, whether you are Jewish, Russian, Black, or White, are the same." It's not true. Before, I didn't realize how bad things were because I was raised by the party—they taught me how to read, think, and teach. Eventually, I started asking myself, "Why am I lying to these children?" With false words, I can't prepare them for real life. I started to talk honestly to my children.

Then things started to be very, very dangerous. One day somebody from the KGB came to my apartment. My husband told me, "Sofya, I don't want to lose you. If we don't do something, you are going to end up in the gulag [prison]." At that time, other Jews were starting to leave. I was 45 years old. It was a tough decision to make. My husband and I ended up leaving Russia for Austria and then to Italy. From Italy we had to decide whether to go to Israel or America. In Italy, a wonderful man advised me to go to America where I could continue my career as a teacher. I couldn't think of doing anything else.

When we first emigrated to the United States we were surprised by all the help we received from NYANA [New York Association for New Americans] and other Jewish organizations. For example, I was given a special ticket to a synagogue in Manhattan. When I presented it to the rabbi, he said, "OK, come with me." He took me to the basement and opened all the closets and said, "Take what you want." I said, "What do you mean?" He said, "Take. You need clothes? Do you need a coat?" I said, "Yes." "Which one do you want? Take it." I was shocked! Why? What did I do for this country or for this rabbi? Did I work for him? Why is he giving all this for free? They paid for 1 month's rent and tuition. They gave us food stamps. I didn't like that feeling of receiving something for nothing. I felt like I owe everybody. Do I work for you? Do I clean your house? Do I teach your kids? Do I babysit them? If you give me your watch, why take it from your hand and give it to me? I can use it a couple of times, but I have to earn my own. Right? My family has never before been on welfare. After that first month, we started working to earn our own way. We are a hard-working family. I cleaned apartments. I babysat. I was a companion for old ladies. I did shopping. Everything. And now I am a professional teacher. My husband was a chief engineer in Russia. He couldn't continue as an engineer here because he didn't have the language. So he started to drive a taxi. He built houses, he painted, he cleaned. People who come now, they accept everything, because they know they can. Now they just seem to be taking more than they give back.

THE RUSSIAN POPULATION IN QUEENS

All the Russian families in our school district are Jewish refugees from Middle Asia, an isolated rural area where there was little education. They come to our district because they are all related. In my class I have sisters, brothers, cousins. They all lived together in their village. A lot of them even have the same last name. Back in Russia some families were professionals. But as refugees they are all on welfare. They stay on welfare for a couple years, until they can get work. Some have jobs on the side, such as taxi drivers, beauticians, shoemakers, or sales people in Russian or American stores. They are struggling financially. I'll give you a very simple example. All my 28 children receive free lunch. If we go on a trip, I pay for the bus fare, because I can't ask them to pay the $2.50.

The families come here for the future of their children. They don't want them to be a beautician, shoemaker, or taxi driver, no. They want them to be a lawyer, a doctor, or a teacher. They want to give them education. Their children can't go to colleges in Russia. These Russian families are here to contribute to the future of this country. That's how I understand my role as a teacher. I want to give them the idea that it's our country now and forever and they must be good citizens. That's all.

Not only must I teach the children, but I have to work closely with the parents. I start with discipline and hygiene. The ladies don't wear undergarments. I tell the parents to bathe more frequently because they smell. When they come here they find the American custom of daily bathing strange. I teach the children discipline of cleaning up after themselves in the classroom. My room is the cleanest in the whole school! The custodian loves me, because my children always pick up everything.

The parents thank God for me, not because I am special, but because I know how to establish the rules and how to organize kids. They ask, "What did you do to my son?" He tells me, "Mother, pick that up! Put things in their proper place!" The discipline children learn in my class is also practiced at home.

TEACHER EDUCATION

Over 22 years ago, I finished pedagogical college in Russia. To transfer that degree I had to take some liberal arts college courses. But I've never had any bilingual courses. The district is sending me for bilingual courses to help me get my permanent state certification. I'm afraid to go to college at this point because I am too old and tired. Also for certification, I still need to pass the National Teachers Examination [NTE], which I'm really scared about.

THE BILINGUAL PROGRAM

I have worked in this district with Russian children for 10 years: 5 years as a paraprofessional at different schools and 5 years as a bilingual teacher at this school. I started the Russian bilingual program from scratch 5 years ago with the help and support of my principal and district bilingual director. From the beginning, because the principal didn't know about how to implement a bilingual program, I was on my own. All my ideas, experience, and education helped me to survive. The district director knew about implementing a bilingual program, but I was never given any special courses about bilingual instruction. So I developed everything by myself. I had to orient the new bilingual teachers about our program. Little by little, the program started to grow.

There are bilingual classes at first, second, third, fourth, and fifth grades. There is no bilingual kindergarten class at the school. The reason is because our principal decided to open a self-contained English as a Second Language (ESL) class at that level. She thinks it's necessary to have those classes. Maybe she's right. She's the boss. That's why we don't have bilingual kindergarten.

For 5 years, I have taught a 1–2 bilingual class. I like working with the young first- and second-grade children because I see them make incredible progress. I find that most newcomer children just swallow up everything I say.

The main goal of our program is to mainstream the children by giving them intensive English. We try to cover all the subjects in English with a summary in Russian. Sometimes the children start to speak better English than Russian. Depending on the child's progress in English, some of them go straight from my class, even during the school year, to an English class. I do this when they don't need me anymore, when they can handle more advanced English. I give them the fundamentals, the foundation. I think they are doing okay in the mainstream. Our children are involved in everything that is going on in school. Eventually the Russian language may be lost because they are not receiving advanced Russian curriculum. But what can I do?

GOALS FOR MAINSTREAMING

I want to help children work, study, and get used to English as soon as possible. I have my theories. I don't know about any other theories. This country is where we're going to live and die. I want to give them my love for this country and to prepare them for life. If I teach them just in Russian, without intensive English, it's going to hold them back for a couple years. I love them too much to do that. As a paraprofessional, I saw the poor children in Spanish bilingual classes who didn't understand one single English word. The teacher was the same. That's terrible. Why do they hold them back? For what reason?

First of all, the Russian families do not intend to go back. They are here for life. Second, all the parents are extremely determined for their children to learn English as much and quickly as possible. So that's our objective. Our district goals are definitely more **transitional** than **maintenance**. Other districts have tried to implement a Russian maintenance program which has failed. Why? Because everything was in Russian with one period in English. And the parents were very unhappy. So we went the opposite way. We started everything in English with a linguistic summary in Russian. For newcomers, I use about two out of seven periods of Russian a day. And we have a separate Russian native language period. If you ask all my parents if they would like to keep the children in my class, they would say "yes" without thinking 1 minute. Why? Because I answer for their needs. They don't want their children to forget Russian native language, but they want them to learn English as soon as possible. The Russian language is maintained in the home.

TEACHING

In the bilingual program, the children learn to read and write in both Russian and English. I start with the Russian alphabet the same way I start with the English alphabet. The work I give them and the strategies I use are the same for both languages. If I do it differently, my children get lost.

What makes it difficult for me is that new kids come in all the time. I have children who are pretty fluent in English because they have been here for 2 years. Tomorrow, when somebody else comes in, I'll have to start all over again. Since I am alone, that's why I present lessons in English and then give a summary in Russian. I would like to give more Russian, but I can't. The system doesn't allow it. We don't have extra teachers or help. I have to keep my eyes on all of them. And not just that, I have to teach and give them some knowledge. And I have more than four levels because I have two grades. In addition, the first-grade newcomers never have attended school before, so it's very hard for them because I must teach them the most basic things.

My approach to reading in either language includes discussing the book cover and the main ideas. Each day for homework, I give them vocabulary words from the story from which they alphabetize, draw, and write sentences. The next day I give them a mini (spelling) test with those words. They get about 15 new words a week. On Fridays, I will test them on all 15 words. They have to know how to spell and use them.

I use **ESL** techniques to teach content areas of social studies and science. In order for my children to learn, they must feel, touch, and see the content. For each lesson, I use lots of visuals and manipulatives such as counting materials, pictures, movies, and songs. I think it helps them a lot. We make big books, small books, charts, and pictures. To make materials, we cut, paste, and draw.

I build the Russian language by studying literature, fairy tales, poetry, and songs from which we have developed puppet shows. We have some curriculum in Russian but not nearly enough. For Russian culture and events, I have children watch the Russian news on cable television. I have them take notes or draw pictures about what they see. Once a week, the children sit in the magic circle and share what they have learned about the cultural and political life in Russia and other countries. They each report on one news story. That makes them feel close to the country where they were born.

CURRICULUM AND MATERIALS

When the program started, we didn't have any subject books or materials to help us. As a Russian master teacher, I was permitted to bring some books from Russia. But I only use them for my own reference because of the Communist ideology represented in them. Most of our materials are in English, but we also have some in Russian, which were developed by teachers here. Our district paid us one summer to develop some Russian materials. We made an alphabet book for first- and second-grade children with stories and everything.

To better establish this program, we need more Russian curriculum to have the same amount and quality of material as we do in English. The

Russians are still coming. And the Russian teachers don't have enough curriculum or materials to work with the children. If we want to keep this program alive, we need more and better curriculum and materials. In a few more years, when I retire, I want the curriculum to be in place so that the children are not going to get lost, because there's nothing to help the teacher. We need somebody to help us with materials to show us how we have to teach English and Russian in the American ways.

TESTING

We use the English _Language Assessment Battery_ (_LAB_-1982) test and a district-designed LAB test for Russian speakers. We also have science, social studies, and math tests for them in Russian. For the most part, the _LAB_ testing is effective because we have an experienced ESL teacher who does it. I find it difficult for many of my students to reach the 41st percentile _LAB_ cutoff score in 1 year. For those who do, I unofficially mainstream them, sometimes even before the end of the year. It's because I feel they can handle more English than I can offer. Their _LAB_ scores usually reflect their progress in the English class after about 6 or 7 months. If the administration knew I was doing this, maybe I would get thrown out of the school. As a professional teacher, I see that the child needs more English. I don't mainstream all of them. But sometimes 2 out of the 14 second-graders are ready for English class, so I send them out.

None of my children are given the other standardized tests because they have been here for less than 2 years. This is a New York City policy that exempts them for 2 years. This gives them time to develop their English before being tested. For classroom tests, I train them for tests through all of our mini-tests. I remember being afraid of tests. When they said "test," even at 50 years old, I started to shake. When I say to my children, "Tomorrow is a test," they're happy and they like it.

SUCCESSES WITH CHILDREN

Throughout the school, my former students are doing well, whether they are in English or Russian classes. Walking through the classes, I could ask any of the teachers, "How are they doing?" And they'd answer, "Great!" They are hard-working, organized, disciplined children who do their class-work and homework. They follow the rules.

With all the successes, I still have a couple of children with special needs. It's not because I am a bad or good teacher, but it's in the family. One of my students is disturbed. But for Russian parents, if the child is to be evaluated, it's like he's completely crazy. And they're against any evaluation! So you have to work slowly with them, giving them the idea that the child needs special help. We start with the resource room. I never put a child directly into special education. Sometimes it might be the language barrier or **culture shock**. Who knows?

ORIENTATION OF PARENTS
AND THEIR CHILDREN

We do a lot of work with parents because when they come here straight from Russia, they are lost. The school offers them free weekly **ESL** workshops. In addition, I help the families on my own for the sake of the children. What happens in the home affects my children. When a child comes to school and is nervous, or steals, or cries, I know something is wrong at home. Many parents get divorced because the families have lots of stress and problems here. They start fighting over money and other things. It's a big adjustment for them to get used to the freedom and lack of control over people here. The parents come to my home, where I give them workshops to help them get along with each other. When I see problems, I invite them to discuss their problems. I give them some suggestions about what to do. I show them some family relationship videotapes. As I translate from English, I say, "That says we have to be friendly in the family. We have to respect each other. Look. This was a broken family and now they are together. Do you want to live with your husband or with your wife?" My husband says I shouldn't do this because I'm not a psychiatrist. They don't pay me to do this. I do it out of care and interest for the family and the children. Through the videotapes and our discussions, parents learn how to be friendly and relate better to one another. I have helped to save several marriages.

Many Middle Asian families show aggressive behavior. Those families see the wife as nothing but a mother and a maid. That's all. The man is the boss. He's like a god. It's very difficult to start working with those children because they don't talk. They fight right away because that's what they see at home. One night, I called one student's parents because he was fighting and cursing in class. The father said, "What? He's doing that? Get a stick and hit him." I also teach parents different ways to deal with their children. Little by little, I explain to parents that beating children here is considered child abuse. I tell them they have to talk to the child and punish him by withholding privileges like TV or games. I have had a couple of children who were abused, which I had to report to my principal. One of them is now in a foster home. That's the kind of children I deal with.

I am very involved with the parents. Parents can call me at home anytime because I give them my home telephone number. They call me during the night with any problem or question. Through my efforts and closeness with them, parents respect me. I love and respect them, too. When I ask them to come to a parent conference, they all come. My principal said, "Sofya, My God! What are you doing to them? I said, "Nothing." I just tell the children that their parents must come because it's very important. So out of respect for me and interest in their children, they come.

At our meetings, I've had to explain what the bilingual program is all about because they absolutely disapprove of bilingual education, especially if it's all in Russian. That's why I took an intensive English approach. I tell them to look at the bulletin boards; half of the work is in English and the other half is in Russian. When I show parents the Russian and English work and books, they feel satisfied.

When a child is ready to go to the English class, sometimes the parents want their child to stay with me in my class. Parents say, "No, Mrs. P., keep them in your class." They like our class because it reminds them of Russia. Before the desks were in rows and my principal said, "Sofya, it's not a concentration camp." In Russia, the desks are in rows, children sit up straight, and stand when they speak. To comply with my principal, I changed the rows to two long tables: one for first and the other for second grade. In Russia, a teacher has a different position than here; a teacher is a god. Here, children respect you, but they sometimes talk while you talk.

The parents like the way I organize the children. I never waste 1 minute of teaching time to organize them. I have to start with discipline. The most important thing is to teach them how to behave, to listen, and to concentrate their attention. If they can listen, they can study. Somebody called me "Major," because I'm like a drill sergeant. It's a free country, so, I designed my own method of disciplining and organizing children. I never scream at them. If they get out of control, which sometimes happens, because I am not magic, then I shut off the lights. I yell, "Step 1!" for them to stop what they are doing. Then I yell, "Step 2!" for them to listen to directions. When I call out "Step 3," they can continue what they were doing. Although it probably sounds like gulag, my class has received many awards for following school rules.

In getting to know about the children, I always ask each parent about their family history and background. I ask parents about the child's health, behavior, and academic progress in Russia. I learned that some children behave terribly at home. For example, one mother said when her son misbehaves she tells him, "You behave like this, I will tell Mrs. P." It's like she put a pot of cold water on his head. I listen and together we discuss what's wrong. Because here in America, you have to talk to the parents from the positive side. In Russia I would say, "Look, you do this and that. Otherwise, I will kick your child out of school." Here we don't talk that way to parents. I had to learn this here. I used to tell them, "Your child is no good. He is not behaving!" And that was totally wrong. Because if you tell people that they're bad, they will start acting like that. So you must treat people with respect and they will respond respectfully. They never say, "What are you talking about? I am his father!! And you are just a teacher." Never. They listen, they accept, they do whatever I say. I admire my parents. They are good. We work very, very closely together. If I need them, they are there. One, two, three. And if they need me, anytime, any day, I'm there.

SUPPORT:
PRINCIPAL, DISTRICT, AND COLLEGIAL

Our present principal is a very educated and humane person. She's like a sister to me. She and the district director support our program. Everybody is very, very positive with this program. Among the bilingual colleagues, we are more connected now than before. We discuss and exchange books, papers, pictures, and ideas. We do assemblies together. We work nicely together. Even though we all are in different grades, we share methods. The monolingual colleagues see us as one family. I'm really lucky to be in this school because it's a cooperative place. I'm not just saying that. It's real life.

5

Manouchka

PERSONAL BACKGROUND

My name is Manouchka. When I was 8 years old, the political situation had gotten so bad in Haiti, that it wasn't safe to live there. So, my parents emigrated to New York City leaving my sister and me with our grandparents. Two years later, in 1971, we joined our parents in New York. In Haiti, I had attended Catholic school where all instruction was conducted in French. When I started attending New York City public schools, I was placed in an all-English mainstream classroom. I also received **English as a second language (ESL)** instruction. No Haitian bilingual education services existed then. Actually, the first Haitian bilingual programs used French as the language of instruction, but that started long after I came. Not until the early 1980s did they start using Haitian-Creole in the bilingual programs.

Anyway, I did okay my first couple of years in school because my teacher knew some French. However, in seventh grade, I started having problems because my teachers understood nothing about my language or culture. I was really on my own because my English wasn't that great yet. I was terrified to speak in front of a group because in English class the children laughed and made fun of me. Psychologically I was at a loss. I remember becoming very introverted. Had I had Haitian teachers who spoke my language and knew where I was coming from, I might have felt more comfortable. That's the reason why I became a teacher, because of all the things that happened to me that I didn't like. I want to be in a position to be an advocate for kids who are coming in.

Somehow with the support from my parents who encouraged me, I was able to successfully continue my studies through high school and college, where I majored in special education. After graduating, I first taught monolingual English-speaking elementary students in a private school. Then, because I still couldn't find a public school teaching job, I started working as a paraprofessional with **Limited English Proficiency (LEP)** special education students in the district where I work now. That job gave me a feel for children in the public school setting. For the last 6 years, I have taught in a Haitian-Creole/English bilingual program in this New York City public elementary school. I started as a bilingual teacher without any bilingual education training. While teaching, I completed a master's degree in bilingual education. I'm still not fully state certified because I haven't yet been able to pass the state-required teacher certification exams.

SCHOOL CULTURE AND CONTEXT

Located in Brooklyn, my school has mostly Black students from diverse backgrounds: African Americans and Caribbeans (Haitians, and West Indian English speakers from Jamaica and Trinidad) and a few Latinos from Puerto Rico and the Dominican Republic. The neighborhood is considered low income. In past years the population used to be more White, but it has gradually shifted. Many veteran teachers, who have been at the school for 15 to 20 years, reminisce about how nice the neighborhood was and well-behaved the students used to be.

About 50% of the student population in my school is Haitian. Haitian parents range from being on public assistance to being college students, taxi drivers, nurse's aides, live-in babysitters, and factory workers. Some parents, who were professionals back in Haiti, have lost the opportunity to work in their professions due to the language barrier and because they cannot afford to go to school. Many Haitian parents are economically strapped and work two or three jobs to support their large families.

The K–5 school has almost 1,500 students and occupies three buildings. The school receives **Chapter I** monies for instructional support to children who need help with reading and math. There are approximately five classes per grade with a Haitian-Creole bilingual class (or combination bridge class) on each grade. The **transitional** bilingual program requires that all subjects be taught in the native language with 180 minutes of **ESL** each week. The goal of the program is to **exit** students into the mainstream. Students usually spend about 3 years in the program, until they pass the 41st percentile on the English *Language Assessment Battery* (*LAB*) test. Some parents choose to have their children stay in the program even after passing the minimum cut-off point. Not all newcomer Haitian children are placed in the bilingual program; some go into the mainstream because their parents don't want their children to learn Haitian-Creole. They prefer that their children learn English and/or French. Some parents, who were educated in French, really don't accept the Creole language. Children placed in the mainstream receive ESL **pull-out instruction.** Some children have a difficult time, especially if they have had limited prior schooling in Haiti, which is common of many of our Haitian children.

Our school has had three principals in the past 6 years. The first one knew nothing about bilingual education. He never came into my room to find out about my teaching. The second acting principal was very supportive by sharing articles on Haiti and giving suggestions on how to improve my teaching. However, many veteran teachers didn't like her direct leadership style and goals for improving the school, so they teamed together and forced her to leave the school mid-year. Now we have another acting principal who seems fairly supportive, as he is learning about running the school and the bilingual program. The district bilingual coordinator also has been supportive in providing some materials and positive opportunities for professional development workshops for the Haitian bilingual teachers.

BILINGUAL TEACHING EXPERIENCES

Over my 6 years, the first year, I taught a fourth–fifth bridge class with 28 students. The last 5 years I've been teaching second grade. This year I have 20 Haitian students, many who are new arrivals and others who were born here.

In the fourth–fifth bridge class, some students had been in the program since kindergarten, however, most were new arrivals. Even though they were in the age-appropriate grade level academically, many couldn't do the work because they had never been to school before. Many of these children lived in rural areas too far away to be able to go to school. Often those children's worlds included country experiences of milking cows, growing vegetables, and picking sugar cane. For them, everything in school was new, they were really like first graders. Many of them had no basic skills. Others, new arrivals from cities or those whose parents had the means to send them to school, had stronger academic backgrounds, which helped them keep up with the work. For them it was easier, because whatever they knew they could eventually translate into the second language. I found that the older kids had so many learning problems. Even after being here a few years, some of them still could not read or write very well. I ended up requesting a transfer from that bridge class to the second grade when an opening became available. I wanted to be able to give children a stronger foundation earlier on. Even though I moved down to second grade, many of the children I receive have never gone to school.

Regardless of the grade I teach, I use many similar approaches. Because there are so many levels and background experiences, I group students into at least three reading and math groups to address the diverse needs. Usually I do a general lesson and then I go around to the groups and reinforce what I have taught. For the children who have never been to school, I also must individualize instruction. I have to teach them even the most basic things like how to hold a pencil and slant the paper to write. Some of these children don't know how to behave. They think school is a place to socialize and play. I patiently tell them that school is serious and not a place to "fool around."

Whatever content I teach, I try to simplify and bring it down to the children's ability levels so they can better master it. My goal is to make the abstract concepts concrete. I teach all content areas (reading, math, science, and social studies) in two languages that I try to keep separate. If I'm teaching Creole, it's only Creole. I do the same for English. I don't translate back and forth because children find that confusing. If I notice a child is having some difficulty in English, then individually I'll review the content in the native language.

In teaching reading, a lot of our children need phonics. In Haiti, they aren't taught to read phonetically. There they mostly teach reading without really breaking down the consonant and vowel sounds. In learning the sound system, children get the language much faster. Even for upper grade children, I taught them basic decoding skills until they felt comfortable with reading. I make an effort to incorporate phonics into everything I teach. For example, if I'm teaching the seasons, I tell the children to focus on the beginning letter of the words "spring" and "summer." For all the sounds, I gather objects and pictures, which helps them experience the sounds. Together we generate word lists for a particular letter and sound. We keep reviewing the lists until they know all of them. With our **whole language** literature stories, I always do this kind of phonics mini-lesson to focus their attention on the sounds. Without these decoding skills, kids often have a lot of problems reading. That's why I try to put everything into units and make sure that they get the skills through these mini-lessons.

Since our district wants us to teach literature-based **whole language,** one problem I have is there are no early childhood Haitian-Creole big books available. So, I translate English big books by putting the Haitian words or phrases below the English text. Because of the colorful pictures, these books are especially great for kids who haven't been here very long. They may be just picking up a few English words but don't yet have enough to comprehend the whole story. I've also made other little books or had the kids make their own books in Haitian-Creole, which the children also like.

To develop writing fluency, I encourage children to write journals in the language they feel most comfortable. Some of them will let me read their journals to the class. Others, who may be shy, don't want to share their personal things. I respect that and have a one-to-one conference to go over it with them. It takes time for them to open up and share their writing.

I do a lot of Haitian storytelling, which develops and reinforces the native language and children's cultural identification. In our culture, especially if you grew up in Haiti, the whole family always gathers around together to listen to grandparents and other family members tell stories. Haiti has a rich storytelling tradition that includes lots of folklore, proverbs, and stories to teach morals. To open the storytelling the elder says, "Cric!" to which everyone else responds in African call–response tradition, "Crac!" As I tell a particular story, children excitedly exclaim, "Oh, I remember my grandmother told me that same one!" Sometimes versions of the stories differ across regions, so we explore those differences. I often chart the differences using a **Venn diagram**. I also use those stories for writing topics. For other writing assignments, I ask students to interview family members about life in Haiti. To encourage writing, I use topics that students are familiar with.

Teaching about Haiti in the native language helps students retain their culture. I place a lot of emphasis on social studies, especially current events through collecting and sharing newspaper articles about political things happening in Haiti. I want kids to know and appreciate what's going on down there, since many still have families back home. Many students have had relatives who have died or are very poor back there. So it's important to acknowledge that and discuss what's going on, because it somehow affects them. Last year, a child, whose financial situation was really rough, shared about being hungry back in Haiti. I related his experience to what's happening here with the homeless. That way children don't feel badly and they are able to see that we have those kinds of problems here, too. I want kids to see the connection that learning in school will later on give them a chance to have a good job and better lives.

In the United States, I find some students often want to forget about Haiti because they want so much to assimilate and fit in. With all the problems in Haiti, lots of mainstream kids meanly pick on the Haitian kids, saying, "Oh, you're Haitian. Why don't you go back home?" So our kids sometimes are afraid to let other children know they're Haitian. They feel ashamed and don't even want to speak the language, so people won't know they're from another country. In trying to assimilate, they are really losing their culture. They start to not care about what's happening back in Haiti or Haitian family traditions. That's why the bilingual program is so important. Children learn to appreciate their culture, as they learn English and the American ways.

That's why I try to set up a comfortable tone in the classroom, so students will like themselves and love where they come from. I don't want them to let others intimidate them or make them feel less because they're from another culture or because they speak another language. I want them to know that in this class, we all are special in some way or another and we're here to help each other. We are one big, happy family. I don't want them to feel inadequate or afraid to stand up in front of the class to express themselves.

I have found the more comfortable the environment, the faster a child learns. The more content he can relate to and manipulate, the better he will retain everything. The majority of our kids come from low-income homes where they don't have many resources such as computers, libraries of books, or games to play with. So, I try to provide all those things that help enrich the background experiences they bring. For example, for our human body unit, I wanted students to learn how the organs work and to care for their bodies. The lesson in the textbook was so abstract that I wanted to them to experience the whole thing, by showing them pictures of the organs, having them cut out the body parts and glue them in the proper places like a puzzle. One day I do the lesson in Creole and the next in English so they get the same terminology in both languages.

Covering the curriculum in both languages prepares students for the exams. If they don't know it in both languages, they're going to have a hard time on the English and Creole tests. I don't have time to teach all lessons in the curriculum in two languages. I mainly teach content area subjects where the vocabulary is new. I do this especially for science because the children have an English-speaking science teacher, so I want to make sure they understand what the teacher is talking about.

Children are required to take the standardized _DRP–Degrees of Reading Power_ test (Koslin, Zeno, Koslin, Wainer, & Ivens, 1987) in English after 2 years in the school system. These tests are not fair because a lot of the vocabulary and topics the children are unfamiliar with. Many words are culturally biased. If children don't completely comprehend one little thing, it could really throw them off. I think children need to be in the system for at least 4 or 5 years to build a better foundation before taking these tests. That policy of having children take the test after 2 years needs to be changed or the test should be changed, which I don't think will happen. I also find the _LAB_ (1982) test very hard. These kids need more time to develop in English before being tested. It's not just the Haitian children who have trouble with it; those from other bilingual programs also have a hard time because they haven't been exposed to the English language that long.

CURRICULUM AND MATERIALS

Sometimes it's difficult to teach all the subjects in Haitian-Creole because there are not the necessary materials. We definitely need more and better books. Comparing what we have with what's available in the regular or Spanish bilingual classes, they have tons more materials than we do. Part of the reason there are so few Haitian-Creole materials is because it is a relatively a new language that was standardized in the early 1980s. Only since then have they started making Creole books. Prior to that, all instructional materials were in French. Most of our materials have to be shipped from Haiti, which takes a long time. For example, I could order something in September and it wouldn't arrive until March.

Many of those Haitian books are not up to the same standard as those in English. Many are paperback books on newsprint with no color pictures. When kids see that those books aren't as beautifully illustrated as the English ones, they are given a message that Haitian is less important. The colorful Haitian-Creole books, if you can find them, are really expensive and the district won't buy sets of them for literature studies. You're lucky if you have one book to use with the whole class. In addition, we lack subject area books, like history books, for the early grades. For math, we must use English books because there's no complete series in Haitian that includes a student book, workbook, and teacher's guide. I think we are limited in a lot of ways.

To address this, out of my pocket I buy as many Haitian materials as I can put my hands on. When people visit Haiti, I ask them to buy books and artifacts for my learning centers. I can easily spend at least $25 a month on materials. If a teacher really wants to do much more in her class, the books and materials provided by the district are never enough. I also make a lot of my own charts, books, posters, and activity sheets to augment what's provided. It's extra work for me, but I don't mind because the children benefit from these materials.

I feel that our Haitian curriculum has a lot of holes. Yes, we have some books but it's not a full curriculum. There's a great need for the Haitian professionals to join together to develop curricula and to publish more materials. We need to get the Board of Education and Haitian professors to support us in doing this. And, it's going to take a long time to do this and unfortunately, there is too much disunity among the Haitian people because each one wants to get on top first. No one is willing to make the sacrifice. They want to be making money right away, and if not, forget it. So, it's a very slow process. In the meantime, I'll still keep collecting whatever I can. Over the years, I have amassed quite a lot, which makes it easier for me to teach than for a new teacher. Whenever colleagues ask me, I am more than willing to share what I have.

COLLEGIAL INTERACTIONS

Some of my bilingual colleagues are like me: they put all their effort into creating a supportive learning environment for kids. Unfortunately, not all bilingual teachers make the extra effort to provide that kind of environment. Using whatever is given to them, they don't want to go out of their way to buy and make materials or bring in other things. They feel, "Hey, that's not my problem." I think that if every teacher would put in the extra effort, the kids would have fewer problems, because they would have greater consistency across the grades.

In addition to having bilingual colleagues who only want to do the minimum, other colleagues and parents believe that Creole should not be used as the language of instruction. Many of them never learned to read in Creole. They want to put down the Creole language because in Haiti, it was put down for a long time. The Europeans enslaved us and forced us to use the French language. The elite in Haiti still feel that way. So, we have all these internal conflicts that prevent us from productively working together as a group.

I wish we (Haitian teachers) could work better as a team. For example, I suggested to the assistant principal that we have a meeting to develop some strategies and procedures for working with the children who come in with limited schooling. I figured, "We're all here for the kids and we need to work together on this." No one showed up because they don't want to have that kind of meeting in front of the administration. They fear they will be criticized for not knowing their stuff. I said, "You don't know everything. We need to learn from each other."

Many monolingual teachers don't understand the goal of our bilingual program either. They feel that bilingual is like special education and assume our children are slow. They don't realize how long it takes children to learn a new language. Those teachers think kids should be placed in ESL. They say, "Manouchka, you didn't have bilingual instruction and you made it. They'll survive the same way you did." But, they don't know the psychological impact on a child, of how it feels to leave your country, when you know no one, when you cannot speak the language, or when no one understands you or has any notion of where you come from. I constantly tell them, "You don't know what you are saying. For kids not to fail later on, they need the bilingual program, because it brings up their self-esteem." They don't seem to understand the effects on a child when he's learning in an environment where people are putting him down and laughing at him. For those teachers who feel that bilingualism is not important, no matter what you do or say, they'll try to knock it down. It's a constant battle and sometimes I feel there's nothing that I can do about it.

The fact that this is mostly a Black school, you can feel the resentment from some of the White teachers in the way they act and treat our children. They resent our Haitian students because they bring down the school's *DRP* (reading; Koslin et al., 1987) test scores. All New York City schools' *DRP*'s scores are ranked. Those teachers say, "It's going to make us look bad, and not show how hard we're trying with our kids." Sometimes they express their negative attitudes toward our Haitian children by yelling nasty things to them. I get angry when they do this, but I won't yell back at them. I use a tone of voice to show them I don't like what they said. I don't like that they portray my children as less than human. A few of kids may have behavior problems, but they shouldn't be treated like that.

Not all monolingual teachers are like that. Others are for bilingual education and recognize that the program is really working. They notice progress the kids have made over the school year, saying, "Wow, what a difference!" Those teachers have asked me for suggestions about how to deal with quiet Haitian children who are placed in their classes. I tell them to do a unit or class project that involves the Haitian culture or to read to the class stories about Haiti. I happily share materials with them if I can. These kinds of activities help the Haitian children's self-esteem and enable the other children to better relate to and understand their Haitian peers. One fourth-grade teacher was concerned about a particular Haitian girl, who was doing fine academically but was very withdrawn. So, she sends the girl to help out in my room for one period a day. The girl reads to my kids, plays games, works with them individually, or translates for newcomers. Coming here makes her feel good about herself because often her classmates pick on her. Also since her parents work late, she doesn't get much adult attention at home. So, I praise her and give her lots of attention. She looks forward to coming to my room. In fact, she often prefers to stay with me when her class goes on trips. I welcome her anytime. So, we have all types of collegial interactions. Some are very positive and others need lots of work.

PARENT INVOLVEMENT

No Haitian parents are involved in the PTA because there is no one to translate. This is a shame because 50% of our population is Haitian. We

need translators to help them in filling out forms and applications. Occasionally, I'm called to the office to translate, but sometimes I can't because
I'm just too busy. I always welcome parents to come in to talk to me
whenever they can.

I've had to talk to parents about bilingualism because they don't fully
understand it. They think the bilingual program is like a special education
program. Many parents don't want their children in bilingual. To them I
explain, if a child is in an English-only class, the child may have problems
understanding and will have to wait until they go home for you explain it
to them. In the bilingual class, however, we can more easily communicate
with the children and parents. Once they see the results of the program,
they usually understand it better and begin to like what we are doing.

I find lots of kids' parents aren't really "on top" of things. Some of these
hard-working parents hold three jobs. The kids are being raised by a
babysitter or by grandparents. And I have several who are "latchkey"
children with keys around their necks. They are home alone waiting until
Mommy comes home. In those cases, nobody's there to attend to them or
go over their homework. I've had children come in for a whole week with
no homework. I try to help those kids with their homework in class. Some
parents didn't even finish school themselves. So, they figure that since they
made it without school, they don't see the importance of their children going
to school. Lots of times they keep their children home to take care of younger
siblings. Those parents sometimes stand in the way of developing their
children's potential because they need them to help out.

Many parents think they are unable to help their children because of the
language barrier. I tell them ways they can help even if they don't understand
English. Not all of them take time to sit down to talk about what their child
learned each day. Haitian parents tend to put a lot of responsibility on us
teachers. I tell parents that I give children as much as I can from 8:20 to
3:00, but at home they have to do their best also. If children go home to sit
in front of the television, they're not learning much. Parents need to at least
read to their children in the native language, which helps children to
become better readers by having positive interactions with parents.

I have problems getting parents to come in for conferences because some
of them work crazy hours. Out of 20 students, I'll be lucky if 12 show up. If
they can't come in, I do my best to keep them informed about their child's
progress and what's going on in school. I call them and they are free to call
me at home, too. Sometimes I regret giving them my phone number, because
they call me late at night. I find for the parents with major problems, their
kids often have tough problems, too.

In addition to helping parents work with their children, I've also helped parents learn better ways to discipline their kids. I talk to them about child abuse. Other cultures handle things differently than here. Haitian parents tend to hit the kids when the kids don't listen. I encourage parents to talk and listen to their children, instead of striking them when they do something bad. So, that's been very important.

6

Diana

BACKGROUND AND
BEGINNING TEACHING EXPERIENCES

I am Diana. Diana is the English name that my father chose for me before I came to the United States. In 1968, I came from Hong Kong when I was 16½ years old to a small city in North Dakota. Why North Dakota of all places? I had wanted to be a librarian and North Dakota was the only college that offered me a scholarship to study librarianship. After three semesters, I didn't like that program. I was panicking about what to do when I graduated. It was just one of those "eeny-meeny-miny-mo" situations. I looked at the courses and education ended up as my choice, purely by accident. I didn't really go into teaching with some long-term inspiration to be a teacher. No. What helped me decide was that, professionally and culturally, teaching is sort of respectable. So, that's how I ended up teaching.

Coming as a foreign student definitely was not the same as that of an immigrant. People would treat you a bit differently. Although I met many very nice, courteous people, I still experienced subtle discrimination. How should I say it? When I worked in the cafeteria, for instance, they didn't say things to your face, but I always ended up being assigned to jobs behind the scenes like washing dishes and making salads, yet others (nonminorities) were assigned to the serving line. At such a young age, I was too ignorant and naive to know those things. Looking back, I asked to be in the front and they'd say, "No, you can't be here." At least I was able to find a job that allowed me to survive and support myself with my scholarship.

Being from Hong Kong, a British colony, I had already learned enough English to get by academically. But social-wise, I just didn't know what to say to people. I didn't even know the commonest things they were talking about, like football, sports, TV shows, hay rides, and Halloween parties. It was a very enriching experience just absorbing the American culture. Absorbing.

I finished college in 3½ years. Then I moved to Northern California to join my future husband, where I've been ever since. I've been in the education field for 19 years: 14 years teaching and 5 years working at a regional **Multifunctional Resource Center** creating bilingual materials and doing professional development training.

I have only taught at the early childhood level because of the devastating advice given to me by my undergraduate master teacher, who recommended that I not teach the upper grades because of my language ability and cultural background. Somehow, I lived that vicious cycle believing that I was not capable to teach that level. I think as a second language learner, my English language ability will never be as proficient as my first language. Sometimes when I'm nervous I make grammatical mistakes. Also because of my accent, I almost didn't get my teaching certificate. Culturally, back home, Chinese teachers are highly respected, so I expected and demanded that same kind of respect from kids. And my master teacher told me, "In this country, respect is earned from hard work." My cultural belief that students should listen to and respect the teacher just because she is the teacher, she saw as a hindrance. Because of these differences, she thought I would have a difficult time working with older children. She felt I would not be able to control them. This scared the heck out of me. For many years, I did not dare teach beyond third grade. Now I might like to try.

I have changed that cultural belief, which I think was wrong. Children should not just accept that whatever a teacher says is right. And I think she saw that weakness of mine. Even though it hurt, she was truthful. Being from the Midwest, she didn't have a lot of cross-cultural experience. And out of her own ignorance, she put limitations on me that really weren't fair. Nevertheless, she was a wonderful teacher from whom I learned so much about teaching, dedication, and commitment. She was at school until 7 p.m. and on weekends. She used hands-on stuff, like learning centers with animals like a boa constrictor. In the 1970s, she was way ahead of her time. I shaped my practice from her example.

I first started substituting here in Northern California because I couldn't find a job. It was terrible. And then one day, I ended up in a Chinese community child-care center that had no Chinese-speaking teacher. To them I was a miracle. Suddenly I was the prize. That's how I became a bilingual teacher, because I happened to speak Chinese. The kids were mainly Chinese-speakers and teachers were English-speakers. They used Chinese-speaking instructional assistants to communicate with the children and parents. So, I was the first credentialed teacher who could speak and read their language. I taught there for 6 years before I moved to the elementary level.

When I started bilingual teaching, I had no bilingual credential, just an elementary education credential, nor had I had any bilingual teacher training. I just passed the **Bilingual Certificate of Competence (BCC)** test. What a joke was that test! I had to write an essay about the Miss Chinatown Pageant. What does that have to do with teaching? I had to do a "demo" lesson in Chinese. The third thing was a multiple-choice test on Chinese-American history. That's about it. I have taken some master's coursework but never finished my degree. Shame on me. I was working on it. I was close, but, after I had my kids, I stopped.

If I had received bilingual training, I would have liked to know how you handle two languages and about timing in introducing the two languages. What do you do when you have English speakers and you are by yourself? How can you be effective in serving one language group without doing a disservice to the other group? How do you make sure that our minority kids do not receive a "watered-down" education? How can we enrich all children's experiences? I would like to know those strategies. So far nobody has been able to give me the answers.

SCHOOL COMMUNITY:
DIVERSE AND CHANGING

I have taught first grade at this school for the past 5 years. The school, located in a densely populated Chinatown, has 740 students consisting of 82% Asian (65% Cantonese, 16% Vietnamese, and 1% Filipino), 12% African American, 3% Latino, and 3% Caucasian. Of the students, 71% are **LEP,** primarily Cantonese and Vietnamese speakers. Eighty-eight percent receive free or reduced meals. Eighteen percent qualify for Aid to Families with Dependent Children. The district in this urban city has approximately 14,000 **language minority** students. For many years, the district has been out of compliance in its services to **LEP** students.

We used to have a lot of immigrant families from Canton Province. Lately, more families from mainland China and Taiwan are coming, bringing speakers of different dialects: Mandarin, Cantonese, Hakka, Choudou, and Say Yup. I've had ethnic Chinese from Vietnam. It's much more diverse than before. And some children have had no schooling at all when they come to me. The families have been here from 3 months to 7 years. And some of the children were born here.

The immigrant families usually have had a big change in socioeconomic status. In China, some fathers were doctors, maybe foot doctors. Now, most of them work long hours in restaurants, as busboys or cooks, or in grocery stores, as cashiers, bakers, or meat cutters. Many mothers are housewives. That's the range. Most of them have lost their former status. Most are fairly well-educated, although I have had a few who were illiterate. I once asked a mother, "Oh, didn't you read my note?" She replied, "I can't read." I was so embarrassed! I never would dare ask that question again. Now I say, "I sent a note home. Did you RECEIVE it?" instead of, "Did you READ it?" This year, I think most of my parents can read at least in Chinese, but definitely not in English too well.

The family structure has changed in that both parents are working. You'll see lots of grandmothers helping to care for the young children. Recently many more single mothers are raising children on their own, too. From recent mainland Chinese immigrants, there are a lot of only children, a result of strict Chinese birth control policies. I find these only children to be more spoiled because they lack socialization skills from not being raised with siblings.

Asian parents definitely want their children to learn English so they can go to college, succeed, and get a good job. You still have those old country and culture values. They want their children to listen to them, to be respectful and obedient, and not to get into trouble.

THE BILINGUAL PROGRAM: PROMOTING MONOLINGUALISM OR BILINGUALISM?

The Chinese bilingual program has two to three classes at the lower grade levels and one class each at the upper grades. Of the 25 teachers, 14 are bilingual and most of the others have **sheltered English** classes. Those teachers usually have their **Language Development Specialist (LDS)** credential. The **sheltered** classes are for upper grade students whose parents do not opt for them to be in bilingual and/or for children who speak languages other than Cantonese (e.g., Vietnamese and Cambodian). We also have a couple of English Only (EO) teachers who do not have their **LDS** credential.

Our bilingual program really isn't Bilingual/Bicultural. That would be a lie. It's **transitional** and bilingual in name only. Mine is called a bilingual class, but am I really maintaining two languages? No, there's no accountability to ensure that the native language gets taught. It's very lax. I honestly think the main goal is to help mainstream children so that they can learn and be fluent in English. The parents want it that way. No one ever questions me if I don't do Chinese. Though parents sign the papers to place their children in the bilingual program, they really don't understand what the bilingual program is.

Our program doesn't promote cultural or linguistic **maintenance** in any way. Lots of times, I notice many American-born Chinese kids grow up and lose their identity even though parents send them to Chinese schools and insist that they speak Chinese. Even though they're Chinese, they just want to be White and in the mainstream. They feel that as long as they speak good English, they will succeed. Somehow they don't identify themselves with or want to serve the community. They don't fight for anything in our community. And they eventually move away from the community. So, it's a real loss.

It's the fault of the school, the system, and society. Because if, in school and society, children do not see role models showing the importance and pride for their heritage, history, or language, then, of course, they get the message that their language and backgrounds are of lesser value. Language and cultural maintenance is not reinforced too well by the Chinese language schools that most children attend. Actually they feel punished by having to go to school in the afternoons and Saturdays when everybody else is out playing. Also children don't enjoy the traditional methods of drill, rote memory, and copying. And sometimes there's even corporal punishment. Parents place their kids in the Chinese school mainly for free babysitting. Some of the schools are sponsored by the Kuomingtan (KMT), a Taiwanese nationalist political party that drills kids that Communism is bad. Parents view the two schools separately. Chinese school is Chinese school; regular school is regular school. They don't see the importance of their language and culture being addressed in the larger society, instead of somewhere on the side.

Children in the bilingual program feel stigmatized. They are there because their English is not good, not because they can speak two languages. They don't see bilingualism as a gift or that they are smarter if they speak two languages. There's a double standard for certain groups. Bilingualism is valued if you speak French or a Romance language, but speaking Chinese is not valued by this society. So, kids don't feel proud of speaking Chinese. I notice fifth and sixth graders don't want their parents to come to school because they are embarrassed that their parents speak Chinese. It's just very sad. In the primary grades, they're still not very conscious of this. They will speak Chinese and laugh about it. But later on, I notice former students speak less and less. When I speak Chinese to them, they reply in English.

As they use it less, then they become less able to express themselves. They're losing it.

Another reason parents enroll their kids in bilingual classes is because they want their children to be with others of the same race. The parents' attitude is that they don't want their kids with Blacks. I'm not making excuses for them. Some of them are afraid because they have been burglarized and victimized, and they bring those fears to their kids.

MANAGING DUAL LANGUAGE INSTRUCTION

Less Native Language Than Before

In the beginning, I tried to teach more native language, but after a while I said, "I give up." Now I devote very limited time to the native language as compared to before. I mainly give directions, do songs, finger plays, chants, storytelling, and discussion time. That's about it. I'm not really teaching new words or writing. I don't do formal native language lessons anymore like I used to in 1985 for the first years. I was very happy doing my Chinese lessons. And then I would do my other lessons bilingually with translations, which I know is not the best way. That was how I could handle it because I also had English speakers, too. I felt badly for those children because when I taught Chinese, they'd just be sitting there. I struggled and I just couldn't do it. I was facing discipline problems with them. I could not teach them Chinese as a second language because I barely had time to teach the native language to primary language speakers. I felt badly about those English speakers, who were also minority students, mainly Black, Afro-American kids. So that was a "toughy." Then, I was doing about 30% Chinese and 70% English. Now, I probably do 10% to 15% Chinese instruction and the rest in English.

I realize I am falling into a pattern. We need to inform and mobilize the parents to support us in changing what is going on. This is wrong. I have no energy to get them together. Actually my colleagues have gone through the same feelings like me. And finally they say, "We are sinking here, doing everything by ourselves." I can't teach all that is expected, so, of course, Chinese gets pushed away.

I feel badly because I'm not going out of my way anymore to teach the native language. But why should I? There is no structure, no accountability, no **standardized** or **performance-based tests** to measure the native language. Now, there's so much to teach, so many grade-level expectations.

And when the children go to third grade, many can't read Chinese yet. I can't really teach Chinese reading, because I don't have that many books. The ones we do have are old or poorly translated. I haven't seen the quality of Chinese materials improve, as compared to other languages. Most Chinese literature we have are folktales. Materials rarely address the Chinese-American experiences that our immigrant children can relate to.

FIRST AND SECOND LANGUAGE INSTRUCTIONAL STRATEGIES

Approaches to Oral Language

It's not so easy to teach Chinese, because some children come from other regions and speak different dialects. I speak Cantonese, and Mandarin is my second dialect. Luckily, those people who speak Choudou can understand my Cantonese. The medium of instruction I use is primarily Cantonese. For example, for Tiffany, who doesn't speak Cantonese, afterwards I'll go quietly over to her and explain the content in Mandarin. Once in a while, I will **code switch** between the two dialects. For kids who speak other dialects, I often have a hard time understanding them. Sometimes, I can guess what they are saying. They usually are able to follow along either by looking at the pictures or watching and copying their classmates. It's not really a problem for them. If they are having a problem, I take them aside and give them a little extra help.

For **ESL**, I also use **Total Physical Response (TPR)**, which I find less boring and more fun for them and me. It's not just "Repeat after me. This is a chair. This a . . ." This method enables them to be more creative with speaking. Because I don't know what their response might be, they do not just give me the words I want. Using their words gives them a sense of ownership.

What I try to do is to make kids feel comfortable to speak Chinese whenever they want. They can address me or their peers in Chinese anytime. It's open and free. That part I have not changed. I try to be responsive to the teachable moments to whatever comes up. For example, today, I spontaneously decided to do a math lesson when I was cutting our Rice Krispie treat into squares. I had them predict the number of cuts that were needed to divide it to have enough for everyone. Basically, I was showing them how multiplication and division fits into their daily lives.

I try to get my Chinese students to speak up confidently when they share with the group. I find that most Chinese kids are good students who are able to write nonstop, but they don't say anything. I hate to generalize that way. For many teachers, they are 'model students,' who never cause discipline problems. I don't want to teach kids just to be good writers. In this country, they have to be able to communicate and verbally share their thoughts. Public speaking will be a useful skill in the future. To motivate them to do this, I have them bring things from home to talk about and have their peers ask questions.

Other classes have been successful with this kind of activity, but this class, I don't know why, just gets up and doesn't say much. It's so funny. They say the same things like, "Where did you get it?" or "How much did it cost?" I even modelled it saying, "This weekend, I went to the beach and got these shells. Does anyone have questions about them?" Even though I did that, they still didn't say much. I need to write a letter to the parents explaining the activity and have them practice at home. It hasn't been going well the last few days. It was a flop! Even after 19 years, I'm still experimenting.

Approaches to Reading and Writing

I've never been able to teach much Chinese writing. Sometimes the parents do writing with them on their homework. I tell them, "Have mommy and daddy write Chinese for you." Some of them can write because they learn it in Chinese school. Unfortunately, I don't have time or training to help them learn it. For example, just because you can drive doesn't mean you can fix a car. Just because I can speak Chinese doesn't mean I can teach it. So that's the sad part. I have the bilingual teaching certificate, but I really didn't have much training in native language teaching. I've never formally learned how to teach Chinese reading or writing. I only remember how I was taught and base my method on how I learned to read and write. The teacher read a word or sentence, then we would just repeat and copy it. Because the Chinese language is not phonetic, copying seems to be the way to learn it. That is the only way I know how to teach it. I write a sentence and have the child copy it. I also have applied comprehension strategies that I learned about teaching English reading to Chinese reading. I get children to talk about what they see in the pictures and tell what happened. Those comprehension and prediction skills are transferable from one language to another regardless of the alphabet system that the language uses.

For English language development, basically I use a **whole language** approach through visuals, patterning, and repetitive language. And I find this most effective for my limited English speakers and even for monolingual

English speakers. Especially for young children, it develops their writing skills and helps them generate ideas and vocabulary.

I also use **inventive spelling,** which is a temporary spelling system until the kids learn how to spell words. Before, I used to spell words for them that they couldn't spell correctly. This made them really dependent on me and afraid to try to spell words themselves. Each week, I'd dictate 10 spelling words and then test them. That has changed. Now, I just give them the words and we talk about the letters that make up the words. The next day, we will do some more words and review them. On Fridays, I test them in a relaxed way to find out how well they can put the letters together. They no longer write each spelling word 10 times for homework. I encourage them to invent words when they write in their journals.

Before, in their journals, they used to write the same sentences everyday, such as, "I have a cat. I have a dog." But now with inventive spelling, they can give the first letter or whatever. When spelling is not as important, this frees them to write much more. The focus is to get their ideas and to know what they are thinking. I try to integrate all the skills: reading, writing, drawing, and speaking. After they read a story, they draw their favorite part. I also have them re-tell the story using their pictures, which gives them a feeling of ownership because it's their pictures and their writing. And I find those strategies very helpful to encourage **LEP** kids to write. Even if they cannot write, they can draw and tell you about their pictures.

In the last few years, I started using heterogeneous grouping for reading. I used to teach the high group in the afternoon and the low group in the morning. After going through some **literature study circles** workshops, I realized that kind of homogeneous grouping traps kids. Some kids will always stay on the bottom, which is really bad for their self-esteem. When my class was videotaped, I saw that mixed groups of non-English speakers and English speakers could still participate in their own ways by just listening. The **LEP** kids were very stimulated by the interaction and seemed to absorb a lot as they listened to all the English role models. The Chinese- and English-speakers somehow find their own ways of talking. With heterogenous groups, kids translate for and learn from each other. In forming the groups, I take into consideration personality, chemistry, gender, and maturity. I try not to put all my "hyper" ones together. The first 2 weeks of school, I don't even waste time, like some teachers do, testing them to find out their skills. I just randomly group them and then regroup them as I get to know them better.

I don't use **basal** readers very much anymore because the stories are boring. They don't have all that good stuff that trade books have: no rich content, plot, illustrations, or art work. If given a choice, kids will never pick up those readers. They'll always select the beautifully illustrated fun books with a plot. I do send the basal readers home, so that the kids have something to read, because often they don't have many books. I just pick and choose some of the better stories from those readers.

Learning about **literature study circles** has greatly influenced the way I teach reading. To start, you need to have sets of trade books. I have been lucky to get lots of books for participating in projects and from writing grants to buy them. Otherwise, I might have no choice but to use the basals. Before getting my sets of _The Giving Tree_ (Silverstein, 1964), I went to five different libraries just to get five sets. It's tiring going to the library to check out sets of books. After a while, you don't feel like doing that again. Because materials, funding, and resources are scarce, a teacher may have no choice but to use the basals. I was just lucky and worked hard to get books.

My greatest success is seeing children enjoy literature and reading. Even though they might not know all the words, they aren't intimidated by reading. Through our small group work in **literature study circles,** they talk about what they like (see sample questions in Appendix C). I no longer ask them to read aloud in turns anymore, like before. To check their reading, I use other informal assessments by listening to the questions they ask and watching what they do. I notice them very involved in the reading corner as they help one another figure out words. They aren't afraid to pick up a book even though they don't know what it says; they just follow the story by looking at the pictures, figuring it out, and enjoying it.

In addition to literature, we do phonics 15 minutes a day, which gives them tools to spell and write. I use the McCracken way, showing them how to put letters together. It works and they like it.

Instruction in the Content Areas and Culture

For content areas, I try to make everything concrete and hands-on. I preview the concept first in Chinese and then I'll teach the lesson in English. In our "Water is Wet" unit, I asked them in Chinese, "What do you use water for?" Then I wrote down their words on a chart. We went over it in English a second time. Even if they don't have the language, they can still experience it and draw pictures. Maybe because it's primary grade, many children don't yet have the language. I find that drawing is the best way for them to express themselves. I teach them to draw through Monart method (Brookes, 1986), which I learned from a training class. Drawing is broken down into steps. We practice drawing things using shapes, straight lines, angles, dots, and circles. Once they learn to draw by this process, they just love it. Many students have become quite good artists.

For math, our school insists we use these stupid books that are not designed for second-language learners. Each skill is presented in two pages, then the book skips around from skill to skill, which doesn't give children enough time to learn and practice a particular skill. Children can't learn subtraction in two pages. No! I prefer to use hands-on programs and kits that have manipulatives like _Connections_ (Charles & Brummet, 1989), _Math Excursions_ (Burk, Snider, & Symonds, 1992), and _Math Their Way_ (Baratta-Lorton, 1976).

I teach culture mainly through stories, myths, and lots of Chinese storytelling. We also talk about and celebrate the different holidays: Chinese New Year, the Moon, Dragon, and Winter Festivals.

ASSESSMENT

Using the _CTBS_ (_Comprehensive Test of Basic Skills_, CTB/McGraw Hill, 1989) **standardized test** isn't fair at all because it's not geared for minority students or **LEP** students. Besides, I don't believe that first graders should be tested with **standardized tests.** It's just too early and traumatic: the format is awful; the content is so beyond and above; and the words and names are unfamiliar. Somehow the questions and purposes seem geared more to trick the kids rather than to really assess them. So I always look at their papers and don't pay attention to the test scores. But unfortunately, everybody else does. Test scores are used for referrals. Because kids have to take these tests, that's why I train my kids in how to take those tests. I make up mock tests, so they learn to fill in the bubbles. Bit by bit, I expose them to the format because I don't want them to panic during the test. I still have to follow the system, even though I don't like it.

For language assessment, I think the primary language scores are fairly accurate, because the people who administer those tests speak the language. I am quite pleased with that. For English language assessment, the _Bilingual Syntax Measure_ or _BSM_ (Burt, Dulay, & Chávez, 1978) is used. The scores don't really show fluency until almost fourth or fifth grades.

A better way of testing is through **portfolios.** I also think we need to do away with report cards, which I hate. **LEP** students seem to get all "Ns" (needs improvement) for the content areas and "Gs" (good) for effort. It's so stupid! And I would like to have more space to comment on what the child is doing, because as a mom, I always looked at the comments. As a parent, I would want to know exactly what my child has been doing, the strengths and weaknesses. I'd like to know what I can do to help them. I would like to see that kind of assessment. Right now, the only time I can communicate about a child's progress is during parent conferences. I think that kind of assessment would be more productive than grades.

PARENTAL INVOLVEMENT

I communicate often with parents about what is going on in class through conferences, phone calls, and by sending notes and information home. Whenever I find useful articles, I have them translated and send them home. The articles give parents suggestions on what to do at home with their children (e.g., dinnertime discussion topics, places to take their kids, lists of books to check out from the library, how to help with homework, how to develop good reading habits, and how to get children to take on more responsibilities.) A lot of times, I have to teach parents how to teach their kids.

Generally, Chinese parents are supportive but in a passive way. I encourage parents to come in and help us in class. Some are comfortable coming on field trips or helping with cooking projects, collating papers, or preparing materials for art projects. However, they are not comfortable sharing more substantial topics such as their immigration experiences or careers. I'm not sure if it's related to their socioeconomic status or that they don't have the skills or feel that what they have to say is not important. They have the Chinese concept that only the teacher knows what to do. They still separate home education from what goes on at school.

They forget that education starts at home. They respect us so much that they don't ever question or challenge what the teacher does, which is sad. I just wish that they would get more involved with their children. When I talk to them during parent conferences, I get the impression that they don't know how to help, nor do they know the resources that they can use. Some are just tired and don't want to deal with it, saying, "You teach my kids to be good and to read. I can't do all that!" I need to communicate more with them about how valuable their experience is to their children and in our class. They need to take on more initiative.

COLLEGIAL SUPPORT

I find that "birds of a feather flock together." I get support from those teachers who share similar ideas and commitment as me. They are the people I can cry to when I have a bad day. I try to stay away from those teachers who don't like or understand what I do. They maintain their distance from me, too. They might feel intimidated or threatened by my willingness to always try new things. Some of them have been teaching 25 years and still use the basals. With them I don't share what I do or my excitement about what my kids are doing. I shy away from them and don't reveal my thoughts.

In terms of a real bilingual program, very few teachers really believe in maintaining the native language. I hate to say it, but many teachers have gotten their job because of the need for Chinese speakers and affirmative action, not because they are qualified or trained in bilingual education. This makes having a consistent and quality program difficult. Some don't teach any Chinese or let children speak it at all. To them, being a bilingual teacher is just a job. And they do not improve themselves by taking courses. Their hearts are not into bilingual education. We, committed bilingual teachers, have gotten tired of fighting to maintain the native language, so we just do our best in our classrooms. To regain some collegial spirit, I would like the administration to give more team teaching planning time for those of us who want to work together.

With the monolingual colleagues, in the beginning there was a lot of resentment about the program, because many veteran teachers were displaced. And sometimes that resentment is expressed both towards us and our children. I feel what all teachers need is to be sensitive to children. Whatever language children speak, accept them and love them the way they are. Kids will blossom. If a teacher who speaks their language is mean and not loving, it's better not to have that teacher. I think the quality of a teacher is more important than the language a teacher speaks.

ADMINISTRATIVE SUPPORT

One thing that has been quite helpful is the support I've gotten to attend professional development workshops. This year we only got $100, but before, anyone who signed up could go. One year, I spent $1,000 attending different workshops, which was wonderful. They never said, "You're taking too many classes." And in an indirect way, when the principal leaves you alone and is not always looking over your shoulder, that's support. They trust you to do your job. And my former administrator used to come in, show an interest in what I was doing, be very encouraging, and give me materials. Fortunately, I had that experience of having a supportive administrator.

Now our present principal is not like that. We need stronger leadership. He leaves us to do our own thing, which can be good. But, at the same time, we need to have consistency among teachers. I guess in any school there will be different teaching styles. Some people will always do the same old thing. I think the leader needs to move us along, keep us up-to-date with new things. When the administration leaves us on our own conscience to take the initiative, some people won't do it. What really bothers me is that there's no guarantee that what I have done with my kids will be carried on by the teacher next year. When I get my kids, I often have to start from scratch teaching them about **cooperative learning** or **literature study circles**. Some children have never even touched a book because teachers won't let them, because they think they'll get the books dirty. That vision and consistency needs to come from the leaders, so that kids don't go crazy and get confused with the different teaching styles. It's the administrator's job to lead us and move us into the best kind of teaching practices and environment.

Our present administrator is not too supportive of the bilingual program either. He just follows whatever the district policy is, which is none. He sees his position as a job. That's all. I have not seen vision, leadership, or even an interest in finding out about what I am doing. For example, one time when I was talking about **literature study circles** and he said, "Oh, I am not familiar with that." Never has he bothered to come to see what it is. Whereas, my other principal came in and showed an interest in what I was doing.

Most principals I've had were mainly hands-off and didn't care what I was doing. My first years when I was struggling to learn what to do, I was so glad he never came into my room to find out how bad it was. A hands-off approach can be a kind of support which lets you find your way and recover. But then there are times that you want someone who cares about what you are doing, who shares your vision, and challenges you. Not in a way of finding fault, but of support. Now more and more, I hope for "hands-on" support, not "hands-off." I want a more coordinated school effort. It will not come from the present administration.

7

Heather

SCHOOLING EXPERIENCES, IMMIGRATION, AND ENTRY INTO THE PROFESSION

I was born in Saigon, Vietnam. I went to Catholic schools where French-speaking nuns taught us everything in French. It was more like an **immersion program,** rather than a bilingual one. By high school, we took two foreign languages: Vietnamese and English. Basically, I know four languages: Vietnamese from home, French from school, Japanese from college, and English from here.

When I finished high school, my parents sent me abroad. If they can afford it, Vietnamese middle-class families usually send their kids to a foreign country for university studies. I had planned to study in Switzerland but couldn't, because the war started getting really bad. In 1974, I ended up going to Kyoto, Japan, where I spent the first year learning Japanese. For the next 4 years, I majored in gifted and talented education and minored in music. After that, I taught the Vietnamese language for a year at a Japanese university.

In 1975, when the Communists took over South Vietnam, my parents moved to Omaha, Nebraska. My dad, who was a doctor in Vietnam, was given a scholarship to study for his medical degree in the United States. In return, he had to work in Omaha as a doctor for 2 years. My mom, who had been a high school teacher in Vietnam, started working at the district office as a Vietnamese community liaison and interpreter. When my father began working, my mom went back to school for her teaching credential.

In 1980, my parents sponsored me to come to Nebraska. When I arrived, I was given an emergency credential to teach at my mom's school, where they were really desperate for bilingual teachers to work with the Vietnamese community. Because of the great needs, my mother and I became bilingual teachers without knowing what bilingual education was. No bilingual teacher training programs were available yet. The administration told me, "Here are the non-English-speaking kids, go ahead and teach them." I never thought I'd become a bilingual teacher.

During the day I taught and at night I studied at a local university to get my credential in Elementary Education. I mostly took American history courses, because I had only studied Japanese history. It really wasn't that much I had to do.

The school had no bilingual program; rather, it used what is now know as a **Newcomer Model**. Our Newcomer Center had about 50 K–6 students all together in a big classroom with two teachers and two teaching assistants. I taught all the Vietnamese kids and the other English-speaking teacher and assistants worked with the children from other language groups. We kept the students all day until they had enough survival English to be mainstreamed into regular classrooms. Children were grouped together, not by age, but by ability level. For example, a non-English-speaking kindergartner would be in a group with a non-English-speaking sixth grader. Because there were no materials, we used regular materials, which I translated into Vietnamese.

As children gained English fluency, they were mainstreamed to the regular classes for about 25% of the time for subjects that didn't require much English, such as PE, art, and music. Gradually, we increased the time as students could handle more. Unfortunately, the mainstream teachers had little knowledge of what to do with these students, so they didn't really want to take them. They expected our kids to fit right in with their classes. Basically, our kids had achieved survival and conversational skills and could not yet handle the grade-level content demands.

I taught at that school for 4 years. During that time I married a Vietnamese man I had met in Japan. In 1985, our family moved to California, south of San Francisco, where we were attracted by the warm weather. I had wanted to take a year off to stay home with my two young daughters. By word of mouth, a local bilingual coordinator found out about me and offered me an emergency credential with a waiver to teach in a new Vietnamese bilingual program. For 7 years, I've been teaching Vietnamese bilingual first grade in this school.

Again, I had to go school to get my California bilingual/bicultural credential and **English as a second language (ESL)** endorsement. I didn't learn much in those courses because the bilingual education philosophy was very general. The course content was completely different from what goes on in the field. Also, much of the information and materials were designed for teaching in Spanish and didn't really apply too well to teaching Vietnamese students. We did have a Vietnamese professor who taught some useful bilingual courses where we made a lot of materials and did field observations. I also had to take the California Basic Educational Skills Test (C-BEST) and the National Teacher Examination (NTE) to qualify for the credential.

VIETNAMESE IMMIGRATION HISTORY: ITS EFFECTS ON CHILDREN

In 1975 when the Communists took over South Vietnam, millions of Vietnamese fled, many to the United States. The first wave were well-educated, middle-class families who gained direct and easy access to the United States because they were sponsored by family members or by their association with the U.S. military. The children of the first wave of immigrants, because of their educational background, didn't take long to catch on and do well in school.

The next wave of immigrants were mostly "boat people." Usually, they were from small villages or farms and had limited access to education. The boat people paid approximately $500 per person for their perilous escape. Many experienced trauma, because they were intercepted by pirates while at sea. They were rescued and taken to Southeast Asian refugee camps, where they often waited for years to be sponsored by a charity or another agency. Their children frequently had problems of being withdrawn, not open, and very scared. In the camps, they wasted lots of time waiting, wandering around, and doing nothing. Not having gone to school much, they had big gaps in their progress.

Refugees don't escape much by boat anymore, because they ended up living in camps for years and never reached America. They were sent back from the camps by the local governments. As things have started to open up with Vietnam, only people sponsored by family members make it out by air travel.

The most recent immigrants are those granted humanitarian departure because they served the U.S. government during the war. They have spent years in prison camps. In return for their efforts, the U.S. government has rescued them from the camps. In those families, while the father was in prison, the single mother took care of the kids. Those children attended Communist schools, which were pretty poor, because after 1975, the country put its resources into rebuilding the infrastructure that was destroyed by the war. Those children received a very political and restricted education where the Communist philosophy of being part of the group was taught. There, individualism is discouraged, and creativity and thinking are stifled. Those kids are really passive. If you ask them to give an opinion, they are scared to say anything. When they come here we must acclimate them to the American way of education.

COMMUNITY DEMOGRAPHICS

In this Northern California city, the Vietnamese community is large with approximately 20,000 people. In the middle-class neighborhood surrounding the school, many Vietnamese families have settled because housing is somewhat cheaper than in other areas. Even so, several families share a single-family house. Sometimes 15 people live in a three-bedroom house, where they all put money together to pay the rent. Often their high school-age children must work part time to help support the family.

Some college-educated immigrant and mainstream parents are engineers and hold jobs in the nearby computer industry. Other immigrant, refugee, and mainstream parents do odd jobs and factory work. Some of them open small businesses, such as auto parts stores or body shops. Others work in grocery stores or nail salons. Usually both parents work, sometimes two or three jobs. Some also receive public assistance. Overall, parents want their kids to have a better life here than what they have. So, they really push their children to achieve.

THE SCHOOL AND ITS PROGRAMS

The school has a large, one-story modern building with several portable classrooms surrounded by spacious, grassy, and asphalt play areas. In Grades K–6, the 690 students are served by 25 teachers in mainstream, bilingual, or **sheltered English** classes. Of the students, 80% are entitled to **Chapter I** services. The largest language minority group is Vietnamese, which makes up 25% of the student population.

In 1986, the Vietnamese bilingual program started with two classes: kindergarten and first grade. Now it has four classes from kindergarten through Grade 3. Presently, the **transitional** program aims for students to go into the mainstream English program by fourth grade. Ideally, the program will be adding one bilingual class in each of the upper grades in the next 2 years.

Because the English standardized test scores are very high, many students have been reclassified as English proficient after 2 or 3 years in the bilingual program. By sixth grade, many of our former bilingual students are on the honor roll. Our program has such a good reputation that some parents from outside the neighborhood want to transfer their kids to our school.

Each of the four Vietnamese bilingual classes has an instructional aide for 1 hour daily. The highly qualified aide, an older grandmotherly type, formerly was a teacher in Vietnam. Her limited English ability and the demanding teacher credential requirements have prevented her from returning to study for her credential. She is particularly important in helping students with native language and **ESL** instruction.

There are also **sheltered English** classes in Grades K–6. Because there are six or seven different languages in these classes, it's more **ESL** instruction than bilingual. Upper grade, newcomer Vietnamese students go to those classes. Sheltered English teachers are in the process of obtaining their **Language Development Specialist (LDS)** credential. New teachers hired in the district now are being required to have this certification.

CLASSROOM COMPOSITION

Of my 33 first graders, 18 children are Vietnamese. Fifteen were born here and 3 were born in Vietnam. All these students understand and speak varying degrees of Vietnamese. Backgrounds of the diverse English-speaking children include Cambodian, Indian, Hispanic, African American, and European American. At least two of the English-speaking students may need special education services.

Children sit in eight teams of four or five students. I try to pair Vietnamese children together so they may converse among themselves in Vietnamese when necessary. Newcomer students are seated with bilingual students who translate for them. At each table, Vietnamese kids are with English speakers so they can learn from each other.

The classroom is attractively decorated with teacher-made charts, graphs, pictures, student work and commercial materials in Vietnamese and English. Weekly poem charts are posted for children to recite. Classroom objects are labelled bilingually.

DEALING WITH VIETNAMESE
LANGUAGE DIVERSITY

Because there is a difference in native language ability and experiences between newcomers and those children born here, my goals are different for those two groups. The newcomers, for the most part, have Vietnamese

Cognitive Academic Language Proficiency (CALP). I want to develop their English **Basic Interpersonal Communication Skills (BICS)** and **CALP,** which will help them later in their transition to English. For children born here, I want them to have a foundation in Vietnamese language and culture. For some of them, it's like teaching them a completely new language. They may speak Vietnamese but have no idea how to write it. I mostly teach them in English with Vietnamese reinforcement. Even if they are bilingual, they have no knowledge of Vietnam. If they are taught about Vietnam, it's not like having the experience of living there. The kids born here have a harder time, because they don't have the native language, vocabulary, or cultural knowledge. For example, you might be talking about bamboo, but they have never seen a bamboo tree before. Perhaps they have seen it in a picture. But if you talk about a Nintendo™ game, they know about that. At the same time, a newcomer will have no idea about a Nintendo™ game. It's hard to teach them together. I'm doing both transition for the Vietnamese speakers and **language restoration/recovery/mainte-nance** for those born here.

In terms of time, I use Vietnamese about 30% to 35% of the time and the rest is English. Usually for any lesson, I pre-teach it in Vietnamese, then I do it in English and again I'll post-teach in Vietnamese. The English is sandwiched by the native language. The aide also works with small groups or individual students on native language development and to translate English texts for them. And if American-born Vietnamese children find a lesson too hard, I'll send an English book home so their parents can review it in Vietnamese. Sometimes I'll use **concurrent translations** because it is much easier and faster to explain it to them in Vietnamese. I know this is not good because the kids just wait for the translation.

In whatever language the child speaks to me, I'll respond. I try to be flexible and patient, especially with children raised here. They seem to understand Vietnamese perfectly, but it's much easier for them to respond in English. It takes them a long time to express themselves in Vietnamese. I have to give them enough "wait time" because they are processing their thoughts in a second language.

TEACHING STRATEGIES

Reading and Language Development

Vietnamese reading and language arts is the essence of our bilingual program. In Grades 1 through 3, we have a split reading schedule where the first hour of day is devoted to Vietnamese reading and language arts. All the Vietnamese students come in the morning. English reading and language arts are done in the afternoons. Since there aren't many Vietnamese reading materials, much of what we use are translated **basal** stories. Vietnamese-speaking students who know how to read in Vietnamese find learning to read easy in English, because the skills, such as phonetic sounds, syntax, spelling, and grammar patterns are transferable. Strong Vietnamese reading skills help them to learn to read in English, even though it has a different alphabet and sound system. Some children also go to Vietnamese community language school, which helps to reinforce their connection to Vietnamese language and culture.

We use both **basal readers** and **whole language** literature, such as big books and tradebooks. From the basal readers, I tape English-speaking parent volunteers reading stories. I have children practice reading along with the tape, either during reading or free time. My Vietnamese-speaking kids need to listen to good English role models. These taped stories also help them connect what they hear to written text. I also lend these tapes for children to practice reading at home.

I use the **whole language** approach in both languages and try to integrate the language skills of reading, writing, speaking, and listening by using a lot of literature, poetry, chanting, charting, and webbing. One of the first things I do is teach children how to track words. Our school uses the *McCracken* method and materials, which immerses children in print throughout the classroom environment.

In teaching English to new arrivals, I understand that they need time to listen to the sounds and connect them with the content. Because they are going through a **silent period**, I both shelter the English instruction and give them lots of enriched language with gestures, pictures from the *IDEA Kit* (Ballard & Tighe, 1989), songs, experience charts, repetition and repetitive stories to help them understand. Using **TPR**, I try to model the language using actions and short simplified sentences. I read them lots of stories and have them read after me. I like to use content that kids are familiar with. After a while, their speaking ability starts to emerge. Because many of those students are very shy, they may feel uncomfortable speaking in front of others. So I encourage them to share when they are ready.

All children must learn to recite a weekly poem in English, which we chant a couple of times everyday. In presenting the poem, I try to make it comprehensible through talking about it and drawing pictures of it. It is part of the weekly homework, so parents can work on it with them. By the end of the week, about 80% of the children can recite it. I bind all the illustrated poems into a poem book, so kids can continually revisit them (see example in Appendix D).

I use the **writing process** in both English and Vietnamese where kids write stories about familiar topics such as holidays, toys, or cultural objects they bring from home. We'll do prewriting **webbing** activities together before they write. For the first draft, I encourage them to use **inventive spelling.** For later drafts, I help them with editing and by having them read their piece aloud. They'll also correct their spelling either by referring to our chart of frequently used words or by looking up words in the dictionary. Finally, they recopy their stories, share them with the class, and put them on the bulletin board.

For new arrivals, I individualize instruction and/or have the other kids help them. Those children stay after school for 20 minutes when I review the day's lesson to make sure they understand. After school is the only time for me to give that extra attention, because during the day there are too many other students needing attention.

Content Areas

At our school we also try to integrate reading with the content areas in **thematic units.** We have developed units on various social studies and science topics such as friendship, mammals, and oceanography. I try to make math and science "hands-on" by using lots of manipulatives, visuals and experiments. We use Bullock's (1992) _Touch Math_, which really helps with computation skills because the students touch dots for each number, which helps them experience the number concept and place value. We are moving away from focusing on computation skills toward developing kids' thinking and problem-solving skills. With manipulatives, I have them come up with their own word problems.

I also try to give students **cooperative group work** so they can help each other. First graders are still learning how to work cooperatively. For example, they had a science classification activity where each team had to find pictures of objects to glue on a big paper under the headings: solid, liquid, or gas. Some kids just glued the pictures without talking to one another. Many kids don't yet understand when they are supposed to work together or alone.

Whatever we do, I try to model it and let them know what I expect. I walk them through the reading, math, writing, or drawing activities using charts or transparencies. With time, they are able to do more by themselves.

ASSESSMENT

When students first come to our program, the **ESL** teacher, who is Vietnamese, administers the _Pre-LAS_ (_Pre-Language Assessment Scales_, Duncan & DeAvila, 1981) to kindergartners and the _LAS_ (_Language Assessment Scales_, DeAvila & Duncan, 1981) to measure English and Vietnamese proficiency of children in the other grades. K–2 children are given vocabulary, listening, and speaking tests. Children in Grades 3 through 6 also have to take reading and writing tests. American-born Vietnamese children usually pass the English test and fail the Vietnamese test and the reverse is true for the Vietnam-born children. So, it's really a mixed bag. This is the only time kids are given those **language proficiency tests** until they are reclassified. In the later grades, they use **standardized tests** to assess academic progress. There needs to be better documentation showing student growth, especially when they **exit** the bilingual program. All we have are the English standardized tests. We need to have a better measure of their native language progress that includes writing and reading.

Because we don't use **standardized tests** in first grade anymore, we have started using writing and science **portfolios** for assessment and parent–teacher conferences. I find the portfolio process much better than standardized tests because you can see the child's progress through work samples. Children select their best work to show their parents what they have been doing. Since it's a new process, we're still learning how to do it right. Now we must figure out what work to keep and where do we put all the student work. Portfolios take a lot of space and time for filing.

I find all of the tests are biased in assuming a child is familiar with certain content. For example, a test question might ask about the American flag and the student may only know the Vietnamese flag. Another item may refer to a story such as, "Jack and the Bean Stalk," which many children aren't familiar with. Even the _LAS_ (DeAvila & Duncan, 1981) has a picture of a couch that the children confused with a chair because they had never seen a couch. More precise tests that are not culturally biased need to be developed. Perhaps teacher-made criterion-referenced tests based on what is actually taught would work better than norm-referenced tests. **Standardized tests** need to be normed on different ethnic groups. In addition, when native language tests are translated from the English version, there are problems. Those tests need to be designed in the native language, rather than just translated.

MATERIAL SHORTAGES:
TEACHERS RESPOND AND MAKE THEIR OWN

The native language materials we use are made here. We "shy away" from commercial materials from Vietnam. We do use them as references. We don't want children checking them out of the library because the content in them is too political. We want to try to be as neutral as possible in representing certain ideologies. As a bilingual teacher, one must carefully select materials for appropriate content, level, and language. Some U.S.-made books are really poor and don't use even standard Vietnamese, because publishers tend to pay low wages for translations.

After all these years, at least for first grade, we have lots of materials. The best ones have mostly been developed by teachers from other school districts with large Vietnamese student populations. We purchase those materials from them so we no longer have to invent the wheel.

Through **Title VII** and district grants, we've been able to develop lots of Vietnamese materials such as charts, translated workbooks, **basals,** and thematic units. Finally, the computer industry now has excellent Vietnamese language word-processing programs, so we are able to make some pretty professional-looking native language materials. I wish I had more time to publish materials myself. Even though we are still short of materials, I have seen a big improvement. I'm happier now than when we started from scratch. The state will soon be coming out with a catalog of bilingual materials in diverse languages. There is hope.

PARENTAL SUPPORT FOR THE PROGRAM

At first, because some Vietnamese parents didn't really understand what the bilingual program was, they opposed it. They feared that too much time would be spent in Vietnamese and that kids would never learn English. As they have learned about what we do and seen their children's success, parents have become more supportive. They are anxious for the program to extend to sixth grade, so their kids can stay in bilingual classes throughout the grades.

The English-speaking parents sometimes are concerned about having their kids in the program. Several English-speaking volunteers, who see what goes on, are supportive about having their children in a bilingual class. I explain to all the English-speaking parents that their kids get the same enriched English reading and language arts curriculum as other first graders. Sometimes the English-speaking children pick up a few Vietnamese words from the environment. Unfortunately, we don't really have enough time to expose those children to Vietnamese as a Second Language. I do try to sensitize all children to issues of diversity through exposing them to cultural units on Vietnamese New Year (Tê´t), Vietnamese foods, cooking, and games.

Both Vietnamese and other parents always support us a lot. Three parent volunteers regularly help us with class projects. One Vietnamese-speaking mother helps children with native language math skills during class and after school. By helping in our class, her English is improving, which she seems to enjoy. For the most part, the Vietnamese parents passively just send their kids to school and leave everything to the teacher. This stems from how teachers and education are viewed in Vietnam. There the teacher is the master and can do whatever she wants. Parents expect their kids to do well, but they don't really help them. They just think the school will do it all. They're not used to coming to school and getting involved, as do parents here. They only come to conferences if the teacher is bilingual, or if they are pushed to come. Also, because many parents work several jobs, they can't come. I really try to make them feel comfortable by talking to them a lot. Parents know there's an open-door policy and they are always welcome to come and chat. For cultural festivals, they usually come and volunteer to make food.

I personally don't have any problems with parents. However, the school generally is not able to reach out enough to parents. I have to make phone calls for other teachers about parent conferences and to get their consent for children to participate in after-school and other programs. Parents need to be convinced to send their children, because culturally, parents are protective and afraid to send their kids out. Parent outreach such as this rests on the bilingual teachers' shoulders. More support for parent outreach is needed.

In the adjustment process, parents are losing their authority over their children. As kids assimilate, parents' values are being left behind. When children learn English, there's less parent–child communication. Plus, parents are hardly even home much, because they're struggling to survive. There is a big conflict between the older and younger generations as kids search for their identity. They don't know if they should be Vietnamese or American. And, it is really hard to keep their Vietnamese heritage while becoming American.

To address this conflict, we can't just teach the kids, but we really have to teach parents new ways of taking care of and dealing with their kids. So, many parents come to me trying to regain control, because they no longer have the power over their children like they did in Vietnam. Parents also need to learn American ways of disciplining children. Some aren't even aware that they are abusing their kids physically and verbally. We really must work closely with the parents to help them take a more active part in their children's lives and education.

SUPPORT FROM ADMINISTRATION

When I first started in this program, there was no support at all. The principal had no idea of what a bilingual program was or how to run it. That all changed 4 years ago when we got our present principal, who was formerly the district bilingual coordinator. What a difference in support! When parents try to withdraw their child from the program, she won't let them. She explains that their kids are lucky to be with excellent bilingual teachers. She assures them that their children are receiving the same curriculum as in other classes. In ordering materials, all I have to do is ask her and she'll buy whatever I can find. I am in charge of ordering Vietnamese texts and library books for the school.

She treats all the bilingual teachers as part of the staff. Sometimes, other teachers are not happy about that, because they fear that the bilingual teachers will take over their jobs. Because our principal is so supportive, many of the teachers who are against bilingual education tend to move to other schools. Then, the principal tries to hire people who will be advocates.

Recently, I received a district award for excellence and commitment for meeting the needs of **language minority** students. So, little by little, the work of bilingual teachers is being recognized and legitimized not only in the school, but on a broader scale.

COLLABORATION BETWEEN
BILINGUAL AND MONOLINGUAL TEACHERS

When the bilingual program started at kindergarten and first-grade levels, the other teacher and I were both new. The monolingual colleagues didn't like me, because another teacher was transferred to create my position. With time, they have gotten used to me. They still don't like it every time we bring in a new bilingual teacher.

In the last few years, as California schools have become so diverse, many monolingual teachers are getting certified as **Language Development Specialists (LDS)**. They do this to assure their job security. As a result, they have started to understand what is needed to teach bilingual students. In learning about the language acquisition process, they have become more sensitive to children. They realize that kids in the **preproduction stage** shouldn't be forced to say something before they are ready. So now they know to give kids more time before they expect them to speak. As those teachers become more aware, hopefully kids won't have to just sit ignored, coloring in the back of classrooms. The teachers can see that allowing children to speak the native language helps their self-esteem.

Those teachers get upset if they don't pass the **LDS** exam. They understand better what we bilingual teachers have been through. Since they are learning about **language minority** students and going through similar training, we have more of a common bond with them. Often, those teachers come to me after school asking for help. I share with them lots of materials, teaching strategies, and solutions to problems.

They realize that we make a difference. Especially by the upper grades, most of our former students are already fluent in English and quite capable academically. Were it not for our efforts in developing the native and second language, those students would still be non-English speakers and much harder for those teachers to instruct. So, they are seeing the results of our work.

Times have changed. We're working together more on behalf of our students. But there are always some people who still don't want to change. Those teachers say, "I'm too old to go back to school to pass my **LDS** test." They just ask to transfer to schools that are mostly White.

For those teachers willing to learn about our kids, they especially need to know why students need bilingual classes. They need linguistics and second language acquisition classes to have a better idea of how kids learn in other languages. Maybe they should also take some foreign language classes, too. Learning in another language is different than what they learned in high school foreign language classes. So they might want to travel. By learning a language and culture in another country, they can experience what the kids do and feel when they don't speak the language.

NEW TEACHER RECRUITMENT AND SUPPORT

Many of the Vietnamese bilingual teachers are new teachers with little experience (1–2 years). As the bilingual program extends into the upper grades, it may be difficult to find qualified Vietnamese bilingual teachers, because young people do not want to go into the field. There's a real need for bilingual teachers so that programs will be in compliance and won't lose the money. To address this, the district goes to the local college to hire prospective teachers before they finish their teacher training. They give them emergency credentials.

Once in the school, those new teachers need more support. The district must provide mentors and fewer responsibilities. Otherwise, they'll get frustrated and leave. Last year, a few new teachers didn't make it through the year, because they weren't strong enough to face the lack of support and understanding about the bilingual program. It's tough because, as a new teacher, one is too busy working with the kids. And that's why young people don't want to become bilingual teachers. Why have that extra burden of teaching in another language to deal with? You're not paid more. They are not willing to go through all the extra college courses to be certified as a bilingual teacher. Often, younger teachers who were raised here don't want to be bilingual teachers. Like the kids, they must struggle to teach Vietnamese language and culture because they weren't exposed to it in their American schooling.

We try to support new teachers with in-house bilingual mentors and an experienced floating teacher, who helps them with classroom management. As do all bilingual teachers, they receive school and district in-services. In addition, all teachers have a couple of days of release time to observe other colleagues in the district. It is a great way to see other programs and learn new strategies. I take advantage of these opportunities to observe and learn from others.

I encourage new teachers to hang in there and stand up for their standards and beliefs. Since there is no concrete written policy to follow and so many bilingual teaching approaches to choose from, one must find what is appropriate by looking at the kids. New teachers need to feel comfortable with what they teach and go from there. Some people will be supportive, but lots won't. The first year, it's so overwhelming that one must live day to day. With time, the results will show how much the kids have learned.

8

Sandra

BACKGROUND AND ENTRY TO TEACHING
IN SOUTHERN CALIFORNIA

I have been a bilingual teacher both in the Los Angeles area and in Illinois, where I am originally from. I was born, raised and educated in south central Illinois. My family, of mixed Western European background, dates back 8 to 10 generations in the United States.

Throughout high school, I took Spanish. During the summer of my senior year, I went to Ecuador as an exchange student and lived with a family. There I learned to use everyday street and conversational Spanish, which complemented the textbook Spanish I had learned in school. When I returned to Illinois I started college. I majored in Spanish because it came easily to me. I love languages and am a parrot. At 21, I finished college and moved to Los Angeles. I had no idea what to do with a bachelor's degree in Spanish. I thought of becoming a bilingual secretary. How silly! They don't need "gringa" bilingual secretaries because there are a million Mexican women willing to work for peanuts. For a short while, I was a regular secretary, which I hated.

Then, I went to a Southern California university to inquire about teaching at the college level. "You need a PhD," they said. They sent me to the Department of Elementary Education where I started taking some classroom observation courses. I didn't think that I liked children. To my surprise, my first day observing in a classroom, this little Mexican girl gave me a present. I was caught! She landed me hook, line, and sinker! I decided that teaching Hispanic children was what I wanted to do.

For a solid 3 months, I took university bilingual education methodology courses in reading, math, and science. The classes were mostly "busy work" where we wrote lots of papers and Madeline Hunter-style lesson plans for every hour of the day. Filling in those little boxes with the anticipatory set, guided practice, independent practice, follow-up, and closure activities was really time consuming and got old really fast. After those classes, I was given an emergency credential and assigned a full-time paid teaching position that they called an internship. After a year, I got the bilingual credential, after passing the California Basic Educational Skills Test (C-BEST), National Teacher Examination (NTE), and the **Bilingual Certificate of Competence (BCC)** tests.

This was in 1986, a time when they were desperate for bilingual teachers. If you spoke any Spanish, they snapped you right up for a full-time teaching position for which they paid you a seemingly huge salary. I essentially was thrown into a classroom with 32 kids after only 3 months of minimal training. It's amazing that this was acceptable to the state, since I had had no student teaching. I supposedly had a master teacher at another school, but I was never able to take time off to watch him. We also had an internship supervisor assigned to help us. This was a joke. He'd watch me, tell me I was doing great, and then leave. Maybe it's that I'm just a natural teacher. Or perhaps he did that with everybody. Some people were just horrible at teaching, so maybe he helped them more. I was basically just left alone.

Fortunately, the kind-hearted **English as a second language (ESL)** teacher in the class next to me took me under her wing and helped me a lot. What a nightmare was that first year! I was too stupid to know that. When you don't know what's coming, somehow you just blunder through and sink or swim. And I guess I was swimming. The day before I started teaching, there was a major earthquake. So, we learned about earthquakes the first day of school.

I taught second grade at that Los Angeles school for 3 years before going back to Illinois. The school had 98% Hispanics (mostly Mexican and Central American) and the rest were Asian. The K–6 school was huge with about 1,200 students on a year-round schedule divided into four cycles. Three cycles, or about 900 students, were present at a given time. Each of the three cycles had kindergarten, first-, and second-grade bilingual classes with about 12 bilingual teachers in all. We also had a couple **Chapter I** teachers who strictly taught **ESL.** We had one or two bilingual third- and fourth-grade classes, which would strangely appear and disappear, depending on who was in charge at the time. During my 3 years, we had three different principals. So our program was real goofy with very little continuity.

The school had been there for years. The community had changed gradually from all White to predominantly Hispanic. The area started going "downhill" with more poverty, gangs, and crime. Some of the original teachers were still there. They were so angry all the time. I hated to promote those poor kids to the third-grade teachers' classes. This was a problem, because there was no bilingual third grade to promote them to on our cycle.

The bilingual program was **transitional** so by third grade, students were expected to go to regular English-only classes. This was really difficult, especially since students were coming in all the time from Mexico. It was assumed that if they were in the second grade that they had gone to kindergarten and first grade in Mexico, which was not always true. There was a strong push to get them into English reading.

The other cycle was for the Asian students (Korean, Laotian, and Hmong) where the teacher did mostly **ESL.** Those classes didn't use native language instruction because there were too many different languages. Native language teaching assistants were available to help the teacher.

My first year, like most beginning teachers, I often stayed pretty late at school until 9 p.m., which was not really smart in that neighborhood. I just couldn't leave because there was just so much to do. Now I realize, I'll never finish and so I just leave it. I probably taught my best ever because I went nuts putting all my energy into doing elaborate cooking and Project AIMS activities every day. It was exhausting carrying in bags and stuff like a cart horse. All the veteran teachers would say, "What's she doing now? There she goes again making us look bad." I have calmed down a bit since then.

Project AIMS are hysterically fun Spanish/English **thematically integrated** science and math hands-on interactive units. Depending on the lesson, some take a couple of days and others take an hour. The units take a lot of preparation. So, I was going crazy preparing and trying them out with the kids.

COLLEGIAL INTERACTION

Monolingual Teachers

Several older monolingual teachers expressed their anger about the changing population telling the Hispanic children, "What are you? Stupid? Speak English. You're in America!!" They just spewed out negativity whenever they opened their mouths. Often, I had huge verbal confrontations with them. I learned to be assertive in that situation. And they didn't want to do anything extra like attending our parties or voluntary workshops.

Bilingual Teachers

The school's bilingual teachers weren't very qualified or unified because as Spanish speakers they were practically hired off the street. One was a psychopath who did inappropriate things in her class. So, I didn't really care to spend time with "wackos." Some bilingual teachers were Hispanics and others were "gringas" like me. Many of the bilingual teachers hung out together in cliques. Several bilingual teachers did not really believe in bilingual education. They would wipe out the kids' primary language by just immersing them in English. I was surprised they went against all the theories and research studies that we'd been learning about building a strong native language foundation. The kids seemed to do okay in the short-run because they loved learning English. But in the long-run, many failed because they didn't have strong comprehension and vocabulary base in any language. They were practically illiterate in two languages.

DISTRICT SUPPORT

There wasn't much district support. Rarely was anyone interested enough to come to see what was going on in our classes. Occasionally, the superin-tendent and his staff would come to check that the required lists of student groups and their composition books were in order. The only support I did get was through workshops, which were helpful.

The district offered monthly workshops and arranged for substitutes, so we could attend. Their goal in providing all that training was to make sure we all taught the same way, not out of interest for the teachers' growth. Usually the workshops were conducted by a mentor teacher, who presented current and remedial strategies, such as _Touch Math_ (Bullock, 1992), and use of literature and **whole language.** And of course, having never taught, student taught, or observed anyone, I needed all the help I could get.

So, at least the district was good at keeping us up on the latest things. Since the workshops and courses were district-sponsored, I didn't get credit for them. Unfortunately, now I have to repeat and pay for almost the same ones here in Illinois to get my bilingual credential and **ESL** approval.

TEACHING

My bilingual teaching approaches have been pretty similar in both Los Angeles and Illinois. They only varied because of the different curriculum emphasis in the two places. When I first started teaching, my Spanish was horrible, so the kids constantly corrected me. They delighted in telling me words I didn't know, or fixing something on the board. It put us on the same level as learners. I think it also helped their self-esteem. I always try to present the concepts first in Spanish. Once they know them, then I start mixing the languages in the follow-up activities. For instance, if I'm teaching subtraction, I use the words "restar/quitar" until they learn the process. And then I start saying "subtract/minus" in English. When they are strong in their language, I start building the weaker language.

I encourage children to **code switch,** which shows me how much they know. If they have to do a task all in English, they often don't have enough vocabulary, so they won't do anything. When they're free to use both languages, I get a lot more from them. I accept their responses in either or both languages. If they say something like, "Give me el vaso [the glass]," that shows me they've learned the "give me" part. When they write, I always accept when they throw in an English word here and there, because it shows they're learning.

In Los Angeles, we were supposed to teach all in Spanish except for the ESL period when, we had to use all English. For ESL, I mostly used **Total Physical Response (TPR)** activities, where children didn't have to respond verbally but they had to show me through actions or drawing that they understood. Here in Illinois, I integrate **ESL** activities across the curriculum, not just during the ESL period.

In Los Angeles, there were always two or three English speakers placed in my class, so I couldn't just speak in Spanish. I had to translate for those kids. Though they didn't study it, they learned some Spanish in this off-hand way from the other kids and the environment. I couldn't really do **Spanish as a second language (SSL)** because I had so few kids. I never really even thought of doing it because it was hard enough keeping up with the regular curriculum.

Since our program was only in K–2, newcomer, upper grade kids had a really tough time in the all-English classes. One fifth-grade Salvadoran boy was placed with me in the mornings for reading and math. He was very smart, even though he had never before been to school. In the war down there, he knew how to put a gun together. At first, he felt badly in our class because he wasn't with kids his own age. I tried to raise his self-esteem by having him help other kids, which immediately made him feel successful. He liked being there. When he went back to the regular class, kids would pick on him and he didn't do too well. In teaching culture, the multicultural curriculum mostly focused around holidays and celebrations such as Cinco de Mayo (The 5th of May, where Mexicans celebrate liberation from the French) and Chinese New Year. We put on bilingual Christmas assemblies. Our programs would include all the cultures represented in the school.

Most of the cultural activities were just on the surface level. That's what we do here in Illinois. It's really hard to get past that.

CURRICULUM AND MATERIALS

In Los Angeles, everything was in English and Spanish. For **ESL,** I was forced to use the _IDEA Kit_ (Ballard & Tighe, 1989), which consists of a thematically arranged picture cards to develop English vocabulary in a very structured way. Math was straight from the text book. They also gave us some manipulatives, like _Unifix Cubes,_ which are small interlocking colorful plastic counters to develop number concepts. Curriculum for social studies, science, and health units were all written by the district and taught during one 3-month cycle at a time. We also had to show the district-broadcast cable television health programs, to augment the curriculum.

In Los Angeles, the district curriculum was very structured. All teachers had to teach the same subjects at the same time. This policy was created due to the high mobility rate. Students would frequently go to several different schools in the district. Students were also homogeneously grouped by high and low ability levels, so we could trade kids for the different subjects. Lists of all the different groups had to be posted in the room.

Since the mandated curriculum was pretty boring, I spiced it up by sneaking in extra creative activities, like _Project AIMS_ and cooking during **ESL,** which was the only free period I had. The rest of the time we used **basal readers** and textbooks. I don't know how effective it was to control the teachers by structuring the curriculum so strictly. When I moved to Illinois and was able to make my own schedule, I freaked out. I had no idea about what to do.

ADMINISTRATIVE SUPPORT
OR LACK THEREOF

In Los Angeles, I had three different principals in 3 years. The first one hated bilingual education and was not supportive at all. After the earthquake on the first day teaching, I asked him about earthquake plans or if there was a kit. He replied, "There's no plan" and that his earthquake kit was his Remington rifle under his bed! Great, if there's an earthquake, he's "gonna" go get his gun! He refused to discuss anything, because he was tired and old and was planning to retire.

The next principal was brand new and had limited teaching experience. She looked like a big Barbie™ doll dressed in suits and 3-inch "tacones" [heels]. Her vision was that children should be in English as soon as possible. She wanted everyone quiet all the time. This conflicted with what children need to learn a second language, an environment where they are able to talk to learn. When she entered the room, she didn't want to hear anyone talking except for me. With that expectation, I couldn't do cooperative groups or anything progressive. So, I trained the kids to be quiet. Pretending to be her, I'd leave the room and return; the children had to be completely silent. I explained that I'd be in trouble if they talked. We practiced this like a fire drill. They loved me, so of course, when she came in, it was "zip the lip." I felt badly to put all that guilt on them. But, I didn't know what else to do because I was getting bad evaluations. I had to teach them to be subversive to preserve my reputation.

Thank God, my last year, we got another principal, someone who was a real "mover and shaker," supportive with common sense and her feet on the ground. I said, "I need an earthquake plan." She encouraged me to create one. She was so inspirational especially in terms of bilingual education! She was part Mexican and spoke Spanish.

She was much more concerned with reaching out to parents. For example, the other principals didn't care about written communication sent home to parents. The notes were poorly translated and mistake-filled. I always objected, saying, "You wouldn't send notes like that home in English. So, don't send them out like that in Spanish." The new principal made sure that notes were properly translated. She knew not to treat parents like that. Before her, there was nothing for parents, no PTA. They rarely came for parent conferences or open house. With her, we started having performances before open house to entice more parents to come to school. She started offering parent training like, _Family Math_ (Stenmark, Thompson, & Cossey, 1986). She got parents a lot more involved. When that happened, the school started to grow. I didn't really get to see that because I went back to Illinois for family reasons.

TEACHING IN ILLINOIS

Community and School Context

For the last 4 years, I have been teaching in my present school located in a southern Illinois suburb. I taught bilingual third grade the first 2 years and for the last 2 years, I've been in second grade. Our district has both very affluent upper-class, White professional families, who live in wealthy areas, like Beverly Hills, and poor Hispanics, mostly Mexicans and Central Americans, who live in a small apartment complex. Two and three Latino families often share an apartment together. Rarely do they own a condo or cars. Many of them are illegal and/or on public aid. When they work, their jobs include food service, landscaping, hotel-, and factory work. The city government and local businesses used to perceive them as a cockroach den to be paved over. Recently, things have been changing and the community has started making an effort to include them.

This K–6 school is not very big. Of the 550 students, about one quarter are Hispanic. The rest are mostly White middle- to upper-class children. The bilingual program is offered in kindergarten through Grade 3 and serves exclusively Hispanic children. After third grade, if those children still need bilingual education, they are transferred to another school that has upper grade bilingual classes. The push is to keep them here, so they don't have to leave the school. This is hard on our kids, because they sometimes have major gaps in their reading and academic abilities. The bilingual program at the other school isn't that strong. What is worse, being transferred to another school or being transitioned out too soon in order to stay in their home school? It's a no-win situation.

Unfortunately, our district uses bilingual kids as fodder to increase the enrollments at other schools. The state pays each school depending on the number of students. If a school has a low enrollment, they'll stick a bilingual or a special education program there. We have had to fight hard just to keep our K–3 program at this school. In fact, this year, we got the bilingual kindergarten here after much fighting. Before, the little ones were bussed to another school where one of these programs was placed. Who knows what they were getting over there? Continuity is important, especially for the little ones.

Our bilingual program is nowhere near as structured and directed as the one in Los Angeles. Even though it's **transitional,** our program seems to give children more time to develop in their native language before mainstreaming them into the regular program. They **exit** when they're ready and have tested at a certain level on the _LAS_ (_Language Assessment Scales_; DeAvila & Duncan, 1981) and English reading tests. Like in Los Angeles, no one is concerned about their Spanish reading progress. Only the English proficiency is considered in putting them in the mainstream class. However, our program is more flexible because the district bilingual director believes in supporting the native language.

TEACHING APPROACHES

I mostly speak in Spanish and occasionally I switch back and forth into English. I don't really have a formula. It really depends on the materials. If I have Spanish materials, I use them. If I don't, then I'll adapt the English materials for **ESL**. There's such a shortage of Spanish materials in certain subject areas. If I want something on China in Spanish, often I don't find it in the library. So, I use a lot of Spanish trade books, which I have collected, from my travels and at conferences.

For literature studies, I look for similar stories to read in both Spanish and English. Recently, I read my second graders _Cenicientas_ (1990) [Cinderella] in Spanish and _Yeh-Shen: A Cinderella story from China_ (Louie, 1982) in English. That story complements our unit on China, and coincides with our study of Chinese New Year. After reading the two stories, we discuss the stories in Spanish. I use a **Venn diagram** on a transparency to explore the stories' similarities and differences. Then, students write something from the diagram. This activity not only reinforces their oral skills, but writing and critical thinking skills. Once children have those skills in Spanish, they are able to transfer them to English, providing they have the vocabulary.

For other reading activities, I sometimes read a book aloud and have students fill out a book report form, where they tell about the book, why they liked it, and draw parts or characters from the story. We talk about the morals from legends and fables. Often I'll have them retell stories either with pictures or puppets. This can be difficult for them, especially if the story is in English. I'll accept either Spanish or English, which shows that they comprehend the story. I'll also have them do sequencing, if the story has a clear sequence of events.

Our **basal reading series** is awful, so I just take stories from them once in a while. I find the Spanish language and punctuation in them weird. Lots of the stories are written in play form, which emergent readers find difficult. Overall, this class has some good readers. I usually have a few who can't read at all. Some are just beginning to recognize the letters. They can bark (mouth the words), but they don't have the comprehension yet. Even though most of them have been in the program since kindergarten, they still need a lot of Spanish instruction.

Over the years, my Spanish has improved, but I still make tons of mistakes. Even so, I don't find that my Spanish errors negatively affect children. They like correcting me, which puts us on more of an equal footing. We often discuss the meanings of words. And if we don't agree, we are constantly looking words up in the dictionary. They'll tell me, "Go look it up, teacher!" Using reference books is an important skill, so I like them to see me and the teaching assistant using these books.

For content areas, I try to do a lot of critical thinking and problem-solving activities (e.g., *Project AIMS*, math games and **cooperative group** activities.) Our school is getting computers, which I hope will help the kids do more advanced problem solving.

CURRICULUM AND MATERIALS

In Los Angeles, I was handed the curriculum and told, "This is what you teach." Here, the teacher has more choice in doing what she is comfortable with. All teachers use **whole language.** For Math we use the *Everyday Mathematics* (Bell, 1992) program from the University of Chicago School Mathematics Project. For science, we use kits for activity-based learning, instead of textbooks, which is good.

The bilingual materials are purchased by the district bilingual director who is in charge of all the bilingual money. Each year, we give him a "wish list." If he decides we need books or other materials, then we get them. Often, the first-year teachers have better chances of getting the materials, because they don't have anything. I got a certain budget to spend my first year.

I wish we had more Spanish literature. It's very expensive. Since the district doesn't have the cash, I've had to buy a lot of those materials and trade books on my own to support the teaching I like to do.

PARENTS' ATTITUDES
ABOUT BILINGUAL EDUCATION

We need **dual language** where English- and Spanish-speaking children are put together and both languages are taught through an **integrated curriculum** and **cooperative grouping.** Research has proven dual language to work. For several years, we had a dual language program in our district, which aggravated some of the rich, upper class parents. They didn't understand the benefits of a bilingual curriculum, since they're not bilingual themselves. They couldn't see that their kids are much better off knowing two languages, like in Europe. They did not support the program because they felt their kids were missing something. They're very traditional and want their kids to start learning another language in high school. Even though the director keeps trying to implement dual language programs, **the** parents keep complaining and the program keeps being moved from school to school.

Unlike those parents, the Hispanic parents mostly are concerned with survival from one day to the next, making sure their kids are clothed and fed. They don't often give input about what is happening at the school. They trust us as professionals who are committed to educating their children. When we approach them, they are generally supportive.

THE COMMUNITY HELP CENTER
FOR HISPANIC FAMILIES

For the last 2½ years, there's been much more Hispanic parent involvement because of our community help center. In the low-income apartments where Hispanic families live, there were gangs, drugs, crime, and prostitution. It was so bad that the apartment manager came to the school and police department offering three apartments. He asked, "What can you do with them?" He recognized the need for community support and involvement. We ended up forming a neighborhood center that has a mini-police station, a bilingual social worker, and a school homework center. The public library provided Spanish books and the local college put in a computer lab for free adult ESL classes. Now after school, the kids have a place to do their homework. The parents have a place to go if they're having domestic problems or if they need help with public aid. When the police moved in, the gangs moved out. The families feel like they can come outside and breathe. They participate in more school activities because they are conducted in Spanish. Before, many parents were not able to attend school activities, since a lot of them don't have cars. They also didn't really feel welcome in school.

As the education coordinator, I'm in charge of the After School Homework Center in which most activities are conducted in Spanish. Each day, I help children with homework, answer questions, play games, and provide snacks. I also do school registrations. Some nights, I also direct meetings for Spanish-speaking parents. These are the same the PTA meetings that are conducted at school about homework, drugs, or charity activities. In the summer, I work with a junior leader group. I got the coordinator job, because I am bilingual and I was the only one to apply. I guess others were scared by the area.

At first, when I used to make "home visits," the neighborhood was kind of creepy. I'd walk around and all these people would yell at me. No more. Parents have learned to trust me because I speak Spanish. They see me with the kids walking around the neighborhood and taking them to the library. I try to use humor in my interactions with them. As they feel more comfortable, eventually, they start coming to school because they know that somebody is there who understands them.

The center is really bringing the community into the school and vice versa. It's making people feel like they are somebody, not just cockroaches to be paved over. Parents know the teachers because they come to the homework center. And they know the police are there to help, instead of seeing them just come beat heads. They take advantages of all the services including translation, social, and health care (e.g., vaccinations and physicals). We just try to meet the community's needs as much as possible. Now the parents actually have a voice, where they had none before.

COLLEGIAL ACCEPTANCE

Acceptance of the bilingual program and its students by the regular education teachers has been slowly changing as a result of lots of hard work. It's been tough because of the extreme prejudice at our school. Lots of English-speaking teachers don't like "those little Mexicans." They're used to teaching White English-speaking kids using traditional approaches. And, if a child can't learn their way, many of them don't want to work any harder or differently.

There are two camps of teachers: those who favor and those who oppose bilingual education. The anti-bilingual teachers feel that the bilingual teachers get special treatment, because we have fewer children and assistants and they don't. They're just ignorant about what we're dealing with, because they've never had to do it. It's like trying to explain mountain climbing to someone who has never seen a mountain. They wouldn't even have a clue. They think they can do a better job by immersing kids in English. They don't understand that not all children can learn that way.

The perception of Hispanics is changing, because some of these teachers have started getting training. This year, through a district grant project, monolingual teachers are learning **ESL,** use of manipulatives, and **language experience** techniques. Teaching them about language acquisition and **sheltered instructional** strategies has made a big difference. In the mornings, I gave some **Spanish as a second language (SSL)** instruction to volunteer teachers. Using the **natural approach,** like **TPR,** I gave the commands, "Stand up. Sit down. Put your right hand here," which made them feel uncomfortable. I purposely wanted them to see and feel what the kids go through by immersing them in another language.

Also, some bilingual and monolingual teachers have been integrating their classes for certain activities like gym, music, science, and art. Another monolingual third grade teacher and I integrate our students one afternoon a week. I teach half her class in art while she teaches half my class in science. After an hour, we switch groups. For years, this teacher taught mostly little White kids. Then as the Hispanic kids started coming in, she hated them. As a devout Christian, she prayed to God to change her point of view. After taking the ESL methodology class and as a result of our sharing, she now loves teaching ESL to Hispanic kids. So that has helped.

The bilingual teachers have worked really hard to reach out to the monolingual teachers through integration. We spend time together planning activities for both groups, which creates a dialog between us that wasn't there before. Now they realize the cognitive complexity of certain activities that requires a higher level of English for the child to fully understand. It is a big eye-opener for them. They say, "You're kidding. They can't read this?" With awareness, the teachers are beginning to better understand what we do and be more understanding of what the children need.

The responsibility rests on us bilingual teachers to keep communication open, which has really helped. I try to be open-minded and nonjudgmental. If the subject comes up about bilingual education, I explain it and if they don't accept it, I try not to get angry, although sometimes that's really hard. I try to stick up for the program.

Integration of Monolingual and Bilingual Classes

When we first started integrating, I did most of the planning myself. Basically, I gave my partner teacher the lesson plan and materials beforehand. I also sent my assistant to help translate for the children who didn't know what was going on. For a few months, my partner was having the assistant concurrently translate whatever she said. I had no idea that this was happening because I was busy teaching in the other room. She assumed translating was more beneficial when really it was detrimental. Lessons took much longer and bored the kids. So, I explained to her to just teach in English and let the assistant walk around, monitor, and help individual students. After that, things improved. The children work in cross-lingual **cooperative groups** or pairs, so they are continually helped by their English-speaking peers and vice versa when the children are working in Spanish in my room.

And, of course, the activities are fun and hands-on. Kids follow directions, construct things, and learn by doing. We use lots of *Project AIMS* activities, like sorting and graphing all kinds of things, like gummy bears. One time, we had kids roll cans of olives down a ramp to predict how far they would go. They did it three ways, with the olives and juice, without the juice, and empty. They really enjoyed seeing the concept.

PRINCIPAL SUPPORT

During my 4 years here, we have had four principals, which has been really hard. The first was not supportive. The second one, an interim principal, was good. The third principal knew nothing about bilingual education. His attitude was "Why can't they just learn English?" He was ignorant and didn't know any better. Though we kept trying to educate him, he never understood the importance that building a native language base has on later learning. Then, he left because he was going to be fired. Our new principal is great. She's "pro-bilingual" and sees our students as important. She has experience teaching dual language and multi-age programs. I'm not sure about her personal bilingual philosophy, but she's much more supportive of what we do and makes sure that everyone gets included. She's also very encouraging about our efforts to integrate.

Dual Language: The Future of Bilingual Education

I believe **dual language** is the future direction for bilingual education. When the monolingual kids learn in two languages, the modeling improves, self-esteem goes up, the segregation disappears and prejudice goes down. Some of the teachers already are beginning to buy into it as they see the benefits from integrating our classes together. They'll say, "I want those kids in my class." I'll say, "Okay, but not one at a time. See what you can do with half a class of bilingual kids." We have no formal integration policy, because the English-speaking parents don't really understand or support dual language. So, we just do it informally without telling them. That way we don't have to get parental permission. When their kids start doing better in school, maybe they'll realize it's important. In a sense, we are taking the policy into our hands.

I wish they'd make this a K–6 dual language school, instead of having the bilingual programs spread out throughout the district. I don't think they'd ever do it because it's too political. They need the Hispanic kids to maintain enrollments in other schools. They wouldn't dare bus the English-speaking kids to those other schools. They only bus the quiet ones who would never complain.

9

Mariana

BACKGROUND

My mother is Puerto Rican and my father was Italian American. In my household both English and Spanish were spoken. Until I was 5 years old, I spoke mostly Spanish with my mother and English with my father. In school, I really became English-dominant, while still maintaining a strong receptive Spanish background. Until the age of 10, we lived in New Jersey, then we moved to San Juan, Puerto Rico. In San Juan, I attended a bilingual parochial school, where certain subjects were taught in English and others in Spanish. I maintained my English fluency while becoming very fluent in Spanish. During that time, Spanish again became my home language. It's the language I still share with my mother and sisters.

In the summer of 1971, I started the university in San Juan with a bilingual education teacher scholarship, offered by the San Juan Board of Education to fluent English speakers. The Board had conducted a research study on Spanish-dominant teachers of English that showed that children modeled their teachers' similar speech patterns (e.g., pronunciation, enunciation, and errors). The Board offered scholarships to English speakers because they assumed that native English speakers would be better English language models for students. That summer, I took 12 education credits which included an 8-week supervised practicum. After the summer, I continued studying evenings and Saturdays while I started teaching at a public school. For a year, I taught **English as a second language (ESL)** to five kindergarten, first-grade, and second-grade classes, under the direction of the cooperating teacher and university supervisor.

In 1973, I returned to the [United] States to continue my undergraduate studies at a private university in New York City. I majored in English literature and theater with a minor in education. While studying, I worked as an assistant teacher in a Head Start program. I had always been interested in early childhood education and teaching.

BEGINNING TEACHING

In 1978, I began teaching English literature and writing in an alternative high school in Spanish Harlem. The students, all dropouts ranging from 16 to 21 years old, attended an intensive year-round GED and work skills program. I did that for several years and then started working as a head teacher in Head Start. In 1982, I took a year off to do my masters degree at a progressive New York teaching college. My majors were teacher education and curriculum, with a concentration in early childhood education. While doing an internship at an innovative early childhood private school, I was offered a head teacher position. I went through a rigorous interview process by a panel of teachers and administrators, who were concerned that the teachers share their progressive vision and philosophy. They wanted teachers to be able to create curriculum. I found that most appealing, the opportunity to create my own theme-based curriculum.

Back then, when other schools used more structured **basal** approaches to reading, this school already was exploring **whole language** and **writing process.** It was an exciting place to work so I stayed there for almost 8 years, teaching various ages and grades: 3- and 4-year-olds, kindergarten, first, second, fourth, and fifth.

BILINGUAL PUBLIC SCHOOL TEACHING

In 1990, while still at the private school, I interviewed at a New York City public elementary school, where the newly hired principal was looking for progressive-thinking teachers. As we talked, I casually mentioned that I was fluent in Spanish. She immediately asked if I wanted to teach in the school's **dual language program.** I didn't have yet enough information to decide whether dual language programs worked. After visiting some district dual language schools and classrooms and talking with teachers, I became very interested. I still had a lot of questions.

What really peaked my interest was the population I would be working with. As I observed in one teacher's room, I saw very little evidence of a child-centered curriculum. Looking at all those little faces, I felt a political calling, as a Latina, to work with those children. I wanted to explore the possibility of applying the progressive teaching I had developed in the private school in this public school setting. I was also very excited because the school was committed to using **whole language** and **writing process.**

The first year, I taught a second-grade class that had three quarters Latino and the rest English Proficient (EP) children (which translated into about 50% each of Spanish- and English-dominant). I believe that education should be a mixture of children who can learn from one another. And, I felt confident about meeting the challenge of teaching the two language groups. With the curriculum constant, I only needed to weave in the two languages so that the Spanish-speaking children would acquire English and the English-speaking children would acquire Spanish. I have learned a lot in my 5 years teaching kindergarten and Grades 2 and 4–5 in the **dual language program**. Presently, I'm teaching a combination fourth–fifth grade class.

COMMUNITY

This New York City community is diverse in terms of languages, ethnicity, and socioeconomic status. The K–5 school has 600 students from Latino, White European, and African-American backgrounds (about one third each). New immigrants also have started coming from Asia and Eastern Europe (Russia and Poland). The dominant community languages are English and Spanish. The Spanish speakers come mostly from the Dominican Republic and Mexico.

Parents' occupations range from educated professionals, like attorneys, doctors, teachers, social workers, small business owners, to factory or restaurant workers. Many of our immigrant parents work very hard, often two or three jobs both day and night. Some families are on public assistance. Children have varied economic resources available to them. In my class, for example, some kids have country homes and others live in crowded one-room hotels, homeless shelters, or Section 8 (Welfare) housing. Our community is very representative of New York City. If you believe that public education is a place where all children should be served, as I do, this is a great opportunity to use the students' diversity for learning.

In the 1970s and 1980s, New York City public schools experienced extreme budget cuts and crises, which led many parents, particularly middle-class parents, to seek alternatives to public schools for their children. Because of the budget crunch and a very autocratic principal at our school, many parents put their children into either private or parochial schools, which left our school with a predominantly Afro-American and Latino student population. When the new principal came, there was a conscious effort to attract the middle-class families from the community back to the school. Since then, there's been a dramatic shift, with increasing middle-class parents placing their children here. The fact that they are looking at our district's schools is telling of the high quality of our school programs. I feel that one reason that the middle-class population is returning to the public schools is because of the great effort the district has been making to involve parents in school and district decisions. In addition, because of economics, many parents can no longer afford the high costs of private schools.

Our immigrant parents are very involved and interested in their children's education. Their children probably have the highest attendance rates. Those parents may not be so involved in PTA activities, because they often feel intimidated by their lack of English. But in the classroom, they consistently come to parent-teacher meetings and maintain close contact with me and other teachers. They supervise homework and are very committed to their kids' success. If there's a special class being offered, they enroll their children. Their kids have had a great many success stories. I've seen those kids really take their education very seriously. Of course, a lot of it is cultural; the Latinos very much value education and trust the teacher, "Lo que Usted dice, Maestra" [Whatever you say, teacher]. They turn to schools for that kind of direction.

Conflicts begin to emerge in this North American setting with a value system that is not theirs. Their kids are assimilating in ways that the parents don't want them to. For example, children start abandoning their native language as they acquire their second language. Children also start responding differently to their parents and to the home culture.

THE DUAL LANGUAGE PROGRAM

Our **dual language program** tries to help children feel good about themselves, their native language, their culture, and their own personal histories. We accomplish this by providing children with strong academic instruction and cultural support. The dual language program was first established at one district school in 1984. The model was so successful that the district bilingual director implemented it in eight other district schools. Our **dual language program** follows a **partial immersion model,** shifting the focus away from **remedial/compensatory bilingual education.** Unlike other bilingual programs, where the goal is for Spanish-dominant kids to ultimately become English-speaking and go into the mainstream, the program really looks at and uses Spanish as a strength for both Spanish and English speakers. We follow an alternate day model, where all talk and instructional activities are carried out exclusively in English one day and in Spanish the next. We make sure that classes have balanced numbers of Spanish and

English speakers, so that children can serve as language role models for each other. Our program not only helps children develop oral bilingual fluency, but biliteracy, which is a tall order. It is very different from a traditional bilingual program. Our program co-exists within the regular school program and has five dual language classes in kindergarten and Grades 1, 2, 3–4, and 4–5.

Our program is one of parental choice: Spanish-speaking children automatically get preference and English-speaking parents may elect to place their children in the program if there is enough space. English-speaking children are permitted to enter the program before the second grade. This ensures time for them to build a foundation in their second language to be able to keep up with advanced grade-level work in both languages. Our program is so popular that there's a long waiting list of English-speaking children to be enrolled in kindergarten. If parents choose this program, they must really be committed to the long-term language learning process. When parents have that mindset and believe in bilingualism for their children, this supports their children in becoming bilingual.

DUAL LANGUAGE TEACHING

My fourth–fifth grade class has 32 children; 17 are English speakers and 15 are Spanish speakers. Most of the children have been in the program since kindergarten. Several Spanish speakers are newly arrived. Children who have been in the program for several years are used to the alternate day format. Even so, students have a wide range of linguistic, academic, and developmental abilities. New arrivals to the program at times require special attention to orient them, especially when instruction is in English. To address these diverse needs, I structure dual language learning opportunities through a variety of means to give children lots of chances to interact with the material and with each other. These learning opportunities include whole-class discussion meetings, individual work, collaborative group work, and long-term projects.

A typical day might include several meetings (for the different subjects of social studies, math, science, geography, etc.), group work time, reading time, journal and report writing. Class meetings are learning time where children are expected to engage in the discussion and listen to one another. Meetings also provide an opportunity for me and the students to track their learning process. Because working and talking together is key to the learning process, all children (e.g., fourth- and fifth-graders, and Spanish- and

English-dominant) are combined for different purposes. Often, there is a lot of movement and productive talking going on to accommodate the different group tasks and projects.

The bulk of our work comes from long-term **integrated curriculum** studies taken from the social studies curriculum. One year, I take the curriculum topics from the fourth grade and the next year from the fifth. This year's studies, on the Native Americans and the Colonial period, are from the fourth grade curriculum and span the whole year. Children engage in many reading (fiction and nonfiction), writing (report, journal, and playwriting), arts (dramatic and visual), social studies, and science projects related to these studies. For mathematics, I tend to use the district-approved math books and curriculum, available in English and Spanish. However, whenever possible, I demonstrate math concepts through hands-on demonstrations and manipulates using *Marilyn Burns'* materials and other innovative programs.

The classroom is a learning laboratory where children are surrounded by real objects, materials, meeting charts, and student work that support their learning. This is especially important because all children need visuals and materials to help them learn in their second language. Related to our Native American study, photographs, lots of books, and artifacts, such as, pottery, beads, shells, tools, and dried corn, are on display for exploration and reference. Student work decorates our room, such as colorful murals and masks, a model of a Native American village, and self-portraits showing each student's Native American name.

Not only does our study stay within the classroom, but I use the broader community through field trips to complement our study. We are fortunate to live in New York City, where we visited a park which helped students see, imagine, and explore the natural environment where the Algonquin tribe once lived. We also visited the Native American exhibits at the American Museum of Natural History and the Native American Museum. All these sources in and out the classroom help them learn.

As a culminating assignment for our Native American study, students complete a very extensive take-home exam, in which they answer many sorts of questions through sequencing, providing information, drawing, and analyzing what they learned through the study. After completing the exam, I conference with each student to discuss their progress on the test and study. In addition, throughout the year, students are required to do two related social studies research projects. They also do other assigned writings, such as fiction or autobiography, depending on the literature genres that we are studying.

STUDENTS' DUAL LANGUAGE PROGRESS

Because I had almost all these students before in second grade, I have been able to track their language development over time. By fifth grade, Spanish-dominant children, who have been in the program since kindergarten, do acquire English. They have strong receptive language, internal grammar, vocabulary, reading, and writing skills. They have definitely crossed over to English and are bilingual and biliterate. Except for the few new arrivals, my Spanish-dominant kids are language peers with the English-dominant kids in speaking, reading, writing, and in content areas. There are some instances when children's second language may not be as sophisticated as that of native speakers, but it is in no way limited. They can organize their thoughts and ideas orally and in writing.

One observation I have made is that some Spanish-dominant children, who were new arrivals in second grade, have acquired English dominance and are quite fluent in their pronunciation and use of **standard English**. I believe this may be because they learn in English in an academic setting from strong language models (the teacher and English-speaking peers). Sometimes these children's academic English is stronger than some Latino children who were born and raised here. This may be because those Spanish-dominant children get lots of support at home. Many of our Mexican parents, although not English speakers, are literate and devote a lot of time to talking and reading to their children. The home native language support helps them with their second language development. When that kind of interest and reinforcement doesn't happen in some households, then language proficiency can be limited.

There is great disparity between Spanish and English speakers' abilities. The English-dominant children, having had only Spanish contact in school, are less fluent in it. Therefore their thinking, organization of ideas, and expression in Spanish is not as sophisticated as that of Spanish-dominant children. The English-dominant kids struggle to put together a basic sentence in Spanish, while Spanish-dominant children, who have been in our program since kindergarten do not have the same struggles in English. What I try to do is really encourage the English-dominant children to use Spanish, even if it's two or three words. In many instances, the English-dominant children do not take the same risks in their language usage as do the Spanish-dominant children. Though the English speakers have made progress, they still are less fluent in Spanish. So, there's a wide range of abilities across the two language groups.

REFLECTIONS ON THE
DUAL LANGUAGE PROGRAM

It's a shame that we only service kids from kindergarten to fifth grade, because the program really needs to go through at least eighth grade. Even though the district has a dual language middle school, many of our children choose to leave the program to attend specialized middle schools that focus on sports, computers, and writing, and literature. It's fine that students have other interests, but to ensure full bilingualism, dual language development needs to be supported longer than just until fifth grade. It somehow stops short. The Spanish-dominant kids seem to cross over to English much faster than the English ones to Spanish. Because the Spanish speakers are in an English-dominant society, they have considerably more input and opportunities to use English all the time. Even though we try to give each language 50% of the time, it's still not an ideal environment where English-speaking kids are immersed in Spanish to the same degree. There are chunks of time when children are not getting Spanish instruction, like during preparation periods or lunch. If you add up how much time students really get in Spanish, it's not equal to English. Spanish needs to be used more consistently throughout the total school context. Unfortunately, Spanish is only happening in the dual language classrooms. If the whole school were a dual language school, students would have more input, opportunity to pick it up, and use it more automatically and naturally.

In addition to having less than 50% of Spanish instruction, available Spanish materials and resources influence how I teach. For example, for our Native American and the colonial period studies, I have a hard time doing a parallel curriculum because of the limited Spanish materials. Sometimes I find some mention of these topics in a history book or an anthology. Social studies is never really covered as deeply in Spanish, except for in general discussions. I find myself translating from English materials more than really teaching with Spanish materials. That's a reality especially in the upper grades. There's a definite imbalance. I find I must do a lot more creating of my own materials than I would if I were teaching only in English. Especially for children who are emergent Spanish speakers, there are few content area materials appropriate to their level of language.

Upon entering the program, I had my doubts about whether the **dual language program** worked. After 5 years, I've learned that some parts work and other parts need work. What works is that we do create a community of children who grow together from kindergarten through Grade 5 and see themselves as language learners. Children develop an appreciation for literacy and languages. The classes have built-in ethnic and linguistic richness, so we use this diversity as part of the curriculum. We don't have to go outside of our setting to find a multicultural environment, because we live it. We appreciate each other and develop sensitivity for other ethnic groups not represented in our classroom, so there are a lot of strengths. There is a definite place for bilingual education. Both groups of kids benefit from the language and cultural exchange that they experience in this program.

What needs work is the program continuity in terms of Spanish language acquisition. All the dual language teachers start with the Board of Education Frameworks and focus on the **content-obligatory vocabulary** (Met, 1994) of the concept that is being taught in a particular language. From a teacher's perspective, it's an absolute challenge to maintain the same district standards and expectations that we have for all children. Because there is so much to teach especially in Spanish, we need clearer and more specific goals about the kinds of language experiences that children need at each grade level. We almost need formal language classes, which is what I try to do. There's much less to support the learning of Spanish. The dual language teachers do work together regularly in weekly dual language planning meetings where we constantly discuss curriculum and the way it relates to language acquisition. We also share teaching materials and strategies that work with all students. We are continually trying to refine our practice to make this program work.

We still need to do a lot of work in developing means to assess kids across the two languages. How do we know what they've learned and what we still need to be teaching? We need other ways of assessing progress, like **portfolios** and checklists showing the skills and language that children should be exhibiting. We need a well-articulated program where progress can be tracked to show the children's academic and language strengths over the grades.

There are lots of language issues that need attention. When Spanish-speaking children move into English, we need to refer their parents to enrichment programs that can support their success in English. I want their English to flourish and grow academically. We need to help children who are having difficulty in reading or writing. For example, some Spanish-speaking students who were born here speak **nonstandard varieties of English**, which really has an impact on how they speak, read, and write. Some will say or write "d-e-r" for "there." So, I'm continually making them aware of the nonstandard and standard codes by showing when it is appropriate to use each. In some Latino communities, there is a mixture of English and Spanish used, which is incomplete. It's not a moral question, because we can go into the debate that language is language as long as they're communicating. But the bottom line is that to be competitive and successful in this society when they reach adulthood, students need to know how to speak, read and write **standard English**. The reality is that because they're Latino or African American, they're going to have to work harder. So, we need to provide certain kinds of learning opportunities for children to be able to do this.

To improve our program, several things are needed. For a language program to work, 32 kids is far too many to serve, especially with the range of linguistic abilities, learning styles, and experiences. I think 25 children should be the maximum. Assistant teachers (not a student teacher) who work with the different groups would be also helpful. A greater commitment toward getting materials is needed. It's not that the material doesn't exist. It does, but it's not reaching the classrooms. It's often hard to find high quality upper grade Spanish materials on a particular subject.

There needs to be a different system of orienting the new teacher. Just because a teacher speaks two languages does not mean that she understands and knows how to implement dual language teaching practices. New teachers need a more seasoned teacher to mentor them. This year, I have been released to go into three teachers' (two dual language and one monolingual) classrooms to help them plan and improve reading instruction. I model reading strategies for them by teaching a reading group. Though this is a step in the right direction, a more consistent mentoring system is needed.

BILINGUAL TEACHER EDUCATION

Although I don't have a formal master's degree in bilingual education, I've had linguistics and ESL training. As an educator, I am always reading professional literature to keep up on the current research. I have attended many Spanish literacy and teaching workshops, including several language institutes. An excellent one was given by Helena Curtain, who presented her book, Language and Children: Making the Match (Curtain & Pesola, 1994). So, bilingual education is not unfamiliar to me. I find it to be a very specific discipline that merits recognition as a practice in and of itself. However, teachers also need to have an understanding of child development, how kids differ developmentally because of culture and language, and how to create child-centered curricula. Whether it's bilingual or monolingual instruction, having a strong grounding in curricula and knowing children is what helps a practitioner be successful.

10

—

Jean

___

BACKGROUND

I am a native of California and have lived and worked in Northern California for most of my life. My family is of European background and has been in the United States for several generations. I've always been interested in languages. I majored in French at the university. As far as learning Spanish, I took some high school and junior college courses, which gave me the basics. I activated my Spanish through traveling and in working with well-educated, Spanish-speaking professionals, who were good language models. My strongly developed first language knowledge has definitely helped me in learning French and Spanish. I believe the theory that your second language can be just as good as your first language. As a teacher, I'm not afraid to use Spanish conversationally with parents or other professionals. Through using it, I have gained fluency. People say my Spanish is really quite adequate.

Traveling to the many Spanish-speaking countries (e.g., Spain, Mexico, Peru, and Costa Rica) has helped me get the "man on the street" language. Before I didn't have command of the social language, only the academic language, which I found I couldn't survive with. The exposure to other ways of communicating and accents, has made my ear more receptive and has helped to improve my Spanish. I've also learned a lot from studying the Spanish teaching materials.

ENTRY INTO THE PROFESSION

In the late 1960s, after finishing college, I stayed home for about 10 years to raise my family. Then, because I needed to get out of the house and get involved in something else, I began volunteering in my children's school. I was soon hired as an (instructional) aide in the district where I have worked with **language minority** students for the last 16 years in varying capacities. Working as an aide, I realized that I wanted to become a teacher, so I enrolled in an elementary education credential program and finished 30 credits past my bachelor's degree. Then I worked as an aide teaching **English as a second language (ESL)** to migrant and international children, who were not getting appropriate curriculum or teacher attention. They rarely participated in class activities and mainly spent their time drawing pictures and coloring. It wasn't that the teacher did not want to teach them, but that she did not have the language, skill, or methodology to know how to teach them. I helped her better serve those children.

When I started as an **ESL** aide, I had no formal second language acquisition training. I first learned about teaching **language minority** students from a resource teacher. I used to spend time picking her brain, asking her about conferences to attend, classes to take, and materials to read. And that's where I acquired a lot of knowledge.

To serve **language minority** students, our district uses state monies to hire a resource teacher and **ESL** aides. The district never had enough students per grade level or funds to create a full bilingual program. Using aides for ESL **pull-out instruction** was a simple solution, because aides did not have to meet credential requirements. Usually they receive some district **ESL** in-service training, but they rarely have academic training per se. Aides are supervised by the site principals, who may or may not know about educating **language minority** students. This was before there was any real definitive state legislation such as California State **Assembly Bill (AB) 1329** which later became **Assembly Bill (AB) 507,** that mandated better service for **language minority** students.

I really enjoyed my work as an aide. Because of my success working with students and staff, I ended up working at almost all of the district schools, running the **ESL** program and presenting in-service training for all new aides. In 1983, I was hired to teach a Spanish bilingual class for children from a resident migrant labor camp. I had received my **Bilingual Certificate of Competence (BCC)** by examination. For 7 years, I taught Grades K–1, 1, and 1–2. My presence at that school started the process of providing primary language instruction to children at that school. Finally, there was someone able to help those students and advise others about how to work with them. I had a lot of support from my principal.

However, the school had no formal bilingual program policy. It was kind of up to each teacher. The district just follows the state bilingual education guidelines that were established from the legislation **(AB) 507** and **(AB) 1329.** Though this legislation was "sunsetted" (allowed to terminate), it still applies. My class was the only designated bilingual class at that school. The other Hispanic students were served by Spanish-speaking teachers, who did not necessarily deliver a bilingual program. The district philosophy was geared to getting students into English as quickly as possible instead of **maintenance,** which is what it should be. Because of the limited commitment to bilingual education and diminishing numbers of **language minority** students at that school, I moved to my present school, where I have been teaching first grade in the Spanish **Immersion program** for the last 2 years.

DEMOGRAPHICS

The district, located in a Northern California interior suburban/rural community, has between 5,000 and 6,000 students in six elementary schools, two junior high, one high school, and two continuation schools. The district schools are modern and quite well equipped. Many of the district's students are children of professors and students from a nearby university. The district attracts very capable teachers and has some of the state's highest test scores. There's a relatively low population of **language minority** students (about 10%–12%) generated largely from migrant farm workers and the university's international students.

The families are from a broad range of professions and socioeconomic status. Many families are advantaged, yet some graduate student families are on restricted budgets. Although those children are very capable academically, their parents are not yet in the job force and have limited spendable income. So, there's quite a disparity. In my class for instance, I have children of lawyers, medical school students, university professors, and migrant farm workers. The area's major crops are rice, hay, tomatoes, and peppers. Some former migrant workers, who are now permanent residents, work as truck drivers or on ranches.

Over half of our **language minority** students are Hispanic, mainly from Mexico and Central America. Most migrant families receive some kind of public assistance. Almost all of them qualify for Aid to Families with Dependent Children (AFDC) and their children receive the free lunch program. Other language groups are from the university's international student community and include Mandarin, Urdu, Uruba, Arabic, Japanese, Persian, Hebrew, and European languages. So, it's quite an interesting mix of students.

THE SPANISH IMMERSION PROGRAM

About 12 years ago, our district started implementing the Spanish **Immersion program,** which was originally modeled after the Canadian Immersion

Programs, where majority English-speaking students were immersed in French. Our English-speaking parents wanted their children to learn Spanish, so they requested to place their children in the Spanish Immersion Program. Many parents camped out overnight to get their children into the program. At first, only a limited number of students could be enrolled. The school board then decided to offer as many classes as the community wanted, which was when the program really started to mushroom. Simultaneously, the district **Title VII** director, who was frustrated with the ESL **pull-out** instructional model used for teaching **language minority** students and the lack of L_1 (native language) instruction, proposed that they be integrated into the immersion classes.

Our Spanish **Immersion program** has both English-speaking children learning Spanish and Spanish-speaking children learning Spanish and English within one classroom. This program differs from dual immersion in that most of the instruction is in Spanish, especially in the early grades. The immersion program is a much better way of meeting language minority students' needs than **ESL** because, as a **late-exit model,** the academics are more comprehensibly delivered in Spanish. It makes sense if you think about it. There is no question that instruction is best delivered in one language. I personally think that immersion is the wave of the future. That's why I'm in the program.

Originally, the program was housed in several school sites. Since 1992, almost 10% of the district students (about 500) are in two schools: one for Grades K through 3 and another for Grades 4 through 6. The program is continuing to grow in popularity.

PROGRAM DESIGN

In kindergarten and first grades, all instruction is in Spanish. In each grade, English is incrementally added: 10% in second, 10% to 20% in third, and by sixth, there's about 40% English instruction. Spanish-dominant students are also provided with English instruction throughout the grades. Our program works pretty well for both English- and Spanish-speaking students. But the **ESL** component still needs to be enriched for our Spanish speakers. When English-speaking students are immersed in Spanish, the majority language (English) is still spoken and supported in the home and community. Their parents read to them in English. They are exposed to all kinds of English language enrichment such as libraries, theater, and TV. When they get to third grade, where English language arts is formally taught, they're ready for third-grade vocabulary and content.

Spanish-speaking students, on the other hand, are immersed in a Spanish environment, so they're not getting the same enriched English vocabulary from home, community, or literature. Their Spanish is enriched from their home environments, which is wonderful. Their Spanish content areas and reading skills are, of course, 100% transferable to their second language. Once you read, you read. They need a stronger **ESL** component that is literature- and content-based, sheltered, and thematically integrated to better prepare them for the upper grade English language arts and reading demands. We're trying to strengthen our **ESL** component through team teaching in Grades K through 3.

CLASS COMPOSITION

I have an interesting ethnic and linguistic mix of my 30 first graders. Of the English speakers, most are Caucasian, but several children are from Chinese and Filipino backgrounds. The Hispanic students are either migrant students or children of university students and/or professors. Six or seven Spanish-dominant students have been identified as **Limited English Proficient (LEP)**, based on **language proficiency tests**. Even though they are classified as LEP, we find their English communication skills and **Basic Interpersonal Communication Skills (BICS)** are quite good. They are quite capable of interacting with English speakers in the classroom and on the playground.

PEDAGOGY

Language and Content Development

The majority of instruction takes place in Spanish. I use a variety of communicative language and second language techniques, such as **whole language, Total Physical Response (TPR), notional-functional,** drama, music, and rhythm/rhyme pattern activities. Vocabulary is developed through literature and content areas. Content vocabulary is pretty specific to each subject and grade. Instruction is content-based and thematically and culturally integrated. For each unit, we do brainstorm charts of what they know, which includes vocabulary and pictures. The charts are displayed around the room throughout the unit, so the children can use the information in their writing.

Even though I model Spanish all the time, English-speaking kids will often talk to one another in English. At first, they seem to understand what is going on. By mid-year, they gradually start expressing some Spanish words and structures. As the year progresses, they are more able to communicate with each other and Spanish-speaking peers.

For the Spanish speakers, in addition to all the Spanish instruction, they get **ESL** instruction for 25 minutes three times a week. Basically, I use the same second-language techniques with a focus on integrated, literature-based **ESL** from trade books and our English reading series. I "shy away" from **ESL** teaching that focuses on isolated, out-of-context vocabulary. I try to give them a strong English literature foundation to prepare them for the third-grade English language arts.

Math and Science

For math, we chart and graph lots of things such as the calendar, lost teeth, and birthdays. Following *Math Their Way* (Baratta-Lorton, 1976) the students count the number of days we've been in school in Spanish. They learn how to handle all sorts of data, which comes from another program called *Used Numbers* (Russell & Stone, 1990). For example, with birthdays, the students wrote their birthdate on a paper that they had to organize in some meaningful way. I told them to look around to see what they could do. They got themselves in groups by their birthday months. I said, "Okay, now let's put that information on the board. How should we do it?" By themselves, they came up with putting the months and days in order!

Two days a week, I teach concept lessons and the other 3 days, children freely explore those concepts with all kinds of materials using tangrams, number lines, and clocks—which they love. I have them count with all kinds of manipulatives, such as *Unifix Cubes* (using suggestions from Richardson, 1984). Most of them can count up to 350 in Spanish! We also count the days of the year with money and graph them on our "¿Cúanto es?" chart. Today shows $103, which means we've completed 103 days of school. Through lots of counting and playing games, they've learned to identify ones, tens, and hundreds place values.

For science, I use the Spanish version of *FO/D* (*Finding Out/Descubrimento*; DeAvila, Duncan, & Navarette, 1987), which focuses on students' social development for students to experientially explore the concepts. The social dynamics of what happens as they work in **cooperative groups** is very much empowering for minority students. Even though the program was actually written for second through sixth grades, another teacher and

I have adapted the same methodology to the first-grade curriculum. For example, we have put together six hands-on experiences to teach the properties of air in the solid, liquid, and gas unit. We have designed other themes on scale and structure for our first graders to explore.

Reading

I do daily formal Spanish reading instruction using literature from trade books and basals. In using **basals,** I pick stories that complement the thematic topic that I am working on. These topics include: living things, body systems, and trash and recycling, etc. I use **basal** stories as I would a literature-based program. We don't just read the books from start to finish. We also do lots of **language experience** kinds of things to complement the units of study. As I work with a reading group, the students read and copy thematically appropriate words and phrases from the pocket chart.

Interestingly, after learning to read in Spanish, children say, "I don't read English." I tell them, "Oh, yes you do! Once you try, you'll see how easy it is." Once they read, they read. It doesn't matter the language. By the end of the year, after learning to decode in Spanish, many are able to begin to read English books without being formally taught English reading.

I often pick literature, not for its language, but for the way it presents the concepts in the theme. I look for books with good pictures that show the concepts. Sometimes when reading aloud I do a lot of spontaneous translations from English texts. I can do that because my students are not reading English yet. They aren't focused on the words in the book trying to figure out what it says, but they get the content. That's a nice strategy, especially when the materials aren't available in Spanish.

Culture

I try to validate the Hispanic culture using as many Spanish-speaking models as I can. I have a native Spanish-speaking aide, who is a university student. For 1½ hours a day, I have him help kids with the heavy academics. I also encourage Spanish-speaking parents to come in, share, and work as volunteers.

I teach customs and concepts from the Hispanic culture, so that every child in this classroom is empowered by the materials and information that I present. In the beginning of the year, we do a chart of students' backgrounds which gets them talking about their heritage with their parents.

This is really important, because I want them to start off with a strong feeling about who they are and where they come from.

During the fall, we study "El Día de los Muertos" [The Day of the Dead] because I have a number of Mexican and Chicano children in the class. I teach about the Mexican ritual of going to the cemetery to honor deceased family members. We make altars with sugar skulls. Children learn that death is a sweet part of life that is not to be feared. The Hispanic children identify with learning about something culturally meaningful and the English speakers also see the importance of different celebrations and holidays. We also recognize and study many American holidays too.

To highlight the Hispanic culture, I use a lot of literature, poetry, and music. As I play guitar, the children jubilantly sing the Spanish songs and nursery rhymes, many of which the Hispanic children already know. This gives those children a sense of pride and a certain level of expertise. I write the lyrics and poems on sentence strips for the pocket chart. Those children quickly recognize the words and are able to model the alliteration and rhythm for their English-speaking peers. The fluent Spanish speakers right away show the success and the joy of learning. Their faces light up like light bulbs. Learning and school is supposed to be fun. If it's not fun, then why should anyone come? Where else can you sit down and just have a good time? And they love it. And I love it too.

Developmentally Appropriate Teaching

I try to motivate students with topics that are age appropriate. For first graders, what could be more interesting than birthdays or lost teeth? I watch for children's academic, linguistic, and developmental readiness to learn new concepts. I want to make sure to teach a concept when they can be successful with it, not when it's out of their reach. Child development is important to consider because all students learn and grow at different rates. Every last one of them is different. From my observations, children also have different **learning styles,** attention spans, and family dynamics. It's best to have a classroom where there are lots of different ways to learn, not just sitting at a desk and copying text from the board. Children need to be able to participate in **cooperative groups** and capitalize on different strengths and talents.

I am kind of loose as far as structure goes. I like children to find their own way. I set things out for them to do, and pretty soon it is all done. I have a room full of teachers. Maybe half of them listened and heard the instructions, so they can help the other half. That's the way life works.

TESTING

Standardized Tests

Our school district does not conduct **standardized tests** until third grade. Children are tested in third and sixth grades with the _CTBS_ (_California Test of Basic Skills_, CTB/McGraw-Hill, 1989) and the _SABE_ (_Spanish Assessment of Basic Education_, CTB/McGraw-Hill, 1991). Because of all the upper grade test requirements, that's why I choose to teach first grade. In the lower grades, there is less emphasis on tests. Only the oral **language proficiency tests** are required. To assess what children have learned, I use criterion reference, teacher-made, and observation assessments. By mid-year, I also give children a weekly spelling list to see whether they can write dictated words and sentences. I keep these results in a booklet, so I have a very concrete measure of what they are doing. We also do **portfolio assessment,** where I periodically review their progress on collected work samples.

Language Proficiency Tests

Spanish-speaking students are all screened for oral English **language proficiency** within 30 days of their arrival to the school. Language proficiency testing follows the state guidelines mandated by the Sunset Provisions of **AB 507,** which are still in effect. Within 90 days, native language assessment is conducted. For English language assessment, the district uses the _IPT_ (_IPT Oral Language Proficiency Test_; Ballard, Tighe, & Dalton, 1991) and the _BSM_ (_Bilingual Syntax Measure_; Burt, Dulay, & Chávez, 1978). We use a lot of different matrices to test English acquisition of structure and vocabulary (such as the _Boehm_, 1986, and the _BSM_, Burt, Dulay, & Chávez, 1978, tests). Sometimes too much importance is given to these tests. It is better to look at what a child knows and can do.

These tests vary in quality and accuracy. Some of the language stimuli are culturally biased and the pictures are horrible. The kids often don't know what they are. The test content is not all that interesting, nor does it reflect students' knowledge. Students react differently to the tests. For example, our **language minority** student population is so diverse that some children find the test content humorous or ridiculous, while others find it okay, and still others have no clue of what to do with it. Teachers need to understand that the background of the population on which the test is normed affects the validity of the test.

The tests are given by the **ESL** aides. When first graders or kindergartners are pulled out for these tests, the results more often measure the child's reaction to the environment or the person giving the test, rather than what they can actually do. Because that happens a lot with young children, I don't find the results are always valid. Actually, testing results might be more accurate if conducted by a professional or the classroom teacher (especially the bilingual teacher) instead of an aide. Testing is still not on par with program design and instruction. Teachers need to know how to design better tests and how to interpret what is being tested.

MATERIALS

In the beginning, when I first started, materials were nearly nonexistent. I did a lot of translating and fishing for materials. I used a lot of teacher-developed materials, especially those from a Los Angeles Consortium called Tortilla Press. As a result of teacher pressure and growing student enrollments, there are many more excellent Spanish materials/programs that were not available before, such as _FO/D_ (DeAvila et al., 1987). The University of California's Lawrence Hall of Science offers some fabulous curricula and training programs in Spanish: the GEMS (_Great Expectations in Math and Science_), _Family Math_ (Stenmark et al., 1986), and _Family Science_ (Noone, in press). These programs include low-cost, in-service teacher training. You can't ask for better support. That's what I use.

Each year, more and more literature and textbooks are available in Spanish. Much English literature is now translated into Spanish. Ideally, I would like to teach only in Spanish from Spanish sources, so that the culture would be totally integrated. Translations are extremely poor. Some are good, though more are poor. I often select literature for the content rather than its language.

SUCCESSES WITH STUDENTS

The **Immersion programs** are very popular. The selling point is enrichment and acquisition of Spanish, which is a growing language in California. All the kids do pretty well in both Spanish and English, because it's an enriched program. Students test as well or better than non-immersion students on nationally normed tests by the sixth grade. If it weren't such an excellent quality program, we wouldn't maintain such high enrollments.

We have found that sixth-grade, immersion English-speaking students have high levels of Spanish oral proficiency, too. However, their grammar and written skills are as not as high. These students are advanced placed in high school Spanish. The immersion program has forced reorganization of the Spanish language classes at the secondary level, which is wonderful because it gives a status boost to those students. Spanish-speaking students also continue their Spanish development in advanced native language Spanish classes. Spanish speakers acquire English **Basic Interpersonal Communication Skills (BICS)** rapidly and well. Not all of them move as rapidly to **Cognitive Academic Language Proficiency (CALP).** There is still a gap for most Spanish-dominant students in our program.

PARENT INVOLVEMENT

I send homework in two languages, otherwise the English-speaking parents can't participate. Some simple assignments that kids are able to do themselves, are in Spanish only. My purpose in homework assignments is to get the families to talk about whatever unit we're working on.

I find all the parents are extremely interested in their children's education. Generally, we have a lot of majority parent involvement in the school system. We involve the Hispanic parents as much as we can. When they have young children at home, it's hard to get them to come in. They mostly come in for a special occasions. Parent volunteers (both language majority and minority) come in regularly to help with different class projects. If I am doing a food unit on breads around the world, they come in and make breads or tortillas from Mexico or wherever they are from.

In terms of outreach to **language minority** parents, I'm lucky that parents of primary grade students are very caring about their children. When parents come after school to pick up their children, I'll invite them in to chat. Then I'll ask the child to show their mom or dad what we've been doing. That gets them in and lets the child know that I expect them to communicate with their parents about what's happening at school.

I communicate with Hispanic parents through my weekly parent newsletter in Spanish, in which I include major points of interest or dates of upcoming school activities. I want them to get the same information that other parents in the school get. Luckily, most of our parents are literate, so they can read it.

For parent–teacher conferences, I always schedule a time for them. If they don't come, I follow up with a phone call to reschedule the appointment or I'll make a home visit to discuss their child's progress. After that, I usually get 100% attendance at parent conferences. But that's because I really push it and let them know how important it is. They're not intimidated to come in; rather, they're very glad to have the information delivered in a language they can understand.

I work hard at parent communication. In all my contact with the parents, I let them know what my philosophy and goals are for their children. I think they believe that bilingual education is successful. I get a lot of good reactions from parents about what goes on in our class. Their kids can't wait to come to school in the morning, and that's where I want them. I have very high attendance.

At the district level, there is some parent outreach. I have conducted parent trainings for our "Family Math Night," where I presented Spanish activities from the State Math Framework. More outreach is really needed because getting the parents to come in is sometimes difficult. Parent education is also needed. They need to know how they can reinforce what's going on at school and how to communicate more effectively with the school. We also need to let them know about how to get services they're entitled to.

ADMINISTRATIVE POLICIES AND SUPPORT

The associate superintendent of instruction, who is not bilingual, administers the Spanish **Immersion program.** Although she's familiar with some of the research, she doesn't have an academic background in second language acquisition and has not worked in those kind of programs. She is, however, working at it.

The principals at the two Spanish **Immersion program** Schools have provided varied support. One principal, from a school with seven immersion classes, was not too skilled in second language acquisition and did not really understand what the program was all about. There were times when he unconsciously sabotaged what we were doing. He excluded the minority students from certain opportunities, which could be interpreted negatively in the **school culture.** His lack of background in the field was harmful. I'm sorry, but I hold him accountable for not seeking the needed information, especially after it was brought to his attention. It is dangerous when a principal is not knowledgeable, because a lot of **language minority** students are misplaced in the regular English-only program. These children often fall behind academically and may get referred for child study.

This year, for the first time, the district has hired a bilingual principal for my school. This is a positive step. And she's knowledgeable. She just hasn't had the actual experience in applying the research, nor the theoretical background that builds over a period of time. She has shown her support in purchasing Spanish library books and professional materials and in providing Spanish in-service training.

TEACHER EDUCATION

In 1991, I completed my master's degree in bilingual cross-cultural education at a state university. I feel really prepared to implement an **Immersion program.** The best thing about my master's studies was the opportunity to network with other teachers, which allowed us to see other programs and teaching approaches. I also got research information that helped me better develop appropriate grade-level curriculum from the state frameworks.

Another good thing was that the professors exposed us to the current politics of education and empowerment strategies for minority students, which I have adopted as a philosophy. Now everything I do, such as **cooperative learning** and _FO/D_ (DeAvila et al., 1987), is designed to empower those students and their families. One Native American professor's classes gave me another perspective on cultural awareness. I became aware of the different teaching and **learning styles** that teachers and kids bring with them. The teacher must provide for these, while recognizing and validating all cultures. Some students are taught to work for the benefit of the group and not to compete individually. We learned that some students need that chance to be a part of that group.

Because I recently have gone through the Master's program, I have dealt with many of these issues and I have thought them through. I try to read and keep up on the current research in the field as much as I can. I was fortunate to have an opportunity and forum to be reflective. But a lot of teachers aren't encouraged to reflect, because the **school culture** doesn't have a lot of consistency or meeting of the minds.

COLLEGIAL ACCEPTANCE AND SHARING

I have been pretty well accepted by bilingual and monolingual teachers. I've established credibility through my years of work in the district conducting in-services for parents teachers, and aides. I've also worked as a mentor teacher. So, I have had a lot of validation and respect in the district. Even though I have credibility, I didn't escape the "scapegoating" of being associated with "that terrible elitist program." In the beginning, the Spanish **Immersion program** was sometimes perceived as taking over the English program, which created a lot of animosity. There were definite problems with implementing it. At staff meetings, general education teachers made real "off-the-wall" comments, putting-down the program and its staff. It made for a very unpleasant situation, which should never have happened. We never have been completely appreciated by some teachers for our work and what we bring to the site.

Perhaps, unconsciously because I am Caucasian, others may be more apt to accept me, but I would not like to think this is happening. We have some native Spanish-speaking immersion teachers whose Spanish, is, of course, poetic. Because they may not have full English proficiency, I have seen some English-speaking staff members say and do unkind things to those teachers.

The fact that the diversity among the staff is not being recognized or appreciated bothers me. Our teachers are incredibly proficient in two languages because they were either born here or came from Mexico as young children. So, there are teachers with a full range of proficiencies and they are lumped together under the pejorative "bilingual" label.

Overall, the immersion teachers work well together and have adapted curriculum for the Spanish **Immersion program.** It's just a very open group of people. We make sure that the curriculum spirals through the grades. We share a lot of materials. One colleague and I have taught side by side for 2 or 3 years. Philosophically, we are in the same groove. Collegial support is important not just for the sharing of teaching ideas and materials, but it's the mental processing and a safe environment to reflect on your teaching that is needed as a bilingual teacher.

THE FUTURE OF BILINGUAL EDUCATION: ADVICE TO TEACHERS

One reason I wanted to teach in the Spanish **Immersion program** is because it's less stigmatized than regular bilingual programs. In the late 1960s, bilingual education was established as a result of civil rights legislation associated with remedial programs that attempted to compensate for a language deficit. Since then, bilingual education programs have carried that negative stigma. Unfortunately, everybody (the teachers, children, and parents) associated with bilingual were "labeled." Stigmas from labels are very damaging and need to be removed. Demographics clearly show that the need for bilingual education programs is not going away. Who cares what we call it? We need to deliver quality instruction and materials for all students, no matter what the language.

If you are going to be a bilingual teacher, you must really love children. And if you don't have that basic dedication to people, why be in the profession? The dedication and love are the common denominators that keep you going when the work gets to be overwhelming. As a bilingual person, you must understand that being bilingual is a unique gift that should be valued, cherished, and shared with others. This way others can also see the advantage of being bilingual. *Ser bilingüe, vale por dos* [Being bilingual is doubly valuable]. There's no better way to empower kids than to make their primary language the valuable one. Bilingual teaching connects the language and culture by valuing their families, their roots, and who they are. Be prepared to work really hard! Get in there and get dirty! Sit on the floor. Work with dirt, stones, and grass. Make the environment the students' learning laboratory. Let them go, so they'll be free to learn. That's the hardest part. Certain things may not work for some students. But, you must believe that every child can find their way and learn, if given the proper learning environment. The challenge and fun is to create that environment so that every child can learn.

This is rapidly becoming a pluralistic society and world. Jobs, technology, and classrooms are different than during our parents or grandparents' times. There is no way that we are going to turn back the tide. The tide is already here. So, to make it work for you in your classroom, one needs to tool-up and stay current with what is happening in the profession, which means being prepared to value and deal with that pluralistic population. If you're now receiving diverse students in your class, don't fight it, join it in a positive way, with a positive attitude. The advantages of diversity will make you and your classroom richer. I am living proof. You can learn, not only from your students, but your colleagues can be great resources. It's simply a false paradigm that **language minority** teachers can really only function well in their primary language and not English. That's simply not true. And here's a place where that misconception can be dismantled. As you interact with bilingual teachers, students, and their families, you will see their strengths. They, too, can enrich what goes on in school, if you're open to them.

11

—

Luz

BACKGROUND AND SCHOOLING
EXPERIENCES

I was born in a tiny Idaho mining town, where only my family and one other family spoke Spanish. I learned English through total **immersion** as I played with my English-speaking friends. I already had some English by the time I went to school. Even so, when I first went to school, I had a hard time expressing myself. Home and school were two separate worlds. School felt so foreign. The food and everything was so different. I went through feeling a lot of shame, anger, and wondering where I belonged. Because I was Mexican and spoke another language, I was made to feel different.

By second grade, through studying hard and lots of memorizing, I got the feel of what school was all about. I was very quiet and didn't say a whole lot. By third grade, I started getting good grades and did pretty well. Then, after junior high school, my family moved to a Northern California urban city, where I have lived and worked ever since.

All through school, I had always wanted to be a teacher. I knew I wanted to go to college. Nevertheless, the high school counselors didn't encourage me about the classes I needed to take. Even though I objected, I was consistently placed in shorthand and typing classes. The counselors also did not inform me about how to apply for college. Luckily, a Chicano nonprofit organization called *La Causa* [The Cause] came to our school to assist Chicano youth with college applications and scholarships. With their guidance, I was accepted at many colleges and decided to attend a local women's college, where I received a scholarship.

In college, all the Latina and Black students experienced discrimination. We were on probation the whole time. The college was always checking our grades to see if we could make it. We were always having to fight for equity issues. The Chicanas formed a chapter of MECHA [El Movimiento Estudiantíl Chicano de Aztlán–A Chicano Student Group] in which I was very involved. Ever since high school, I have always been committed to struggling for my community and to giving back to it in any way I could.

TEACHER EDUCATION

During my early schooling experiences, I had no role models. Not having that someone who speaks your language, who understands and respects you and makes you feel that you belong is what motivated me to become a bilingual teacher. Since I always saw myself working with children, after college, I took a fifth-year credential program for the bilingual certification.

What I found most helpful about the bilingual training were the classes about the linguistic aspects of first and second language acquisition. I've noticed certain common language patterns are influenced by a student's first language, be it Chinese, Vietnamese, or Spanish. As a teacher, you have to be able to recognize the different linguistic resources that students bring in order to help them to learn English.

Though the quality of the coursework was okay, we weren't really very well prepared for the responsibilities, realities, and challenges of urban education, such as the masses of unnecessary paperwork and not having sufficient teaching materials. Teacher education courses give a beginning foundation of certain theoretical information, but it's up to you to learn the rest. Even after teaching for 16 years, I find I still have so much to learn.

PARENTS IN THE COMMUNITY SCHOOL

In 1975, our school started as a K–3 alternative school. It was a feeder school for primarily Latino children who had attended a bilingual Children's Center. Unlike other schools whose population comes from the neighborhood, interested parents throughout the district could choose to place their children in this bilingual/multicultural community school. My children attended the Children's Center and went on to attend the alternative school. As a community member, I was involved in starting the school. By 1978, I was eventually hired as a teacher, after being interviewed by the committee of parents and teachers.

The vision of the school was to provide students with more than just a Spanish **maintenance** or **transitional** program. Parents wanted children involved in and learning from community struggles. We invited lots of prominent and progressive people, such as César Chávez, as well as doctors, lawyers, authors, and illustrators, to come to the school and share. Our goal was (and still is) to bring the world to our students, so they can see it's not unreachable. Bringing the world into the school makes students feel less isolated.

In the beginning, *la mesa directiva* [the governing board], made up of parents and teachers, ran the school. We had an off-site administrator who came in occasionally from another school. This left us space to make the most of the decisions, much like what is happening now with shared decision making. We had no secretary to answer phones or do the paperwork. As a head teacher, I had to do a lot of that, which was really hard, while having full classroom responsibilities. After a few years of being a K–3 bilingual school, we added Grades 4–6. The demands became so great that we eventually got an on-site administrator to do those bureaucratic things. When the first administrator came in with her own agenda, the parents lost a lot of their control and decision-making power. The parents and teachers no longer ran the school as they once did.

Over time, the parents became more involved in the school again. A program's success is measured by the involvement of the parents. Our school would have been "long gone" without such strong community involvement. Parents, many times, have spoken up at Board meetings on behalf of the school. We've been able to bring out diverse community members from Latino, Asian, White, and African American backgrounds. They believe in the school and are continuously advocating for it.

CHANGING DEMOGRAPHICS:
IMPACT ON THE PROGRAM

The school is located in the downtown area of a fairly large Northern California city. The 11 temporary portable buildings are decorated with student-painted Latin-American murals. The school's diverse population is 70% Latino (Mexican, Central American, Caribbean, & Latin American), 20% Asian (Chinese, Vietnamese, Lao, Cambodian, Philippine, & Thai), 8% Black (African American & African), and 2% other. There are 355 students from Grades K–6 of whom 75% are **Limited English Proficient (LEP)**. Some children, who speak languages other than English or Spanish, become trilingual, because when they leave us, they speak their own language, English and Spanish. The neighborhood used to be predominantly Mexican. Now it's more diverse with Mexican, African American, Vietnamese, Chinese, Lao, and Central American children. There's a range of parents' socioeconomic status (SES) and education levels. Most of the students come from low-income families, with 80% qualifying for free meals.

With the change in demographics, the school started accepting neighborhood children, whether they wanted to be in a bilingual program or not. The student population is now more reflective of the neighborhood. The diverse population has been enriching for the staff. It's actually easier to teach multicultural education, because you have a multicultural group. However, the language aspect is more difficult to address because we don't have the teachers or assistants to provide for all our children's native languages. Only two classes either have a Chinese or a Vietnamese bilingual teaching assistant helping English-speaking teachers.

THE TEACHING STAFF

Of our 12 teachers, 10 have bilingual certification. The other two have their **Language Development Specialist (LDS)** credential and teach the **sheltered English** classes. Among our staff, we have professional writers and artists who share their different talents. Fortunately, the staff is small enough so we can collaborate. We often sit down and discuss with one another what works with particular students. Unlike other schools, where teachers rarely talk to one another or want to try anything new, we all are constantly sharing ideas and curriculum, trying new things, and looking for what works best for children. We are committed to this kind of collaboration. Schools need to be places where teachers can plan, share, and talk to one another.

The teachers' concern for children is felt throughout the school. Due to our school size and ambiance, there's not a lot of fighting on the playground. They're all *our* students at the school. Children are not seen as "those fifth graders" or "those bilingual students." Whatever the grade, all teachers know most of the students and watch out for them. We are all part of a large family.

THE EVOLVING BILINGUAL PROGRAM

Over the years, we have adjusted the program and approaches, depending on our students and teachers. At one time, every teacher and the office staff was bilingual. The program had an alternate day approach with Spanish on one day and English on the next. Everyone in the whole school, on the playground and in the office used the designated language of the day. Now that our population is so diverse, that is no longer the case.

Our program philosophy is not **transitional**; our goal is language **maintenance** and **enrichment**. Multilingual communication is valued within the school. We model that acquiring other languages is important. In the early grades, we focus on developing the child's primary language, especially in reading. Groups of children are divided by language for reading instruction, with English taught in the morning and Spanish in the afternoon. In the upper grades, language instruction is both maintenance of Spanish for Spanish-speakers and second language enrichment for the speakers of other languages. In the afternoons, all the fourth, fifth, and sixth graders are divided into four language arts sections based on their needs: **English as a second language (ESL)** for non-native speakers of English, beginning and advanced **Spanish as a second language (SSL)** for native English speakers, and Spanish reading and language arts for native Spanish speakers. I do the Spanish for native speakers. Departmentalizing like this allows us to work with the same kids throughout their upper grade years. This enables us to see children's long-term language growth over 3 years.

When some of the non-English or Spanish speakers become fluent enough in English, then they start **SSL**. We encourage them to make the transition when they are ready. Some of those children come out speaking three languages. It depends on each student. There's flexibility and choice to fit kids' needs. We've had some English-speaking children who struggle so much with English, that we don't put them in **SSL**. It would be too much for them. You've got to look at what's best for each child.

MULTILINGUAL CLASSROOM COMPOSITION

In my fourth-grade bilingual class, 20 out of the 30 children are designated **LEP**. It's really multilingual with Spanish speakers, Spanish–English bilinguals, speakers of other languages, and English speakers. Of the Spanish speakers, only two are monolingual Spanish-speaking and the rest are bilingual. The speakers of other languages come from all over (e.g., Laos, China, and Ethiopia). In past years, I've had kids who don't speak *any* English. This year most of my kids speak some English.

By fourth grade, many Spanish-dominant kids, who have been in the program since the beginning, are already strong in both English and Spanish. By this grade, a lot of transition goes on where kids who were primarily reading in Spanish begin to feel confident enough to speak and read in English.

There are a few Spanish-dominant children, however, who are losing their Spanish. They forget how to say things when they live in a society that emphasizes and validates English. Children need to see that Spanish is valued and recognized in the school; otherwise, they're not going to retain it. Our goal is to go beyond maintaining the level of Spanish. We want their Spanish to be growing, as is their English. If my class only had children from two language groups, I would teach differently than I do now. I'd be able to utilize both languages in a 50–50 ratio, the way we used to. Since we have speakers of so many other languages, I've had to modify the program and use a lot of **sheltered English** strategies. These strategies help all kids, even English speakers, because of the visuals and the hands-on activities.

Although I don't speak languages other than Spanish or English, I encourage children who speak other languages to speak and enrich their native languages. For my class library, I buy books in many languages so those children can have access to their native language. I utilize many strategies to open the door for communication. For example, if a child does not speak English or Spanish, I try to find someone bilingual in the class or from another class who is able to speak to the child. I try to acknowledge and support all native languages however I can.

TEACHING APPROACHES

Reading and Language Arts

Reading is either all in English or Spanish. As I said, Spanish reading and language arts are departmentalized in the afternoons. English reading has all different levels. I give grade-level materials to students who are beginning to read in English because using primer reading books would be an insult. My goal is to encourage students to read and enjoy various literature genres. I use various strategies to help them live, feel, and understand the story in a nonthreatening way. Partner reading, discussion, and the arts allow them to experience the story and be successful. Just because they are learning to read English, I don't see them in a deficit mode. I understand that they may not learn all the words in the books, because grade-level books are not easy to read. They do, however, understand a great deal. For children with limited vocabulary, I focus on vocabulary. For other children, I focus on different comprehension skills. In addition, I have **core**

literature in both languages which all children read. I select several books for the year, such as _Island of the Blue Dolphins_ (O'Dell, 1960), which I have available in both English and Spanish.

To address diverse language needs, I seat children at tables heterogeneously so they can help each other to understand the language and content. I ask more fluent students to translate and/or summarize what has been said in either language to a particular student or to the whole table. Oral and written summarizing and paraphrasing are skills that they need to develop. Each group has translators. When we have guest speakers, the translators may be asked to tell their group what's going on.

The language I use depends on the subject. I try not to use **concurrent translation,** because they'll just turn off to the other language. Concurrent translation takes a lot of time, so I avoid it unless I'm saying something really important that I want everybody to understand each word, like for a test or emergency instructions. Usually I'll just summarize, because I like them to be able to hear the words in either language. I do write on the board bilingually to reinforce the two languages. If I say something in English, I'll definitely have it written in both languages.

Writing Development

For creative, expressive, or journal writing, students can write in whatever language they feel most comfortable. To develop vocabulary, students do several activities to help them learn the meaning of words, such as drawing pictures or using visuals. They keep a word bank of new and commonly used words. They use Spanish-English dictionaries all the time for both reading and writing. In their journals, to develop writing fluency, I just try to get them to write. I tell them not to worry about spelling. They underline words they are unsure of and then we go back to them later. I respect that their journals are personal, so I don't touch the content of journals, only the underlined words. If they have 10 misspelled words and only one is underlined, I only give the spelling of that word. This gives students control over their learning and power to ask for help. They know that I will respond in writing in their journals. This way they know they are writing for an audience.

Students do a lot of writing for different purposes: pen-pal writing, letters, projects, stories, and poetry. Before they write anything, we do lots of prewriting activities, such as brainstorming and word **webbing** to develop vocabulary and ideas. For certain writing pieces, they go through the **writing process** with editing and response groups. I teach them how to monitor and review each other's work. I try to have them focus on specific language skills in their editing such as indentation, spelling, and punctuation. Only with the final published work do I do the final edit and correction. I use their writing as a guide to show me skills that I need to teach them.

Content Areas

Content areas are thematically **integrated** across the curriculum and in-clude literature, storytelling, arts, and cooking. The goal is always to make whatever we are studying relevant to the students by building a bridge between the concepts and the children. I try to present content areas in the child's stronger language. Students usually work in groups on various integrated projects.

In math, for instance, we study different number systems across cultures seeing the contributions and differences from the Mayan, Chinese, Arabic, and Roman systems. For our human body unit, children measure and compare their different body parts using the metric system. They also measure the room and objects at home. Science also involves projects where children do experiments and build things. They also learn about the differ-ent inventors.

In studying history, I get children to understand and analyze it from the historian's perspective. I make them aware of the neglected perspectives of Mexican Americans and other minority groups that may not be addressed in history books. I teach them how to analyze the perspectives presented in books and examine the biases of the writer. Just because it's in print doesn't mean it's true. Children need to be able to see both sides and make decisions for themselves.

Culture

Regardless of the class composition, I integrate culture in everything I teach through history, music, science, and math. I acknowledge the contributions of diverse cultural groups. Children need to value people who are different and understand that being different doesn't mean that it's bad. When a cultural stereotype comes up and children start laughing, I'll stop whatever I'm doing and we'll talk about it. For example, in our California history unit, when we listen to Native American music, children often laugh. I use various ways to help children learn about stereotypes through modeling and literature. Through our work, they learn to have respect for others and value each others' languages and cultures. It doesn't matter what color we are; we all have the same needs and deserve to be respected.

I also bring in parents and community members as role models, enabling children to see the wealth of community resources available. Parents frequently come in to share their strengths in the arts and their professional lives. Parents have taught our children dances (e.g., modern, African, & Mexican Folkloric), as well as choir and drumming. There are so many ways parents can contribute through cooking, typing, playing music, sewing, and lots more. Having community members such as authors, doctors, and farm worker organizers, come in to tell their stories has enriched the children's lives. Parents and other community members should not just contribute in this way, but their voices need to be heard in the school's educational programs and decisions.

Children need to see that multicultural curriculum is not just eating tacos or having a piñata, but it is integrated throughout the whole year. Any theme can be presented cross-culturally. For the theme of celebrations, I stress that people celebrate things differently. For example, Christmas in Mexico with *Las Posadas* is celebrated differently than here in the United States. I want children to know and understand about different traditions and lifestyles. No one culture is better than any other. It's just what's important to you. The teacher must have sensitivity and respect for differences and help children feel it's okay to be whoever they are.

Grouping Strategies

I'm careful about forming groups. Some children, who are just natural teachers and helpers, work with others very well. Children who are hesitant should not be placed next to someone who is really critical. Sometimes children are on the verge of becoming bilingual and just need that little "umph" of hearing the second language to feel comfortable in it; then, I may put them next to someone monolingual. Frequently, they become really good friends, which helps them both acquire the other language. I do not put all students who are having difficulty in the same group. During the day, I have all different kinds of groups: random, by table, by number, or rotating. I also work individually with kids.

LACK OF QUALITY SPANISH MATERIALS

Many great programs (such as the *Bay Area Writing, Bay Area Science, Bay Area Math Projects,* and social studies units) are only available in English.

Unfortunately, those materials are not provided in Spanish, so I translate them, which requires a lot of work and time, of which I have very little.

Although we have a lot of Spanish books, they are not the same quality as English ones. They might be paperbacks versus hardbacks and are not as beautifully illustrated. The publishers don't seem to give Spanish books the same priority. Many are poorly translated or are in Castilian Spanish, a dialect unfamiliar to our Latino children. Children's literature written by Latino authors or in local dialects are hard to find. There aren't many books that address the experiences of Mexican American or Latin American upper grade children in this country. There seem to be more beautiful picture books for early childhood K–2 grades. Translated books (e.g., _Las Telarañas de Carlota_ [_Charlotte's Web_]—White, 1990; and _Una Arruga en el Tiempo_ [_A Wrinkle in Time_]—L'Engle, 1985) often cost more than the English versions. So it's more expensive for the bilingual teacher to purchase materials, which is what I do. I've been collecting Spanish literature for years. I've attended many workshops where I've gotten lots of materials.

The programs available in Spanish rarely use the newest learning strategies, such as **whole language.** You're lucky if you get a text and workbook, which are the boring "drill and kill" kind of stuff. Many new teachers in other schools don't even have the **basal** reading series or teacher's guides from which they could pull stories and activity suggestions. Rarely do they have Spanish literature, unless they make the extra effort or the principal makes a commitment to purchase native language literature. Then they wonder why kids don't succeed. I am finally beginning to see more materials coming out, but many teachers still don't have access to quality materials and programs. It's difficult.

ASSESSMENT

Standardized Tests

When the school first started, children didn't take **standardized tests,** because the parents and teachers didn't want to be linked to the system like puppets. With tests like the _CTBS_ (_California Test of Basic Skills_; CTB/McGraw-Hill, 1989), all kinds of strings are attached that dictate how teachers are supposed to teach. Eventually, we decided to have the students tested just to get funding. Only the English tests (not the Spanish ones) counted for money. If the English test scores fall below the 50th percentile, then the program gets a certain amount of funding. If the students do well, the school gets punished and doesn't get money. Think about it!

A lot of **LEP** kids have trouble with the tests, which don't really measure what students know in reading, language, or math. To test math, kids have to write and explain their problems in English, which is not just testing math; it's testing their English. They say they're testing one thing, but they're really testing another. There's no way I'm going to know if a child understands a problem, if I don't ask him to explain it in his own language. That's not a true assessment of what a child knows. He may know the concept, but with English testing we'll never know that. We've been doing all this work developing **portfolios** and then the children are judged with the **standardized tests.** It's not consistent. The children probably realize it too.

The district has placed far too much importance on those tests. At one point, they were pressuring teachers to teach to the test. I knew teachers who actually gave children the same test questions, although they were not supposed to. In some schools, children practice test-taking skills, so they can improve on **standardized tests.** Testing is a reality all through school. Until that changes, test-taking skills are important for kids to learn. They need to know how approach timed-tests to pace themselves and not spend too much time on any one problem. I don't think that the whole curriculum should be based on the test and preparation for it. The district is at fault to place so much emphasis and evaluate teachers with test scores. Being judged by students' scores makes teachers feel their job is on the line. If the kids score poorly, the teachers are blamed. Instead of the tests, the district should focus on **authentic assessment** that reflects student learning.

Dual Language Assessments

We used to use the _Bilingual Syntax Measure_ (_BSM_; Burt, Dulay, & Chávez, 1978), but now we use the _IPT_ (_IPT-Oral Language Proficiency Test_; Ballard, Tighe, & Dalton, 1991) which is frequently used in a lot of California districts. That test assesses English proficiency to classify whether a child is **LEP** or not. To assess Spanish academic ability, our students take the _SABE_ (_Spanish Assessment of Basic Education_; CTB/McGraw-Hill, 1991), which they've just started using. Formerly, we used _CTBS Español_ (CTB/McGraw-Hill, 1978) that used a Castilian Spanish dialect that was unfamiliar to our students. Both the _SABE_ and _CTBS Español_ are similar. Neither test is a particularly good assessment. They test Spanish as if it were English. It's not comprehensive.

There are all kinds of problems with these Spanish tests. Instructions for some tests are given in Spanish, while others are given in English. Teachers who score them may not be bilingual, so the results may not be accurate. All the testing takes so much time away from instruction and then you don't do anything with it. I prefer to assess children's language strengths in Spanish and English by listening to how they read and talk, and seeing how they write. I want to have a broader understanding of their capabilities.

Better Ways to Assess Learning

Many of the new curriculum programs have different ways of pre-and posttesting children. For example, after completing our California history unit entitled "The First Californians," students are asked to imagine, write about, and draw the environment where the Native Americans used to live. For all subjects I use a variety of **alternate assessments,** such as open-ended questions, drawing, and integrated writing, to see if children understand the concept or process. I have them explain orally or in writing their approaches in solving math problems. That's a window to their thinking. I ask them to talk about something we've done and I jot down notes of what they say. Sometimes I watch them solve a problem. At the end of each report card period, they put their three best writings that they've taken through the writing process into their writing folders.

If the teacher can focus on learning, eventually the children will do better overall, even on the **standardized tests.** Teachers should be able to build the program to help kids succeed and learn as much as possible. What they're learning should be the measure. Teachers, especially new teachers, have to feel they can do that. One needs the freedom to do what you think is right for the kids.

We want to develop a school-wide **portfolio assessment** system where the portfolio follows the child. A lot of us use portfolios, but we're all at different stages. For our next staff development day, we will be discussing our writing program to decide what should go into the portfolio at each level.

Eventually, we want to move toward assessing the whole child, not just English, reading, and math, which is what is tested in this system. One must take into consideration the different **learning styles** and test those. Even if students are tested in English and Spanish, the child's creative side is not being considered. It all goes back to the **seven intelligences** concept that children have a variety of strengths. Realistically, how can we get a picture of the whole child, see the development, and help with that? A teacher has to be able to pinpoint and research the strengths and weaknesses of each child. Teachers may know that a program or particular strategy is ineffective, but we don't have the time to sit down and document what works or doesn't work for children. Time for that kind of planning, investigation, and reflection needs to be incorporated into the school program.

SUCCESSES WITH STUDENTS

I've had "Aha" moments with individual students. One Spanish-dominant Mexican boy came from another school, where he had been placed in a monolingual class. He had been isolated in the back of the room working with the Spanish-speaking aide. He just hated school and started getting sick. When he came to me, his self-esteem was really low. Although orally fluent in Spanish, he couldn't read even the simplest Spanish words. I spent a lot of time building his Spanish before starting ESL. He felt supported by all the Spanish spoken in school. What a difference! By year's end, he could read Spanish well and he started to learn English in a healthier environment. I just wanted to get him to read. Eventually he graduated from high school and went on to college.

A lot of our students have gone on to college. Those students often visit us and share their successes. As they share with our students, they tell about their positive experiences of having role models and teachers who understand them. They have developed self-respect, pride in themselves and their heritage, and to value others. It's that intangible inner strength that helps students become most successful. Hearing former students' stories and seeing their success encourages our students.

Our success rate is higher with Latino students than other schools in the district. Many Latinos at other schools give up and drop out. Since they really don't get much support, school isn't meaningful to them. Then they get a low-paying job and that's it. I can't believe it.

Not every teacher is going to reach all children. I feel like a failure when a student doesn't graduate. My students know I really want them to learn. My expectations are high, maybe sometimes too high. But low expectations are like death. I want to find the balance. When a student is dragging, I don't blame the child. I ask myself what can do I do to reach the child? If they don't want to learn, they're not going to. So, if I can just get the "wanna" part, the "gonna" part will come. Each child is like a puzzle and it's my job to find the pieces that will motivate them to learn.

LACK OF DISTRICT SUPPORT

District policies do not support native language or cultural development. Their concern is that students have enough English when they finish sixth grade. If they don't, they're tracked into **ESL** classes and excluded from prerequisite college classes. The district needs to recognize the significance of the native language resources and understand that students will eventually learn English. Teachers need to be able to develop the native language fully so children can make the transition to English from a stronger base. We don't have as much success with children who don't have a strong base in their native language. They're being pushed so quickly into English that they don't end up speaking, reading, or writing either language well.

The district and society have that English-only mentality. It's like a skeleton that takes away the flesh and leaves you just raw. Language is so much a part of your culture and a part of you. Hopefully, we won't have to go back to having our kids experience the punishment, like when I grew up.

ADMINISTRATIVE SUPPORT, COLLEAGUES, AND FUTURE TRENDS

Our present administrator used to be a teacher here. He went into administration and then came back. At first, it was a struggle because he wanted to prove that he was "the boss." His focus was more on routines and paperwork (lesson plans), rather than on teaching and learning. At first he did not involve parents much in the school. The administrator can either discourage or encourage parents. Our parents are willing to listen, but they need to be informed. They may not know a lot about bilingual education or **sheltered instruction**, but they can be very supportive to the teachers if they are included. After the first few years, the principal's focus changed to include parents more. Now that he's more competent as an administrator in terms of fulfilling the district requirements, he's more supportive and able to work with the parents and teachers.

Shared decision making and site-based management looks good on paper but in practice it's very difficult to do. Although it's time-consuming and requires considerable willingness, it is essential for an effective program. The principal has to be able to let go and share that power. I consider a leader, not by title, but if people listen to that person. We don't have too many leaders as principals. Sometimes teachers are leaders. Schools are not set up so teachers can pool their strengths together. When there's unity it's so much better, because everyone's working together and making the effort to build a quality program.

Often times, when the principal evaluates the bilingual teachers, many teachers get misevaluated because the administrator has no idea about bilingual education. Maybe the administrator hasn't taught for very long and hasn't received the proper bilingual education training. They need training about linguistic needs and cultural sensitivity. They often don't understand the value of the primary language in acquiring maintaining and developing two languages. When the administrator comes in to evaluate, you don't want to hear just about what you didn't do. Evaluation can be very threatening. Schools aren't organized so colleagues can observe one another in a nonthreatening way. We have to be able to help each other in the spirit of friendship, growth, and collegiality. We need time to sit down and reflect on what we do, our goals, our strengths, and how these develop the students. For example, I'm trying to get students to appreciate and respect all cultures. I want to be self-critical of what I do or don't do. There's very little time for that kind of reflection. I want to spend time to do my own research. I can't do it in isolation. Sometimes you can find colleagues at your job or at other schools to help you in that process. It's really important to build that kind of support. It's tough, because not much time is provided for teachers to work together to build those kinds of connections.

We need to be compensated and appreciated for our efforts. Schools need to be places where everyone can grow. Besides the stipend, bilingual teachers get no benefits. In our district once you are a certified bilingual teacher, you no longer get an instructional assistant. After you pass the certification exams and get tenure, there's no incentive to keep growing professionally. Most bilingual staff development is limited and geared for uncertified teachers. There's not much for us veteran teachers. All teachers need more staff development and support. They should also be compensated for it.

Things are starting to change. Last year, I went to the California Association for Bilingual Education (CABE) conference where I heard Paulo Freire speak about **critical pedagogy**, which I learned about in college. Wow! Bilingual education has come a long way in acknowledging **critical pedagogy** and its direct relationship to teaching and learning. But what's happening at the state and district levels? Their eyes are closed to the significant changes necessary for all students to succeed.

Changes in the existing educational system are urgent now with threat of vouchers, the passing of Proposition 187, English-only legislation, and proposed cuts to **Title VII**. Those are warning signs to us. Society is no longer based on agriculture or manufacturing as it was long ago. Technology is the future. Our children start out with outdated stuff. Many teachers still don't even have a computer or other basic quality materials in their classrooms. Teachers are the last ones to get trained. If we're so concerned about the future, then why don't we show that concern though our actions? *El mejor modo de decir es hacer* [The best way to say something is through example]. What is the California education system saying by spending so few dollars on public education? Students should have state-of-the-art computers and well-stocked schools. We should really invest in our children's school experiences by providing the best human and physical resources possible. It's time to listen to teachers and students and make a commitment to education, monetarily as well as morally. Teachers need to become catalysts for that change. Our responsibility goes beyond the classroom. We impact the future.

12

Themes and Issues
Emerging From the Narratives

A COMPARATIVE LOOK AT THE TEACHERS:
THEIR STRENGTHS AND CHALLENGES

In this section, issues and themes from the teachers' stories are discussed comparatively. It is difficult to generalize about bilingual education based on such a small number of teachers, but much can be said about these teachers' stories. Through energy and commitment, these teachers made their classrooms comfortable learning environments for children and welcoming places for parents. The teachers responded individually to their classroom and school contexts using the internal and external resources that were available. They were all fighters, persistent, with a strong sense of self and of their missions as bilingual teachers.

These teachers, as other bilingual teachers, are a very diverse group, diverse in language resources, reasons for becoming teachers, and in training. The word bilingual in the United States is commonly thought to mean Spanish-English, when in actuality, bilingual can mean any two languages, as is represented by these teachers. Regardless of the two languages spoken, the teachers faced similar attitudes and misunderstandings about their language and culture because of the prevailing monolingual–monocultural societal norms.

THE TEACHERS' LANGUAGE DIVERSITY

The teachers themselves had different levels of bilingualism because of their different language learning experiences. The teachers learned their second language either by being born in the United States or by immigrating, as an adult or as a child. Some were balanced bilinguals, and others were more dominant in their native language (which for Jean & Sandra is English).

These experiences shaped them as people and as teachers, helping them to empathically identify with the transition experiences of their students.

The teachers, who learned English as their second language as children (Manouchka & Luz), recounted the pain of not being understood or accepted because of their cultural or linguistic differences. They knew what it felt like to be different for speaking another language and how it felt not to have role models. This made them want to be role models and advocates for language minority children and communities. Although Mariana also learned Spanish and English as a child, she did not express similar pain in her adjustment. Her bilingual–bicultural experiences "politically called" her to work with language minority children, almost as if she were coming home to something familiar after working for so many years with middle-class children in private school. Generally speaking, what helped these teachers as children in their language learning and adjustment were supportive home and family environments, a model that they strive to establish within their classrooms.

The teachers who learned their second language as adults (Diana, Sofya, & Heather) did not have to fight to maintain their native language and culture, which were firmly in place. But they did also experience being different in this culture. To counter this feeling of difference, they worked extremely hard to be accepted. As a lone young foreign student, Diana's case clearly shows the pain of discrimination (in the cafeteria and being advised to work with early childhood students) that she experienced and how she adapted herself by accepting and making the best of her situation. All the teachers seemed to use similar strategies of accepting and making the best of the situation. Through their resilience and multiple adaptations, they have survived, flourished, and are successful in helping their students.

Interestingly, Sofya and Heather immigrated as a result of unsafe political conditions in their countries. Neither woman had the option to return to their home country. In addition, both women had the support of family members in immigrating. Even before immigrating, both teachers worked hard to succeed in their settings: Sofya, as a Jew in Russia; and Heather, as a Vietnamese speaker learning Japanese for her university studies. With them, they brought this will to their adjustment and teaching experiences here. Sofya never lost sight of her mission as a teacher, which drove her to work hard to be accepted first as a paraprofessional and then as a bilingual teacher. Heather's quiet persistence surfaced as she began bilingual teaching even though her colleagues were less than accepting.

The European-Americans (Jean & Sandra) made a conscious choice to learn Spanish as a foreign language. Learning another language and experiencing other cultures through travel gave them a window to other worlds, which profoundly enriched their lives and enabled them to understand others. Bilingual teachers (as do we all) come to bilingual teaching from different angles and bring different strengths from their experiences. These teachers' stories remind us that all individuals are intricately and uniquely connected to their biographies and contexts.

ENTRY INTO THE PROFESSION, CERTIFICATION, AND TRAINING

The teachers' decisions to become bilingual teachers were not always conscious, thought-out ones. Many of them just fell into bilingual teaching by chance, based on being in schools and communities where their native language resources were needed. They gained bilingual certification and training along the way. Certification requirements are external policies that intersect with the bilingual (or any) teachers' lives. Usually the bilingual teacher has other certification requirements in addition to those required of the mainstream teacher.

Different state certification requirements affect the amount of training a bilingual teacher receives. Some of the teachers had finished master's degrees, but most had not. For example, most of the California teachers became bilingually certified by taking the **Bilingual Certificate of Competence (BCC)** exam and passing the California Basic Education Skills Test (C–BEST). Entering the profession by passing these exams only slightly prepared the teachers for the demands of bilingual teaching. Formal training, although somewhat helpful, also did not help prepare the teachers very well for bilingual teaching. Jean seemed to find her training most beneficial as a means to reflect on her years of practice. It should be noted that she also completed her master's work in the early 1990s when current bilingual education research had matured. Teachers taking earlier bilingual teacher education courses may not have found them very beneficial because the research was evolving simultaneously with the practice.

The need for bilingual teachers in some states and districts is so great that there are alternate routes and emergency credentialing procedures that allow individuals to teach without much education or bilingual education training. Like California, where teachers are allowed to enter the profession with limited training, in New York City, for example, teachers may provisionally start teaching with only a bachelor's degree. Teachers then have 5 years to obtain permanent certification by completing a master's degree and passing the state certification exams. The state teacher exams posed a problem to certification for Sofya and Manouchka. These exams are problematic for many bilingual teachers, who may be nonnative English speakers or may not have been schooled in the United States. Teachers may face the same issues of test bias that their students face. These tests and certification requirements may further exacerbate bilingual teacher shortages.

These alternate routes to credentialing teachers may serve to hire teachers who speak a particular language, but they do not ensure that teachers are qualified or even mentally stable. Sandra and Diana alluded to problems in hiring anyone who speaks the non-English language required in a particular setting. They both confirmed that just because one can speak a language does not mean that one can teach in another language. The lack of consistency in teacher quality is a great obstacle in developing a strong corps of teachers who are able to work effectively on behalf of students.

These teachers' stories show that to be a teacher one must be committed to on-going learning. As learners, their greatest teachers were their students and their parents. In the absence of much formal training, the teachers learned on-the-job as they taught. Diana and Sandra showed their growth and development as a result of the many workshops and courses they attended. The most beneficial training and workshops seemed to be ones that most related to their teaching needs. Unfortunately for Sandra, the workshops she took in Los Angeles, although extremely helpful to her teaching practice, did not count toward her permanent certification in Illinois.

INTERACTIONS WITH COLLEAGUES

Collegial support varies among and between bilingual and monolingual colleagues. Pockets of collegial support exist depending on the school leadership, who the teachers are, and the nature of their interaction together. The lack of consistency of teacher quality due to hiring untrained teachers at times prevented these bilingual teachers from working with other bilingual colleagues. This is especially evident in Sandra's, Manouchka's, and Diana's stories. Bilingual teachers felt isolated by the different ideologies and practices of their colleagues. Due to the lack of support for teaching the native language, Diana lost enthusiasm for teaching and devoted less time to it. With similar commitment and visions regarding bilingualism, as in Luz's, Mariana's, and Jean's schools, teachers seem less isolated and more able to productively work together. Teacher collaboration seems most positive, when there is a small number of teachers with similar visions about the program, philosophies, and bilingualism. Administrators may support teacher collaboration by providing time for teachers to discuss bilingual curriculum (as in Jean's & Mariana's schools) and to help one another (as in Mariana's, Luz's, & Heather's schools).

Because bilingual programs were often implemented in response to population changes in communities, some bilingual teachers recounted being treated with hostility by monolingual colleagues. Colleagues, administrators, and parents often did not value bilingualism, nor understand bilingual education program goals, the nature of bilingual teachers' work, and the language acquisition process. The good news is that over time, some of these bilingual teachers have been able to turn around this negativity. In some cases, as bilingual teachers worked with their monolingual colleagues, the hostility diminished through co-teaching bilingual and monolingual students, teaching **Spanish as a second language (SSL)** to colleagues (Sandra in Illinois), lending materials, sharing strategies (Heather & Manouchka), taking language minority students from other mainstream classes (Manouchka & Sandra in California), and mentoring new monolingual teachers (Mariana). On numerous occasions, these bilingual teachers served as bilingual education ambassadors, disseminating useful information and practices about language acquisition, culturally responsive pedagogy to parents and other teachers. Bilingual teachers' knowledge is being valued and sought out by others, thus broadening understanding and support for teaching diverse students.

ADMINISTRATIVE LEADERSHIP

Administrative leadership and support can make or break a program. When there is support, vision, and understanding about the program, teachers can focus more on teaching. How the bilingual program is implemented and supported depends on who is at the helm, especially the principal and/or district coordinator or superintendent. Changes in leadership greatly affects the **school culture** and teachers' ability to work, as in Manouchka's and Sandra's schools. Frequent principal turnover, often endemic in lower class, more ethnically diverse schools, is extremely detrimental to students and teachers. Principals may see these schools as stepping stones in their career paths, rather than having the long-term commitment that it takes to lead effectively. Sandra's frustrating experience of having seven different principals shows her commitment to work for the benefit of the children, regardless of who was in charge. When her commitment to cooperative learning and student talk clashed with the principal's vision for a quiet classroom, she found ways around these limitations. She noted a qualitative difference in the program when the principals were supportive. Administrators need not only to be school managers, but educational leaders, familiar with curriculum and learning to support what teachers know are the best practices for students.

As Jean said, administrators must be accountable to their clients, not the reverse. When clients are limited English-speaking parents and children, they may not know how to make schools accountable to their needs. Administrators need to learn about the language acquisition process and develop cultural sensitivity about their clients. Unfortunately, as Sandra mentioned, language minority parents did not protest when their children were bussed to different schools to be used to increase dwindling enrollments. There is a role for the bilingual teacher to inform parents of their rights and teach them how to protest these abuses.

The parents can play important leadership roles in school decision making as in Luz's school. In the early years, the parents exercised their rights and power by creating the bilingual school, showing that leadership can emerge from the bottom and move up. The parents shared active governance responsibilities with teachers. The parents and teachers eventually succumbed to the ever-increasing bureaucratic demands of running the school and elected to hire a principal to assist them in managing the school. Unfortunately, that principal's top-down leadership style undermined the parents and teachers' control over the school. There is no doubt that leadership is necessary, but it needs to be enlightened and open to genuine school/community participation.

The teachers sometimes found support where little direct leadership existed. Diana and Sandra gained much through workshops which helped them learn new teaching strategies. Although indirect support like this gives teachers freedom to learn, leadership voids leave teachers frustrated. Vision and commitment to language as well as action are needed to make a cohesive program. When there is strong leadership, as in Heather's school, some of the nonsupporters of bilingual education tend to transfer from the school, leaving room for advocates to be hired in their place.

Administrators can show their support by committing funds to buying native language materials and/or paying teachers to develop native language curriculum (Sofya & Heather). Having sufficient and appropriate curriculum and materials would lift a great burden off bilingual teachers who otherwise must create or purchase their own materials.

INTERACTIONS WITH PARENTS

Bilingual teachers, as cultural liaisons, are in an important position to communicate across the family, school, community, and society contexts. The teachers reached out to parents through various means: making phone calls, providing their home phone number (Manouchka & Sofya), writing and translating home language newsletters, and translating articles of interest (Diana & Jean). The teachers made visible to parents what schools expected from them. The teachers built open, comfortable, personal relationships with parents in the interests of children (e.g., Sofya's marital interventions). Teachers wanted to validate parents as children's first teachers and help parents provide instructional support for their work. They communicated with parents some ideas about how to appropriately discipline children in the home (Manouchka & Sofya) and how to support what goes on in school. Getting language minority parents to attend school functions, such as parent–teacher conferences, was sometimes difficult.

In some cultures, as expressed by Diana, Heather, Manouchka, and Sofya, parents deferred authority and respect to teachers and the schools. Teachers communicated to immigrant parents what parental involvement means in this country. Through mutual respect and caring, Sofya got 100% attendance at school functions. For other teachers, though many of the parents may have desired to take part in school activities, many were unable to because of childcare difficulties, busy work schedules, and their efforts to support their families. The teachers were understanding of the family's situations. The teachers wanted more from parents than just the minimum attendance at parent-teacher conferences. They encouraged parents to share their knowledge and experiences in their classrooms (Jean & Heather). Luz's story showed a positive example of respecting and using the richness of parent and community resources as part of the school curriculum.

In spite of the teachers' efforts to reach out to parents, as Jean mentioned, schools still need to be more responsive to language minority families' concerns and needs (e.g., ESL, health, and housing). Flexible services are needed. When those services were provided, as in the case of Sandra's comprehensive family service center, parents and teachers learned more about each other. This meaningful mutual interaction of students, parents, and teachers prompted greater involvement for parents in the school and community. At issue here was caring, the community invested in helping its residents rather than shunning them.

The bilingual teachers often had to explain to parents the bilingual program goals and how native language learning supports second language development. Teachers in more additive programs, such as Jean's and Mariana's schools, had less pressure to justify to parents their work of teaching the non-English language. When bilingualism was seen as an enrichment, parents were anxious to enroll their children in these special programs. It was understood and desired that children would be learning two languages. When bilingualism is valued within the school (and hopefully the societal context), the bilingual teacher may feel more support. The double standard of bilingualism still applies. For the rich it is desired to be bilingual, for the poor, the native language is often seen as a deficiency to be eradicated and replaced.

Many language minority parents have "bought into" this notion. What they do not realize is that in wanting their children to learn English and North American ways, children may gradually lose their native language, leaving parents unable to communicate with them. Parents also struggle with the loss of authority and control over their children. Sadly Manouchka, Mariana, and Diana recounted this loss of cultural connection between parents and children. Children so desperately want to fit into the mainstream that they deny their heritage. Bilingual teachers in their classrooms are trying to fight against these assimilation forces by encouraging children to value their heritage. Though helpful, it seems they are fighting an uphill battle.

Sofya designed her bilingual program to accommodate parents' wishes to encourage rapid English acquisition. The quick transition method apparently did not have adverse effects on students, because they continued to do well in the school. These children, perhaps because they were White, may have had greater potential of melting into the mainstream society, as did other Jewish immigrants in the past. Perhaps it was because her Russian-Jewish parents, who came as political refugees and would never return to their home country, were satisfied to maintain the Russian language in the home. Sofya expressed an inconsistency in wanting to both maintain the native language while at the same time giving her first and second grade students the maximum English for them to succeed. This is the dilemma that many bilingual teachers face.

CHANGING COMMUNITIES
AND SCHOOL ACCOUNTABILITY

Schools and communities are experiencing great diversity for which they need to be prepared to meet the needs of these changing populations.

Flexibility is needed to create student-sensitive instructional and programmatic designs. As in Luz's school, a departmental model was created to shelter second language instruction and to reinforce and enrich Spanish.

California is experiencing incredible diversity. This diversity was reflected in Heather's, Luz's, and Diana's classes, where the bilingual teachers not only had children with differing degrees of native and English language abilities, but those teachers also received students who spoke a range of languages and dialects, not to mention the European American and African American children who were placed in their classes. Even though these teachers did not know the other languages or dialects that children spoke, their sensitivity, caring, and experience enabled them to acknowledge these children's language and cultural resources through seeking out translators and materials and giving them individual attention. In creating comprehensible language-rich classroom environments, language and content were sheltered to help all children learn. As diversity increases, (which is a reality) though teachers may not know the languages spoken by some of their students, the bilingual teachers are in key positions to share what they know with others in addressing this diversity. Schools need to be places where this kind of sharing is valued and encouraged.

INSTRUCTION

Teachers have made students feel comfortable in their classes. They supported students' linguistic and academic growth through a variety of culturally responsive teaching strategies. These strategies seem to reflect current practices that see language and cognitive development as interrelated complex processes. As such, teachers mentioned using individualized instruction, **cooperative learning,** peer teaching, **whole language,** literature-based reading approaches, hands-on integrative content-based **thematic instruction,** projects, and **authentic assessments.** The effectiveness of these practices cannot be determined through interviews or the limited observations I made. Nevertheless, the teachers did believe that these approaches were helpful to stimulate student learning.

Teachers alluded to student academic success, in making the transfer to English (Mariana, Heather, & Sofya) and being put into advanced placement in Spanish (Jean), and a larger portion of Latino students eventually going on to college (Luz) than in other district schools.

Use of the Two Languages

Use of the students' native language varied depending on the teacher, the students, and the program model. Use of the native language for teachers in transitional programs seemed less than in the additive programs of Jean, Luz, and Mariana. In classes where schools had transitional programs, there was flexibility and acceptance of the native language. Teachers were open to use/respond in the language that children spoke to them (Heather, Manouchka, Diana, Sofya, & Sandra). Teachers (Heather & Diana) used **concurrent translation,** even though they knew that some researchers have found it a less effective strategy (Legarreta-Marcaida, 1981; Wong Fillmore & Valadez, 1986). Sandra, in encouraging her children to **code switch,** showed a sophisticated understanding of the language acquisition process and how two languages can be used as a scaffold for meaningful communication.

Diana more recently gave less emphasis to native language instruction than she did before. For her, native language teaching was even more difficult because of the multiple Chinese dialects that her students spoke, of which she did not have command. In addition, because she had never learned formally the teaching of Chinese reading and writing, she lacked confidence in her ability. Because of its different writing system with numerous characters, it was much more complex to teach than English. For these reasons, Diana mostly focused her native language instruction on oral communication. In addition, because native language was given a lesser priority by the administration and colleagues and because she had English speakers in her class, she gradually reduced the amount of native language instruction time.

Programs such as the **dual language program** and Spanish **Immersion program** allowed for more instructional time to be given to develop non-English languages. Regardless of the program, it seems that native language is still not given sufficient emphasis to develop higher threshold levels of bilingualism (Cummins, 1994). **Dual language** and **Immersion programs** seem most promising in their enriched commitment to the non-English language. However, as Mariana mentioned, development of full bilingualism was prematurely arrested. Even more time, commitment, and parellel curricula for developing native language are needed.

Culture

Teachers understood where children came from (home country schooling expectations and cultural background knowledge). They accepted children and oriented them to what was expected here. As culture negotiators, teachers tried to validate what children bring. Bilingual classes were safe havens where it was accepted to be different. This respect for culture enhanced children's self-esteem (as mentioned by Manouchka & Sandra in Los Angeles).

As in many schools, cultural holidays were celebrated. But multicultural exploration did not stop there. Use of students, parents, community members as culture bearers can make multiculturalism come alive, rather than reducing it to a superficial "hero/holiday" focus of studying other cultures. The teachers approached the study of culture holistically by not only exploring heros, holidays and artifacts, but by using authentic sources from people, history, current events, the arts, and literature for deeper cultural understanding.

Curriculum and Materials

The bilingual teachers unanimously complained that limited and appropriate native and second language curriculum and materials were great obstacles to their teaching. Due to the lesser emphasis on languages other than English in this country, publishers have not invested in creating a wide variety of quality multilingual materials. Materials purchased from foreign countries are equally problematic because of expense, and inappropriateness of language, content, and ideology. Repeatedly, materials were either inferior in quality or insufficient in number. Translated materials often were mistake-ridden.

Nevertheless, to meet this challenge, teachers creatively used numerous avenues. Teachers bought their own materials when they could find them. They translated English books and units and/or adapted or created their own. Because Spanish is the second largest language group after English, Spanish materials are most prevalent. Even so, those materials are not as available as English ones, and are less sophisticated in terms of pedagogical strategies (as mentioned by Luz). Getting parallel curricula in upper grades for subject areas is especially difficult. For languages such as Chinese, Vietnamese, Haitian, and Russian, quality native language materials are almost impossible to obtain. The teachers (Sandra & Mariana) shaped what they taught from available materials.

Curriculum continuity emerged as another problem due to different teachers' beliefs and/or experiences with bilingual education. A teacher could never be sure that what she taught in one grade would be followed up by another colleague (Manouchka, Diana, & Sandra in Los Angeles). Native language development might not be supported and built upon from year to year depending on whether the receiving teacher understood the value of maintaining and using the native language. Unfortunately, some bilingual teachers though called "bilingual" teachers use English-only approaches (as mentioned by Diana). There is an implication for hiring qualified teachers who understand the importance of developing the students' native language. Also teachers need ongoing training about current research and to work through these curriculum continuity issues. Small schools or groups of bilingual teachers (as mentioned by Jean, Luz, & Mariana) may be the best contexts for bilingual teachers to work through these continuity issues. Even so, as in Mariana's **dual language** planning meetings, language and content objectives still needed to be even more clearly spelled out.

Testing and Assessment

Language and academic testing requirements come from state and local directives. Native and English **language proficiency testing** was conducted for placement and exit from the program. A variety of instruments was used. Overall, English testing is given primary importance (except in Jean's class), which influenced what the teachers taught. Since lower-grade classes (K–1) were exempted from English testing, this freed teachers from feeling the pressure to test, which allowed them to focus more on instruction.

Manouchka, Diana, Jean, Heather, and Luz found standardized language and academic tests biased in terms of the content and language that were normed on other populations. Test results were often invalidated by the person administering the test. Testing students' content knowledge by using English tests did not accurately measure subject area knowledge, but rather the language. As Luz most eloquently expressed, testing needs to be more closely aligned with instruction. Since the teachers geared instruction toward hands-on, thematically integrated projects, critical thinking and process types of instruction, assessment needs to reflect those kinds of activities. Many of the teachers mentioned using **portfolios** and **alternate assessments** through watching students perform a task, having them explain their problem-solving processes, and through projects.

CONCLUDING REMARKS

What can be learned from these teachers? These teachers have survived and flourished despite their problematic environments. In their dedication and commitment to students and families, they have found many creative solutions. Support does exist. But greater support is still needed in terms of reversing the negativity attached to speaking a language other than English. These stories also show how much can be learned from listening to teachers about what goes on in schools in order to make schools better places for everyone.

13

Epilogue:
The Stories Continue . . .

These teachers' stories represent a moment frozen in time during the 1993–1994 academic year. In finishing this book, I thought it important to tell how the teachers' lives and work have evolved since I initially started interviewing them. So, in September 1996, I contacted each teacher about the changes, developments, and final thoughts about bilingual education.

Sofya is still teaching in the same school and grades (first and second). She has been taking some bilingual education classes toward her master's degree, but she still has not passed the state certification exams. Lately, she senses that the Russian population has changed. Children seem to be coming with less education, which makes it harder to teach them. Parents are often busy struggling to make money to establish themselves. They seem to be ignoring their children more. She thinks maybe she might be too pushy, wanting the children to know everything. At age 60, Sofya is becoming tired after teaching for 34 long years. For her, teaching is not a job where you can take it easy; it's a life. You have to care. She plans to retire in the next few years. But, she hopes to be able to volunteer in the school to continue to help her children, because they need her.

In the last few years, Manouchka continued teaching the Haitian bilingual second-grade class while studying for a master's degree in administration. This year she is working extremely hard as an interim acting assistant principal at her school. She is involved in all decisions of running the 1,800 student pre-K–5 school, including those regarding the bilingual and ESL programs. With her input to the new principal, she helped save the bilingual program from being disbanded at the school. Because of dwindling numbers of new Haitian students, due to the change in government in Haiti, there was an attempt to eliminate the program and implement only ESL programs. Manouchka's years working as a teacher have given her an insider view to implement change. She knows what wasn't working and wants to make sure the bilingual, ESL, and special education programs are run properly through hiring qualified teachers, making sure classes have enough materials and computers, providing training workshops for teachers and parents, and getting Haitian parents more involved in school activities and the PTA. She states, "I may be making some enemies in the process. But it's for a good cause, so the children receive the services they deserve." She finds it exhilarating to be able to learn so much and to be in a position to advocate for children and parents in a different way.

Diana is beginning her third year of teaching in the Chinese–English bilingual kindergarten class. She enjoys teaching at this level for several reasons. First, she seems to be able to use more native language because that is the language that most of her young students speak. Also, because at the kindergarten level she has a partner teacher, she feels less isolated. She and her partner use each other as a sounding board to share ideas and materials, and to get feedback on their teaching. She has continued her passion for learning and recently has taken courses on Developmentally Appropriate Practices (DAP) that she uses in her teaching. One of the challenges of teaching kindergarten this year is that they have extended the day from 3 hours and 20 minutes to 4 hours, which on paper sounds educationally beneficial. But, because the kindergartens share classroom space, there is a problem overlapping time when both classes are in the room. In addition, there has been a change in leadership. The new principal is more organized and more supportive of the bilingual program. In her more hands-on leadership style, she listens to the teachers, asks for their input, and is generally more concerned about what is going on. This principal wants to make sure that all teachers are performing optimally. The principal supports teachers by giving them a piece of the financial pie. Teachers no longer have to spend their own money to buy materials. Each teacher receives $300 to buy literature and books and $200 for instructional supplies.

Heather has continued to teach first grade. Her school has now extended the Vietnamese bilingual program through the sixth grade, making it the only one in the area with a Vietnamese bilingual program throughout the elementary grades. Another change that will impact Heather is class size. This year Heather has 33 students, which within the next month will be reduced to 20 students. California state legislation has offered money to districts as an incentive to reduce classes to a maximum of 20 children for Grades 1 through 3. These changes are being made in an effort to give children more individual teacher attention to better help them learn to read and to improve test scores in order to be on grade level by the third grade (the benchmark year). Although reducing the student–teacher ratio is a promising practice, the logistics of implementing such a change takes time and has caused problems. Some of these temporary problems are due to limited classroom space and lack of qualified bilingual teachers. Heather says, "It is scary because they are giving emergency credentials and waivers to get anyone in there to teach."

Jean says a lot has changed in terms of legislation and attitudes toward immigrants. Unfortunately, there seems to be much more stereotyping and singling out of Mexicans than before. Proposition 187 has made many families fear harassment if they use the primary language, especially if it is Spanish. Because of the anti-immigrant sentiments and state Official English legislation, there has been some flight from the Immersion program by Hispanics because the families perceive instruction in Spanish as a delay in the acquisition of English. Jean states, "We certainly need to do a better job of parent education. Does this mean there will be a resurgence of subtractive bilingualism? I certainly hope not." Despite this, Jean continues to teach in first grade in the Spanish **Immersion program.** She is also enjoying the benefits of a reduced class size of 20 students. Unlike Heather's school, her school was able to make the arrangements prior to the beginning of the school year. Having a 20:1 student–teacher ratio, Jean is able to listen to each child read every day. She is still extremely happy and intellectually stimulated teaching in the Spanish **Immersion program.** She plans to continue teaching in that program.

Many innovations have been made in Sandra's school. All bilingual classes are now multi-age, multigrade. This is her second year teaching a first–second grade class. Bilingual teachers are team-teaching, which cuts down on the isolation. The school has more involvement with computer technology for its students and teachers. Sandra wrote a grant which funded the training of teachers who work with at-risk students so they can better use technology. The school also has developed and is implementing school-wide thematic units. After 3 years (miraculously) with the same principal, there seems to be more support, but there is still limited administrative understanding of the bilingual students' needs.

Mariana, after teaching fourth–fifth grade in the dual language school for another 2 years, was ready to explore a different area in her career. This year she accepted a position teaching humanities at a new girl's alternative junior high school. It is the first single-sex school to open in New York City after 10 years. This year the school started with seventh grade and will add eighth grade next year. Mariana has not lost touch with a diverse population because the majority of the students are Latino and African American. She still uses Spanish to communicate with parents. She sees this move as another step in her career and is finding it fascinating to observe girls at this age, their social and academic development, and their concerns. She is enjoying the change.

Luz still teaches fourth grade at the same community school. She is concerned with the problem of over enrollment in the school, district, and state. Classes tend to be large and there is a problem of space. Plans to reconfigure the elementary schools to Grades K–5 are being considered. More money needs to be invested in building schools and to train teachers. Luz finds that there is a push toward more accountability where schools are being evaluated by the number of LEP students they transition into English. Unfortunately, many bilingual teachers are on waiver, which means they often do not speak the children's native language very well or at all.

Meanwhile, Luz is extremely busy in many school and district activities in which she is learning new content and having an impact on teachers. She continues on the executive union board. In her second year as a mentor teacher, she has been working with new teachers who are overwhelmed by the amount of work and lack of materials. She has been developing fourth-grade California history curricula with a team of teachers. She has also participated in the National Science Foundation-sponsored Project LITES, designed to enhance teachers' knowledge and teaching of science. She has piloted much of this new history and science curricula in her own class. She has also been a Program Quality Review (PQR) consultant where teams of teachers critically evaluate their schools for improvement. With all these commitments, Luz feels overextended. As these projects come to a close, next year she plans to focus more on her classroom.

The stories continue . . .

III

BILINGUAL EDUCATION RESOURCES

14

Theoretical, Background, and Practical Information

ANNOTATED REFERENCES ON THE CONTEXT OF BILINGUAL EDUCATION

In this section of the chapter general foundations texts, history of multilingualism, history and politics of bilingual education, and program model sources are provided. These books have informed my practice as a teacher educator and may be useful to teachers.

General Foundations Texts

1. Baker's (1996) book, *Foundations of Bilingual Education and Bilingualism*, is theoretically comprehensive and practical in its coverage of language acquisition, cognition and intelligence, program models, politics of bilingualism, and effectiveness of bilingual education programs.
2. Lessow-Hurley's (1990) *The Foundations of Dual Language Instruction* briefly summarizes many concepts and issues associated with dual language instruction and programs: the history, politics, models, language acquisition theories, and language development suggestions.
3. California State Department of Bilingual Education (1981 & 1994) has sponsored two editions of *Schooling and Language Minority Students: A Theoretical Framework*. Both are "a must" for teachers in providing a comprehensive understanding of theoretical perspectives and pedagogical applications of first-and second-language acquisition and development that lead to quality instruction and social justice for the empowerment of language minority students. Articles by noted researchers, Cummins, Krashen, and others make this an invaluable resource.

History of Multilingualism in the United States

1. Conklin and Lourie (1983) in *A Host of Tongues: Language Communities in the United States* describe U.S. language diversity from a sociolinguistic perspective. They trace the social history of linguistic pluralism, the evolution of English and its dialects, and demographic factors that influence language use and variation. Policy implications are provided.
2. Grosjean's (1982) *Life in Two Languages: An Introduction to Bilingualism* covers bilingualism in the world, in the United States, in society, in children and adults.
3. McKay and Wong's (1988) edited collection, *Language Diversity: Problem or Resource?* explores general issues of language planning, diversity, and historical perspectives. Specific language situations of language minorities groups (e.g., Mexican Americans, Puerto Ricans, Cuban Americans, Chinese Americans, Filipino Americans, Korean Americans, and Vietnamese Americans) are also discussed.

History and Politics of Bilingual Education

1. In *Bilingual Education: History, Politics, Theory, and Practice,* through a journalistic style, Crawford (1995) thoroughly examines the history and political struggles of bilingualism and establishing bilingual programs. This book also covers the English-only controversy, California's attempts to cope with diversity, alternatives to bilingual education, two-way programs and Indian Education. Useful appendices explain current Title VII regulations bilingual and other legislation.
2. Stein's (1986) book *Sink or Swim: The Politics of Bilingual Education* gives a fascinating analysis of national, state, and local politics and the impact on implementation of bilingual education programs through the 1980s.

Program Models

1. Lessow Hurley (1990) in *The Foundations of Dual Language Instruction* concisely outlines the characteristics and outcomes of several program models (e.g., transitional, maintenance, enrichment, and immersion).
2. Crawford's (1995) chapter on two-way bilingual education programs describes the history, criteria, and variations of one of the more promising models that aims to promote additive bilingualism for both language majority and minority students.
3. Berman's (1992) important study highlights exemplary schools' program adaptations where they used ecletic program model designs, capitalizing on staffing strengths, to meet the diverse student populations' needs.

DEMOGRAPHIC INFORMATION

Language Diversity from the 1990 Census Data

Provided in this section are two charts showing the diversity of language groups in general and the numbers of language minority students (both English- and non-English-speakers). Suggestions for obtaining demographic information are provided.

TABLE 14.1

The Numbers of Speakers of the Top 25 Language Groups and Changes from 1980 to 1990

Language Used at Home	Total Speakers Over 5 Years Old		Percentage Change*
	1990	*1980*	
Spanish	17,339,000	11,549,000	50.1%
French	1,703,000	1,572,000	8.3%
German	1,547,000	1,607,000	-3.7%
Italian	1,309,000	1,633,000	-19.9%
Chinese	1,249,000	632,000	97.7%
Tagalog	843,000	452,000	86.6%
Polish	723,000	826,000	-12.4%
Korean	626,000	276,000	127.2%
Vietnamese	507,000	203,000	149.5%
Portuguese	430,000	361,000	19.0%
Japanese	428,000	342,000	25.0%
Greek	388,000	410,000	-5.4%
Arabic	355,000	227,000	57.4%
Hindi & Urdu	331,000	130,000	155.1%
Russian	242,000	175,000	38.5%
Yiddish	213,000	320,000	-33.5%
Thai	206,000	89,000	131.6%
Persian	202,000	109,000	84.7%
French Creole	188,000	25,000	654.1%
Armenian	150,000	102,000	48.3%
Navajo	149,000	123,000	20.6%
Hungarian	148,000	180,000	-17.9%
Hebrew	144,000	99,000	45.5%
Dutch	143,000	148,000	-2.6%
Mon Khmer	127,000	16,000	676.3%

Note: *Calculations are from numbers before rounding. Source: Census Bureau (cited in Barringer, 1993).

Numbers of Language Minority Students

English speakers from the Caribbean and non-English-speaking language minority children are on the rise.

TABLE 14.2

Estimated Language Minority Population and Percentage Change, by Age and Home Language in the U.S. in 1980 and 1990

Age by Group and Language Spoken	1980	1990	Percentage Change
Total	34,679,000	47,122,000	+35.9
Less than 5 years	2,562,000	3,856,000	+50.5
Ages 5–17	8,096,000	9,985,000	+23.3
English	3,555,000	3,662,000	+3.0
Non-English	4,541,000	6,323,000	+39.2
Ages 18 and older	24,021,000	33,281,000	+38.6
English	6,130,000	7,759,000	+26.6
Non-English	17,892,000	25,522,000	+42.6

Note: Percentages calculated on unrounded numbers. Source: 1990 Census (cited in Waggoner, 1994).

Uses for and Access to Demographic Information

You are encouraged to learn about your community's language minority population in order to develop curricula, write funding/grant proposals, and to advocate for program implementation and community needs.

For more information about demographic information, contact:

1. Your local Chamber of Commerce
2. The United States Census Bureau
3. *Numbers and Needs,* an informative newsletter written by Dorothy Waggoner, specifically focuses on linguistic minorities with the intent to remind representatives and policymakers of the need to provide education and other services to all special populations.

Numbers and Needs
Box G1H/B
3900 Watson Place, NW
Washington, DC 20016
(202) 337-5055

4. *District Information on the Internet*—Public information from 15,000 school districts (showing enrollments, racial/ethnic information, and numbers of at-risk students are provided at no cost by Sunspace Internet at http://www.sunspace.com

CURRICULA, TESTS, AND LITERATURE

The following curricular texts and programs, tests and literature, mentioned by the teachers, were italicized in the stories. Their descriptions, addresses, phone, facsimile, and ISBN numbers are provided when available. Entries are arranged alphabetically by author, program, and/or title.

Curricula

The Bay Area Math, Science, and Writing Projects are university–school collaboratives based at the the University of California, Berkeley. These projects provide teacher education workshops and curricula to promote student-centered integrative learning. For more information contact:

Bay Area Math Project
Lawrence Hall of Science, Room 247
University of California
Berkeley, CA 94720
Phone 510-642-9757

Bay Area Science Project
Lawrence Hall of Science, Room 257
University of California
Berkeley, CA 94720
Phone 510-642-0191

Bay Area Writing Project
University of California
School of Education
5511 Tolman Hall, #1670
Berkeley, CA 94720-1670
Phone 510-642-0971

Ballard and Tighe's (1989) *IDEA Kit* (Individualized Developmental English Activities Kit) is an English as a Second Language (ESL) curriculum consisting of picture cards and ideas for lesson related to literature. ISBN 1-55501-025-3

Available from:
Ballard and Tighe, Inc.
480 Atlas Street
Brea, CA 92621
Phone 800-321-4332

Baratta-Lorton's (1976) *Math Their Way* is a flexible math program for grades K–2 that uses a discovery and exploration approach to develop mathematical understanding. ISBN-0-210-00494-1

Available from:
Addison-Wesley Publishing, Inc.
Phone 800-322-1377

Bell (1992) and other authors from the University of Chicago School Mathematics Project developed the *Everyday Mathematics* series, which is an enriched spiralling K–6 math curriculum concentrating on problem solving and thinking skills. ISBN 1-877817-53-8

Available from:
Everyday Learning Corporation
Phone 800-382-7670

Brookes' (1986) book, *Drawing with Children* presents the Monart method developed by Mona Brookes that teaches children to draw systematically. ISBN-0-87474-396-2

Teacher workshops and materials are available from:
Jeremy P. Tarcher Publications, Los Angeles, CA

Bullock's (1992) *Touch Math* is called the "invisible" math manipulative, which teaches a system of numeration using touch points on the numbers.

Innovative Learning Concepts, Inc.
6760 Corporate Drive
Colorado Springs, CO 80919-1999
Phone 800-888-9191

Burk, Snider, and Symonds' (1992) text, *Math Excursions K: Project-Based Mathematics for Kindergartners*, has thematically organized, developmentally appropriate, hands-on mathematics units in English with reproducible appendices. ISBN 0-435-083457

Available from:
Heinemann Educational Books, Inc.
361 Hanover Street
Portsmouth, NH 03801-3959
Phone 800-541-2086

Charles and Brummet's (1989) *Connections* integrates the use of manipulatives with math topics for Grades 1–4. Includes resource books and manipulative kits.
Available from:
Creative Publications
Phone 800-624-0822

DeAvila, Duncan, and Navarette's (1987) *Finding Out/Descubrimento (FO/D)* blends current knowledge in the areas of psychology, sociology, and classroom experience. Science and math concepts are presented interactively through cooperative groups for Grades 2–6.
Available from:
Santillana Publishing Company, Inc.
Phone 800-245-8584

GEMS-Great Explorations in Math and Science
Guided discovery and constructivist math and science curricula, with accompanying teacher workshops and leadership development opportunities.
For catalog and information, contact:
GEMS
Lawrence Hall of Science
University of California
Berkeley, CA 94720-5200
Phone 510-642-7771
Fax 510-643-0309

McCracken and McCracken's (1982) *Spelling Through Phonics* provides a developmental program that teaches children how print works through small doses of phonics with immediate applications to their writings. ISBN 0-920541-00-3
Programs are available from:

McCracken Educational Services, Inc.
P.O. Box 3588
Blaine, WA 98231
Phone 800-447-1462

Marilyn Burns Education Associates is dedicated to improving mathematical education from the perspective of mathematics as a way of thinking and tool for solving problems. The organization has developed curricula, courses, and other services in order to help teachers and administrators implement such a problem-solving curriculum.

For more information about services, contact:
Marilyn Burns Education Associates
150 Gate 5 Road, Suite 101
Sausalito, CA 94965
Phone 415-332-4181

Noone's (in press) almost-final draft of *Family Science* has parents and children interactively learn science concepts both at school and home. Through hands-on science activities, it increases children's science education and parental involvement.

Available from:
Northwest EQUALS Project
Portland State University, P.O. Box 751
Portland, OR 97207
Phone 800-547-8887, ext. 3045

Project AIMS is a series of teacher-developed, hands-on activities integrating math and science (AIMS) curricula for Grades K–9.

For catalog and information, contact:
AIMS Education Foundation
P.O. Box 8120
Fresno, CA 93747
Phone 209-255-4094 or 888-733-2467
FAX 209-255-6396

Richardson's (1984) *Developing Number Concepts Using Unifix Cubes* helps children understand numbers through manipulatives. ISBN 0-201-06117-1

Available from:
Addison-Wesley Publishing, Inc.
Phone 800-322-1377

Russell and Stone's (1990) book, *Used Numbers: Real Data in the Classroom*, gives classroom-based, problem-solving activities. ISBN 0-86651-517-8
Available from:
Dale Seymore Publications
P.O. Box 10888
Palo Alto, CA 94303

Stenmark, Thompson, and Cossey's (1986) *Family Math* is a program designed to involve families in home activities that reinforce math concepts. ISBN 0-912511-06-0
Available from:
EQUALS/Family Math Publications
Lawrence Hall of Science
University of California
Berkeley, CA 94720
Phone 510-642-1823 or 510-642-1910

The Wright Group offers teacher workshops and integrated early childhood literature on themes.
Available from:
The Wright Group
19201 120th Avenue NE
Bothell, WA 98011
Phone 800-648-2970
FAX 800-543-7323

Tests

Ballard, Tighe, and Dalton's (1991) *IPT Oral Language Proficiency Test* assists in the initial identification, designation, and redesignation of limited English proficient students through measures of vocabulary, comprehension, syntax, and verbal expression. Available in English and Spanish in three levels from pre-school to Grade 12.
Available from:
Ballard and Tighe, Inc.
480 Atlas Street
Brea, CA 92621
Phone 800-321-4332

Boehm's (1986) *Boehm Test of Basic Concepts–Revised* is designed to measure young children's (K–2) basic concept mastery in the areas of quantity, space, and time. Tests are available in English and Spanish, though no norms are available in Spanish. Validity and reliability data are provided.
  Published by:
  The Psychological Corporation in San Antonio, TX
  Phone 800-211-8378

Burt, Dulay, and Chávez's (1978) test, *Bilingual Syntax Measure*, has two levels that are designed to measure second language proficiency with respect to syntactic structures in English and Spanish using cartoon-like pictures.
  Published by:
  The Psychological Corporation in San Antonio, TX
  Phone 800-211-8378

CTB/McGraw-Hill's (1978) test, *CTBS-Comprehensive Test of Basic Skills, Español* was a Spanish-translated version of the CTBS that was replaced by the *SABE* (see below).

CTB/McGraw-Hill's (1989) test, *CTBS-Comprehensive Test of Basic Skills* is a standardized norm-referenced group-administered exam, designed to measure achievement in reading, language, spelling, mathematics, and study skills.
  Available from:
  CTB/McGraw-Hill
  2500 Garden Road
  Monterey, CA 93940
  Phone 800-538-9547

CTB/McGraw-Hill's (1991) test, The *SABE-Spanish Assessment of Basic Education*, consists of a series of norm-referenced tests for Grades 1–8, designed to measure achievement in Spanish basic skills (reading, language arts, and mathematics). This is a discrete point test that uses multiple choice and cloze test items. It was normed using Spanish- and English-dominant groups.
  Available from:
  CTB/McGraw-Hill
  2500 Garden Road
  Monterey, CA 93940
  Phone 800-538-9547

DeAvila and Duncan's (1981) test, *Language Assessment Scales,* purports to determine Spanish- and English-dominance through measures of auditory discrimination, vocabulary, phoneme production, sentence comprehension, and oral production. These few types of language samples limit determining full range dominance. Spanish and English test norms are provided.
Available from:
CTB/McGraw-Hill
2500 Garden Road
Monterey, CA 93940
Phone 800-538-9547

Duncan and DeAvila's (1985) test, *Pre-Language Assessment Scales,* is the Kindergarten version of the *Language Assessment Scales.*
Available from:
CTB/McGraw-Hill
2500 Garden Road
Monterey, CA 93940
Phone 800-538-9547

Koslin, Zeno, Koslin, Wainer, and Ivens' (1991) test, *DRP–Degrees of Reading Power,* is a standardized group-administered series of tests constructed to measure how well students are able to contruct meaning from prose material while it is being read.
Available from:
Touchstone Applied Science Associates
Fields Lane, P.O. Box 382
Brewster, NY 10509
Phone 914-277-8100

Language Assessment Battery (1982) purports to measure language proficiency in Spanish and English. It was specifically designed to identify non-native speakers of English who are not sufficiently proficient in English to participate productively in a general education conducted in English. Each of the two versions consists of four levels. It employs an integrative approach to measuring speaking, listening, reading, and writing. Validity, reliablity, and norming information are available. The tests were renormed in 1989.
Available from:
The New York City Board of Education
Division of Assessment and Accountability, SCAN Center
44-36 Vernon Blvd., Room 207
Long Island City, NY 11101 (Phone 718-349-5600)

Literature

The teachers' classrooms were full of native language and children's literature in English. Unfortunately, I did not specifically ask for their favorite books. In the discussions, however, the teachers mentioned these books in speaking about their approaches. These few titles are not an exhaustive list of suitable literature that the teachers use. You may want to create your own list of favorite native language and multicultural children's literature:

> Cenicientas (1990) Spanish well-loved tales series
> L'Engle (1985) Una Arruga en el Tiempo [A Wrinkle in Time]
> Louie (1982) Yeh-Shen: A Cinderella Story from China
> O'Dell (1960) Island of the Blue Dolphins
> Silverstein (1964) The Giving Tree
> White (1990) Las Telarañas de Carlota [Charlotte's Web]

PROFESSIONAL ORGANIZATIONS AND NETWORKS

Bilingual educators are continually asked to prove the efficacy of bilingual education, so the need for accurate information, research, and support becomes extremely important. Support is available through professional organizations and more recently through electronic networking. The following are a few sources for teachers to gain access to information, support, and avenues for advocacy.

National and International Organizations

NABE—National Association for Bilingual Education.   National information and advocacy organization that addresses the needs of language minority Americans. Sponsors annual conferences. Disseminates *NABE NEWS* and the *Bilingual Research Journal.* It is important to support the national organization because it lobbies against attacks on bilingual education at the federal level.
NABE National Office
1220 L Street, NW, Suite 605
Washington, DC 20005-4018
Phone 202-898-1829
FAX 202-789-2866
E-mail: NABE@nabe.org

TESOL–Teachers of English to Speakers of Other Languages.   The mission of this international professional organization is to strengthen the effective teaching and learning of English around the world and respecting individuals' language rights through policies, conventions, institutes, and publications (*TESOL Quarterly, TESOL Journal,* and *TESOL Matters*).

Teachers of English to Speakers of Other Languages, Inc. (TESOL)
1600 Cameron Street, Suite 300
Alexandria, VA 22314-2751
Phone 703-836-0774
FAX 703-836-7864
E-mail: mbr@TESOL.EDU

State Organizations

State Bilingual Associations.   State-level organizations advocate for language minority students through annual conferences and dissemination of information. It is important to join your local association to support bilingual education and to gain support through networking. Several state addresses are provided. Contact NABE for the addresses in other states.

CALIFORNIA
California Association for Bilingual Education (CABE)
CABE Headquarters
320 West G Street, Suite 203
Ontario, CA 91762
Phone 909-984-6201

ILLINOIS
Illinois Association for Bilingual Education (ILABE)
Attention: Josie Yanguas
1855 Mount Prospect Road
Des Plains, IL 60018
Phone 847-803-3535

NEW YORK
New York State Association for Bilingual Education (NYSABE)
St. John's University
Bilingual/ESL Center
8000 Utopia Parkway

Marillac Hall 304
Jamaica, NY 11439
Phone 914-945-0235
(Phone number changes yearly with each new president)

TEXAS
Texas Association for Bilingual Education (TABE)
6323 Sovereign Dr., Suite 178
San Antonio, TX 78229
Phone 210-979-6390

State TESOL.   States and/or regions have TESOL associations that advocate for English-language learners, sponsor conferences, and disseminate information. Contact international offices of TESOL for these local organizations.

Electronic Networking

Cyberspace is increasingly an important way to stay connected to other bilingual professionals and to gain updated research and information about bilingual education policies and practices. For more information and uses, see Cummins and Sayers' (1995) book, *Brave New Schools: Challenging Cultural Literacy Through Global Learning Networks.*

Here is a sampling of a few E-mail and Internet addresses that might be useful to teachers:

1. National Clearinghouse for Bilingual Education (NCBE)–NCBE Newsline mailing list for the latest announcements from the Office of Bilingual Education Minority Language Affairs (OBEMLA) at majordomo@cis.ncbe.gwu.edu (subscribe newsline).
   To access NCBE library files through the internet, point your browser to http://www.ncbe.gwu.edu
2. TESOL–bilingual teaching–Discussion on issues concerning language learning programs in bilingual education, teaching strategies, materials, and teacher education:
   tesol-bilingual@lmrinet.ucsb.edu
3. Practice talk–Discussion of school and classroom issues affecting the delivery of services to K–12 language minority students:
   practicetalk@lmrinet.ucsb.edu
4. ERIC Database–Search documents from 1989 to present on the World Wide Web.
   http://www.ericir.syr.edu/ERIC/eric.html

Appendix A:
Glossary of Terms

The terms, variations of terms, and acronyms are those mentioned by the teachers are defined and discussed. This is by no means a complete list of terms related to bilingual education, only those referred to by the teachers. Many of these terms may represent a complex field or discipline; for that reason, lengthy discussion and related references are included for further information.

Assembly Bill (AB) 1329 (Also termed The Chacon–Moscone Bilingual–Bicultural Education Act)—In 1976, California established the legal framework for a mandatory bilingual education program. The main requirements of the Act were to collect census information at each school, to identify all Limited English Proficient (LEP) students, provide a transitional bilingual program where 10 or more LEP students were enrolled on a particular grade level, and to assign a bilingual teacher to each transitional bilingual education classroom. In addition, reclassification procedures were established as well as provisions to waive monolingual English-speaking teachers assigned to bilingual classrooms if they agreed to participate in staff development. In 1980, "AB 1329 was amended and became known AB 507. All of the major programmatic and staffing requirements remained" (Dolson & Mayer, 1995, pp. 5–6).

Assembly Bill (AB) 507—The Chacon–Moscone Bilingual–Bicultural Education Reform and Improvement Act of 1980 continued provisions established under AB 1329 until 1987, when Governor George Deukmejian allowed this legislation to "sunset" or expire (Powell, 1995). Under the "sunset provisions" of AB 507, funds are used "for the intended purposes of the programs, but all relevant statutes and regulations adopted thereto regarding the use of funds shall not be operative" (California State Dept. of Education, 1995). Under AB 507, the California Department of Education has nevertheless continued to uphold the bill's principles. School districts are still required to identify LEP students and provide them with English-language development, core curriculum, and cross-cultural and self-concept instruction delivered by qualified teachers (Dolson & Mayer, 1995).

Alternate Assessments (Also termed **Authentic**)—Ways of judging student progress through many measures more closely aligned with what students are learning and how they are taught.

Basal Reading Series (Also termed **Basal Readers,** or **Basals**)—These commercially published, traditional, skill-based reading series usually consist of a teacher's manual, collections of stories, accompanying workbooks, and assessment systems.

Bilingual Certificate of Competence (BCC)—California state bilingual certification is granted to certified teachers through examination. The exam consists of three parts on history and culture of the target group, bilingual–ESL teaching methodology, and the native language. The native language test includes and oral, written, and reading comprehension sections. In recent years, the BCC certification has been replaced with the Bilingual Cross-cultural Language and Academic Development (BCLAD) certificate (Walton, 1992).

Biliteracy—The ability to read and write "using two linguistic and cultural settings in order to convey messages in a variety of contexts" (Pérez & Torres-Guzmán, 1992, p. 51).

Basic Interpersonal Communication Skills (BICS)—Are the face-to-face (often, surface) second-language skills that language minority students acquire in a relatively short period of time (1–2 years) from a variety of social contexts (Cummins, 1981). It takes language minority students considerably longer to acquire the language skills needed for academic achievement in English (see CALP below). Educational personnel have often erroneously mistaken social language proficiency for academic language proficiency; in so doing, they have created academic deficits. While Cummins' later work no longer uses the terms BICS and CALP, practitioners in the field still use these terms (Lessow-Hurley, 1990).

Cognitive Academic Language Proficiency (CALP)—Cummins (1981) suggested that it take 5 to 7 years for second-language learners to acquire the cognitively demanding and decontextualized language needed to perform well in English academic settings. Learning the cognitive skills in the native language can lay a foundation to build cogitive skills in the second language. Recent research by Thomas and Collier (1996) indicated that it may take even longer (from 7–10 years) for second language learners to achieve grade-level norms in English, depending on their prior schooling experiences.

Chapter I (Since 1994, termed Title I, under the Improving America's School Act)—Federal legislation (from the Elementary and Secondary Education Act–ESEA) that provides funds to schools and districts for extra services (usually English reading and mathematics instruction). These block grant funds are allocated based on student poverty indices. Title I, at times, has provided ESL to LEP students. Efforts have been made to provide LEP students with more Title I services under the new Improving America's Schools Act (Crawford, 1995).

Code Switch—The juxtaposition of two languages (codes or varieties) between participants within a social context (Gumperz, 1982, cited in Romaine, 1995). The language interchanges are rule-governed (semantic, syntactic, and phonological). Attitudes about the competence of speakers are assigned by those who do not understand the complex nature of the phenomenon of language-mixing (Romaine, 1995).

Compensatory/Remedial Bilingual Programs—Bilingual program models designed to replace the native language with English as rapidly as possible. These programs evolved from the "cultural deprivation" era of the 1950s where native language and cultures were seen as a deficit to be compensated for (Crawford, 1995; Stein, 1986).

Concurrent Translation—A translation strategy used by teachers with heterogeneous classes of students of varying language abilities. The teacher says a phrase or sentence in one language and then translates the same information in the second language. This back-and-forth translation can have negative effects both on students and teachers. Students tend to tune out their weaker language and wait for the information in their stronger language. For the teacher this "linguistic gear shifting" has tiring effects (Legarreta-Marcaida, 1981).

Content-Obligatory Vocabulary (Met, 1994)—The necessary language that is intimately connected to understanding and mastering a particular concept or task. This is contrasted to content-compatible vocabulary that is generally used for communication.

Cooperative Learning (Also termed **Cooperative Groups,** or **Group Work**)—Planned learning activities designed for students to work collaboratively on tasks and projects. Cooperative work is especially helpful for second language learners because students can pool talents, skills, and knowledge as well as serve as language role models and content teachers for one another (see Cohen, 1994).

Core Literature—This approach is based on the assumption that children learn to read and write through reading quality authentic literature. Phonics, sight vocabulary, and comprehension skills are taught within the context of meaningful and interesting texts (Williams & Snipper, 1990).

Critical Pedagogy—Consciousness-raising teaching practices geared toward student–community empowerment (Freire, 1970). Students are guided in problem-posing, analyzing, and challenging the social, political, and economic influences in schools and society in order to transform them.

Culture Shock—The disorientation and feelings of anxiety or stress that an immigrant experiences in adjusting to a new language and environment. These feelings may be exacerbated by societal perceptions about immigrants and speakers of different languages.

Dual Language Program (Also termed **Dual Language, Two-Way,** or **Developmental Bilingual Education**)—This enrichment–additive bilingual program model aims to give prestige to the native language and English for all children (both language majority and minority). These programs, usually implemented in elementary grades, ideally have balanced numbers of English and minority language speakers, enabling students to serve as language role models for one another. These programs are grounded in language acquisition theories and see dual language development as a long-term process. Content and language instruction are intertwined.

Enrichment Programs—In contrast to compensatory programs, enrichment programs are additive in that the native language and culture are respected and supported while incrementally adding the second language. Enrichment programs often are associated with two-way programs suitable for all students including majority students (Lessow-Hurley, 1990).

English as a Second Language (ESL)—This term is frequently used to refer to the Teaching of English to Speakers of other Languages (TESOL). English as a Second Language is an entire discipline grounded in second language acquisition theories, methodologies and approaches. ESL is a subject taught to bilingual education students. Students learning English as a second language are sometimes referred to as *ESL students.*

Exit— A criterion or set score based on a language proficiency test used to reclassify students into the mainstream English program. Usually in Transitional Bilingual Education programs (TBE), students are expected to reach this level within 2 to 3 years of bilingual instruction. According to Cummins (1981 and 1994), this limited amount of native language instruction does not allow the learner to develop a firm cognitive base upon which to transfer cognitive skill into the second language. Premature exit from the bilingual program allows the learner to reach a partial threshold level of bilingualism, which can put the learner at risk of academic failure.

Immersion—This term is often confused with submersion or sink-or-swim where the language minority speaker is placed in the second language environment and expected to acquire it without out any special assistance (Crawford, 1995).

Immersion Program (Also referred to as the Spanish Immersion Program and the Canadian Immersion Program)—These programs have been most successful in promoting second language learning for language majority students. A model that promotes additive bilingualism and biliteracy, both primary language and second language instruction are carefully planned and incrementally taught through meaningful hands-on materials and activities (see Curtain & Pesola, 1994; Wink, 1992). The teacher, who is bilingual, uses the second language as a medium of instruction. (For videos on Immersion teaching, contact Montgomery County Public Schools, 850 Hungerford Drive, Rockville, MD 20850.)

Integrated Curriculum (Also termed **Thematic Units** or **Instruction**)—Units of instruction where subjects areas are combined holistically. For example, a social studies or science study is taught through literature and hands-on activity.

Inventive Spelling (Also termed **Invented Spelling**)—The emphasis on correct spelling is relaxed in initial stages of writing to encourage fluency of expression. This temporary spelling system, often associated with writing process, allows students to take risks in developing their ideas without focusing on the correct spelling of each word.

Language Development Specialist (LDS)—A California credential, designed in response to the growing numbers of culturally and linguistically diverse students, consists of courses in language acquisition, sheltered language, content instructional methods, and cultural awareness. This credential, though still valid, has been replaced by the Cross-cultural Language and Academic (CLAD) credential (Walton, 1992).

Language Experience—A reading approach where children's words are written down to show the connection between the spoken and written word. Students can generate their own stories or narrative accounts of a shared experience in either language. This approach is often used with young children or learners in the beginning stages of second-language learning. This approach can be used to create materials in the native language when few appropriate level materials are available.

Language Minority—A term used to identify students from diverse ethnic groups who speak languages other than English to receive special educational services, such as a bilingual education or ESL program. This term, like Limited English Proficient (LEP), may have a negative connotation where the student or group is seen as limited or having a deficient language when compared to the majority.

Language Proficiency—Because of the lack of agreement about the definitions of proficiency and communicative competence (Cummins, 1981), there is wide variability as to how to determine and measure it (Valdés & Figueroa, 1994). From an educator's perspective, proficiency in a language may be seen as the ability to process language in the four areas of reading, writing, speaking, and listening. Though determining bilingual language proficiency is problematic, it is nevertheless required for educational decisions.

Language Proficiency Assessment (Also termed **Tests** or **Testing**)—Language tests used to place or reclassify students in or out of bilingual or English as a Second Language programs. These tests (usually in English, but sometimes in the native language), often group-administered, measure reading or discrete points of syntax, vocabulary, or pronunciation. Language proficiency should include broader measures of communicative competence.

Language Restoration/Recovery/Maintenance—The process of providing native language and culture instruction to students who have lost their native language through assimilation to English and American culture.

Late-Exit Model (A recent term for a **Maintenance Bilingual Education** program)—Students receive native and second language literacy and content instruction for a long period (usually throughout grades K–6). As an additive program, the late-exit model promotes biliteracy, biculturalism, and positive parent involvement in the instruction process (Ramírez et al., 1991).

Learning Styles—The information processing and problem-solving modes that a learner uses. Teachers need to be aware of the learner's strengths in designing instructional and assessment activities. (A useful acronym for these different modalities is VAKT: visual, auditory, kinesthetic, and tactile.)

Limited English Proficient (LEP)—One of many terms to identify or label children who speak languages other than English; this term has been and is used for grant and funding purposes (e.g., federal Title VII-see below). Researchers, state policy-makers, and practitioners have objected to pejorative labels of terms such as LEP and language minority. They have opted to use more positive terms such as: English Language Learner (ELL), Potentially English Proficient (PEP), and Culturally Linguistically Diverse (CLD).

Linguistic Summary—A bilingual teaching strategy where a lesson or portion of a lesson is presented in one language, followed by a summary of the key vocabulary and concepts presented in the other language. This use of two languages is similar to what González & Lezama (1976) call the preview-review approach (cited in Ovando & Collier, 1985).

Literature Study Circles—A literature study circle is a time when a small group of students (less than eight) comes together to share, discuss, or talk about a chosen or assigned story, novel, or poem they are reading. (See Samway & Whang, 1996, for an explanation of this method.)

Maintenance (Also termed **Late-Exit Maintenance Bilingual Education**)—An additive program where language minority students maintain and strengthen their native language and content as they learn language and content in English. Maintenance programs have been criticized as segregationist (Crawford, 1995). Ideally, maintenance programs should extend from K–12, but they mostly only extend through the elementary grades (Thomas & Collier, 1996).

Multifunctional Resource Center (MRC)—A technical assistance and professional development training center funded by Title VII to assist professionals in the implentation of its programs. As of 1996, with the reauthorization of Title VII under the Improving America's Schools Act, these centers have been phased out and reconfigured into Comprehensive Regional Assistance Centers. With federal budget cuts, the future of such centers, and assistance to bilingual teachers and programs, is in jeopardy.

Natural Approach—Second language instruction is assumed to be learned best in a low anxiety acquisition-rich learning environment, similar to the way a child acquires the first language. Language input is comprehensible, yet challenging (Krashen, 1994). Learners are classified at different acquisition stages (preproduction, early production, speech emergence, and intermediate fluency), and various teaching techniques are matched with each stage (Terrell, 1981).

Newcomer Model—This program model is used by some schools or districts experiencing a large influx of immigrant students. To better address the needs of these students, the newcomers are grouped together for a short period (6 months–2 years) before going to a regular school environment. The programs provide students with basic English and academic instruction and help them adjust to the school environment. This model can be beneficial for students who have never been to school before. Critics oppose this model because it segregates and isolates immigrant students (Natale, 1994).

Nonstandard Varieties of English—When two languages are in contact, traces of one language emerge in the other, producing a variation. For example, Black (or African American) English maintains some of the linguistic features from African languages and follows systematic linguistic rules. Speakers of nonstandard varieties are judged by the language (and its status) that they speak.

Notional-Functional—Second language instruction syllabus that identifies topic areas and language functions to be developed as related to those topics (e.g., learning to greet and take leave in casual situations). The focus is on meaningful communication in different contexts (Baker, 1996).

Partial Immersion—These programs, usually for language majority students, provide literacy and content instruction through each of the equal amounts of the two languages (Curtain & Pesola, 1994).

Performance-Based Assessment—Student learning is assessed through having "to construct a response, create a product, or demonstrate application of knowledge" (O'Malley & Valdez Pierce, 1996, p. 239). Performance assessments may be used in the native or second languages.

Portfolio—A collection of student work showing academic growth over a period of time in a subject area(s).

Portfolio Assessment—An alternative to standardized tests (or often used in addition to standardized tests) to assess student academic progress over time through collections of student work, teacher observations, and self-assessments (O'Malley & Valdez Pierce, 1996).

Preproduction Stage (Also termed the **Silent Period**)—A beginning second language acquisition stage where the learner is encouraged to develop receptive skills before being expected to produce utterances in the second language. (Terrell, 1981)

Pull-out Instruction—Students (individually or in small groups) are taken out of the classroom for instruction for a short time for subjects such as English as a Second Language instruction or to a special education resource room. Pull-out instruction often has limited efficacy because it may not relate to or reinforce the classroom curriculum.

School Culture—The interaction of everyone and everything (e.g., the physical plant, the human and material resources, policies and power relationships) that shapes what happens within in the school context.

Seven Intelligences—The theory of multiple intelligences (derived from Howard Gardner, 1983, cited in Lazear, 1991) states that students have various cognitive strengths (or intelligences) that need to be acknowledged and enriched within the classroom and school environment. The seven intelligences are: verbal/linguistic, visual/spatial, body/kinesthetic, logical/mathematical, intrapersonal, interpersonal, and musical/rhythmic.

Sheltered English (Or termed **Sheltered Instruction**)—Content is taught in the second language through comprehensible input, hands-on, cooperative groups in a low anxiety environment. Sheltered English classes may be self-contained classes with children from various different language groups. The teacher may not know or use the students' native languages.

Silent Period (See preproduction).

Spanish as a Second Language (SSL)—The teaching of Spanish to monolingual English speakers in heterogeneous Spanish/English bilingual classes, usually Transitional Bilingual Education (TBE). Because of the great instructional demands of teaching Spanish-speaking students to learn English, English-speaking students usually only learn basic vocabulary (e.g., colors and numbers) and simple phrases in Spanish.

Standardized Test—Easily scored (usually multiple choice) tests designed to compare the achievement or language proficiency of one group of students with another group. These tests often do not reflect what teachers have taught or students have learned.

Standard English—The prestigious code of English spoken by those who have wealth, power, and education (Labov, 1966). This supposedly "grammatically correct" variety is used in written texts, government, the media, and the schools.

Submersion (Also termed **sink-or-swim**)—Language minority students are placed in classrooms where all instruction is conducted in English. This negligent practice has caused much academic failure for language minority students (Crawford, 1995).

Thematic Instruction (Also termed **Thematic Units**)—See Integrated Curriculum.

Title VII—Federal funding and legislation, originally under the Bilingual Education Act of 1968 of the Elementary and Secondary Education Act (ESEA), presently is designed "to ensure that limited English proficient students master English and develop high academic attainment in content areas" and to develop "bilingual skills and multicultural understanding" (Crawford, 1995, p. 250). These funds are granted on a competitive basis to schools, school systems, and institutions of higher education (prior to 1996) to meet the purposes of the legislation. Policies and funds are also designated for research and dissemination of information. (See Crawford, 1995, for history, politics, and legislation).

Total Physical Response (TPR)—Asher (1982) originated this second language learning method to develop receptive language through actions. Students listen and follow commands without being expected to speak. This method is a variation of the natural approach and is appropriate for second language learners at beginning second language learning stages because it is dependent on vocabulary to be learned within context of actions, props, and realia.

Transitional Bilingual Education Programs (TBE) (Sometimes termed **Early-Exit Bilingual Education**)—Compensatory programs that give short-term native language instruction with the goal of exiting students into the English mainstream classroom as soon as possible. The transition is usually after 2 to 3 years of bilingual instruction, based on a test that measures English language proficiency. This minimum amount of native language instruction may not provide students with a sufficiently strong native or second language foundation to be able to perform at the grade level in the all-English classroom. Transitional programs have been the major bilingual education program model implemented in general and funded by Title VII.

With the new reauthorization of Title VII, transitional programs are no longer a program category that is funded. Nevertheless, many transitional programs are still the norm and advocated by certain states such as New York, (The New York State Education Department, 1990) and local mandates (e.g., *Aspira v. Board of Education*, 1974, in New York City, Santiago Santiago, 1978).

Two-Way Programs (See **Dual Language Programs**).

Venn Diagram—A graphic organizer that uses overlapping circles to compare and contrast two related areas or pieces of literature.

Webbing (Also termed brainstorming or semantic maps)—A discussion or writing technique used to generate ideas and vocabulary related to a particular topic. Webs or maps are often used as part of the prewriting process to develop ideas and organization structure.

Whole Language—A philosophy for reading and language arts instruction where speaking, reading, and writing processes are interrelated. These processes are developed from whole-to-part, as opposed to part-to-whole, phonics-based approaches within a meaningful social context. Reading and writing skills are taught within the context of authentic literature and texts (Goodman, 1986).

Writing Process—A collaborative process of drafting and creating written works for varied and authentic purposes. The author gives and receives feedback and support in developing a written piece. The steps include: prewriting, drafting, sharing, revising, editing, and publishing (Pérez & Torres-Guzmán, 1992). Not all written work is taken to final publication stages.

Appendix B:
Sample Interview Questions

1. How and why did you become a bilingual teacher? How long have you been a bilingual teacher? What grades have you taught?
2. What bilingual teacher education did you have? Discuss the quality. What was most helpful about your courses/training? What would have been more helpful?
3. Give some background about the community where you teach (immigration changes, SES, and education levels of parents, occupations, languages/dialects spoken, visions for their children). How has this changed over the years?
4. What bilingual program model is implemented at your school? How well does it serve language minority students? How much time is devoted to the two languages?
5. Talk about the strategies/approaches you use (or have used) in teaching first and second languages, culture, and content areas.
6. Talk about some of the successes you have seen with your students.
7. How are language and other academic achievements tested? Are there problems with testing procedures? What practices could improve the assessment of language minority children's language and skills?
8. What support have you received from others (administrators, colleagues, and parents)? What could better help you in your work?
9. Talk about curriculum and materials. What could improve them?
10. How involved are parents in their children's education? Discuss your approaches in involving parents. What could help to improve their involvement?
11. What advice would you give to a new bilingual teacher about bilingual education? What advice would you give to a veteran monolingual teacher about teaching language minority children who have recently been placed in her class?

Appendix C:
Diana's Literature Study Circle Questions

1. Does this story make you think of anything that happened to you?

2. Does this story seem real or imaginary? Why?

3. How do you think this story shows what's important to the author?

4. Does this story remind you of another story we have read?

5. If you had written this story, would you have changed anything?

6. What do you think the story might be about?

7. What is the problem that the character has? Why is he or she in trouble?

8. Based on what you've read, what do you think will happen next? Why do you think so?

9. Do you agree with the character's response? Why or why not?

Appendix D:
Poem for Heather's First-Grade Class

FIRST SCHOOL DAY

I had a lovely walk
to school on this first day.
I met so many friends
as I went on my way.

I had not seen my friends.
There was so much to say
when we all met this morning
on this happy first school day.

References

Ada, A. F. (1986). Creative education for bilingual teachers. *Harvard Educational Review,* 56(4), 386–394.

Ambert, A. N., & Meléndez, S. E. (1985). *Bilingual education: A sourcebook.* New York: Teachers College Press.

Asher, J. J. (1982). *Learning another language through actions: The complete teacher's guide* (2nd ed.). Los Gatos, CA: Sky Oaks Publications.

Baker, C. (1996). *Foundations of bilingual education and bilingualism* (2nd ed.). Clevedon, England: Multilingual Matters.

Ballard W., & Tighe, P. (1989). *IDEA Kit.* Brea, CA: Ballard and Tighe, Inc.

Ballard, W., Tighe, P., & Dalton, E. (1991). *IPT Oral language proficiency test.* Brea, CA: Ballard & Tighe, Inc.

Baratta-Lorton, M. (1976). *Math their way.* Reading, MA: Addison-Wesley Publishing.

Barringer, F. (1993, April 28). For 32 million Americans, English is a second language. *The New York Times,* p. A18.

Bell, M. (1992). University of Chicago School Mathematics Project. (1992). *Everyday mathematics.* Chicago, IL: Everyday Learning Corporation.

Berman, P. (1992). *Meeting the challenge of language diversity: An evaluation of California programs for pupils with limited English proficiency.* Paper presented at the annual American Educational Research Association Conference, San Francisco, CA.

Boehm, A. E. (1986). *Boehm test of basic concepts-Revised.* San Antonio, TX: Psychological Corporation.

Brookes, M. (1986). *Drawing with children.* Los Angeles, CA: Jeremy P. Tarcher.

Bullock, J. (1992). *Touch math.* Colorado Springs, CO: Innovative Learning Concepts, Inc.

Burk, D., Snider, A., & Symonds, P. (1992). *Math excursions K: Project-based mathematics for kindergartners.* Portsmouth, NH: Heinemann.

Burt, M. K., Dulay, H. C., & Chávez, E. H. (1978). *Bilingual syntax measure.* San Antonio, TX: Psychological Corporation.

California State Department of Bilingual Education. (1981). *Schooling and language minority students: A theoretical framework.* Los Angeles, CA: California State University.

California State Department of Bilingual Education. (1994). *Schooling and language minority students: A theoretical framework* (2nd edition). Los Angeles, CA: California State University.

California State Department of Education. (1995). *LEP program guide: Organizing a compliant program for students of limited English proficiency.* Sacramento: Author.

Carter, K. (1993). The place of story in the study of teaching and teacher education. *Educational Researcher, 22*(1), 5–12, 18.

Castellanos, D. (1983). *The best of two worlds: Bilingual-bicultural education in the U.S.* Trenton: New Jersey State Department of Education.

Cenicientas. (1990). Spanish well-loved tales series. New York: Penguin.

Charles, L. H., & Brummet, M. R. (1989). *Connections: Linking manipulatives to mathematics.* Mountain View, CA: Creative Publications.

Cohen, E. G. (1994). *Designing groupwork: Strategies for the heterogeneous classroom* (2nd ed.). New York, NY: Teachers College Press.

Conklin, N. F., & Lourie, M. A. (1983). *A host of tongues: Language communities in the United States.* New York: The Free Press.

Connolly, F. M., & Clandinin, D. J. (1990). Stories of experience and narrative inquiry. *Educational Researcher, 19*(5), 2–14.

Corchran-Smith, M., & Lytle, S. L. (1990). Research on teaching and teacher research: The issues that divide. *Educational Researcher, 19*(2), 2–11.

Council of the Great City Schools. (1996). *The urban teacher challenge: A report on teacher recruitment and demand in selected great city schools.* Report prepared by Recruiting New Teachers on behalf of the Urban Teacher Collaborative. Author.

Crawford, J. (1992). *Hold your tongue: Bilingualism and the politics of "English Only."* Reading, MA: Addison-Wesley.

Crawford, J. (1995). *Bilingual education: History, politics, theory and practice.* Los Angeles, CA: BES.

CTB/McGraw-Hill. (1978). *Comprehensive test of basic skills, Español.* Monterey, CA: Author.

CTB/McGraw-Hill. (1989). *Comprehensive test of basic skills* (4th ed.). Monterey, CA: Author.

CTB/McGraw-Hill. (1991). *Spanish assessment of basic education* (2nd ed.). Monterey, CA: Author.

Cummins, J. (1981). The role of primary language development in promoting success for language minority students. In *Schooling and language minority students: A theoretical framework* (pp. 3–49). Los Angeles, CA: California State University.

Cummins, J. (1994). The role of primary language development in promoting success for language minority students. In *Schooling and language minority students: A theoretical framework* (2nd ed., pp. 3–46). Los Angeles, CA: California State University.

Cummins, J., & Sayers, D. (1995). *Brave new schools: Challenging cultural illiteracy through global learning networks.* New York: St. Martin's Press.

Curtain, H., & Pesola, C. A. B. (1994). *Languages and children: Making the match* (2nd ed.). White Plains, NY: Longman.

DeAvila, E., & Duncan, S. E. (1981). *Language assessment scales.* San Rafael, CA: Linguametrics Group.

DeAvila, E., Duncan, S. E., & Navarette, C. (1987). *Finding out/Descubrimento (FO/D).* Miami, FL: Santillana Publishing.

Dobbert, M. L. (1982). *Ethnographic research: Theory and application for modern schools and societies.* New York: Praeger.

Dolson, D. P. (1994). Introduction. *Schooling and language minority students: A theoretical framework* (2nd ed., pp. vii–ix). Los Angeles, CA: California State University.

Dolson, D. P., & Mayer, J. (1995). *Schooling immigrant children: Current practices and policies.* Paper presented at the annual conference of the American Educational Research Association, San Francisco, CA.

Duncan, S. E., & DeAvila, E. (1985). *Pre-language assessment scales.* San Rafael, CA: Linguametrics Group.

Fitzgerald, J. (1993). Views on bilingualism in the United States: A selective historical review. *Bilingual Research Journal, 17*(1 & 2), 35–56.

Freire, P. (1970). *Pedagogy of the oppressed.* New York: Continuum.

Goldstein, B. L. (1987). *The interplay between school culture and status for teachers of immigrant students.* Paper presented at the annual meeting of the American Educational Research Association, Washington, DC.

Goodman, K. (1986). *What's whole in whole language?* Portsmouth, NH: Heinemann.

Grosjean, F. (1982). *Life with two languages: An introduction to bilingualism.* Cambridge, MA: Harvard University Press.

Hargreaves, A. (1996). Revisiting voice. *Educational Researcher, 25*(1), 12–19.

Headden, S. (1995, September 25). Tongue-tied in the schools. *U.S. News & World Report, 119*(12), 44–46.

Jackson, P. W. (1968). *Life in classrooms.* New York: Holt, Rinehart & Winston.

Koslin, B. L., Zeno, S., Koslin, S., Wainer, H., & Ivens, S. H. (1987). *The DRP: An effectiveness measure in reading.* New York: College Entrance Examination Board.

Krashen, S. (1994). Bilingual education and second language acquisition theory. In *Schooling and language minority students: A theoretical framework* (2nd ed., pp. 47–75). Los Angeles, CA: California State University.

Labov, W. (1966). *The social stratification of English in New York City.* Washington, DC: Center for Applied Linguistics.

Lambert, W. E., & Tucker, R. G. (1972). *Bilingual education and children: The St. Lambert experience.* Rowley, MA: Newbury House.

Language assessment battery. (1982). Brooklyn, NY: The New York City Board of Education.

Lazear, D. (1991). *Seven ways of teaching: The artistry of teaching with multiple intelligences.* Palatine, IL: Skylight Publishing.

Legarreta-Marcaida, D. (1981). Effective use of primary language in the classroom. In *Schooling and language minority students: A theoretical framework* (1st ed.). Los Angeles, CA: California State University.

Lemberger, N. (1990). *Bilingual education: Teachers' voices.* Unpublished doctoral dissertation, Teachers College, Columbia University, New York.

L'Engle, M. (1985). *Una arruga en el tiempo–A wrinkle in time.* Miami, FL: Santillana Publishing.

Lessow-Hurley, J. (1990). *The foundations of dual language instruction.* White Plains, NY: Longman.

López, R. (1995). The moment of truth has arrived: Education funding hinges on budget deal. *NABE News, 19*(3), 1, 27–28.

Louie, A. (1982). *Yeh-Shen: A Cinderella story from China.* New York: Philomel Books.

McCracken, M. J., & McCracken, R. A. (1982) *Spelling through phonics.* Blaine, WA: McCracken Educational Services, Inc.

McKay, S. L., & Wong, S. C. (Eds.) (1988). *Language diversity: Problem or resource?* Boston, MA: Heinle & Heinle Publishers.

Met, M. (1994). Teaching content through a second language. In F. Genessee (Ed.). *Educating second language children: The whole child, the whole curriculum, the whole community.* New York: Cambridge University Press.

Mishler, E. G. (1986). *Research interviewing: Context and narrative.* Cambridge, MA: Harvard University Press.

Molesky, J. (1988). Understanding the American linguistic mosaic: A historical overview of language maintenance and shift. In S. L. McKay & S. C. Wong (Eds.), *Language diversity: Problem or resource?* Boston, MA: Heinle & Heinle Publishers.

Montero-Sieburth, M., & Pérez, M. (1987). Echar pa´lante, moving onward: The dilemmas and strategies of a bilingual teacher. *Anthropology & Education Quarterly, 18*(3), 180–189.

Natale, J. A. (1994, January). Homeroom to the world. *The Executive Educator, 16*(1), 14–18.

New York State Education Department. (1990). *Guidelines for programs under Part 154 of Commissioner's regulations for pupils with limited English proficiency.* Albany, NY: Author.

Noone, P. (in press). *Family science.* Portland, OR: Northwest EQUALS Project, Portland State University.

O'Dell, S. (1960). *Island of the blue dolphins.* Boston, MA: Houghton Mifflin.

O'Malley, M. J., & Valdez Pierce, L. (1996). *Authentic assessment for English language learners: Practical approaches for teachers.* Reading, MA: Addison-Wesley.

Ovando, C. J., & Collier, V. P. (1985). *Bilingual and ESL classrooms: Teaching in multicultural classrooms.* New York: McGraw-Hill.

Pérez, B., & Torres-Guzmán, M. E. (1992). *Learning in two worlds: An integrated Spanish/English biliteracy approach.* White Plains, NY: Longman.

Powell, K. (1995). The history of bilingual education and California's response. *CABE Newsletter, 17*(6), 14–17.

Ramírez, J. D., Yuen, S. D., & Ramey, D. R. (1991). *Longitudinal study of structured English immersion, early-exit and late-exit transitional bilingual education programs for language minority children. Final Report to the U.S. Department of Education. Executive Summary.* San Mateo, CA: Aguirre International.

Richardson, K. (1984). *Developing number concepts using Unifix cubes.* Reading, MA: Addison-Wesley.

Romaine, S. (1995). *Bilingualism* (2nd ed.). Oxford, UK and Cambridge, MA: Blackwell.

Russell, S. J., & Stone, A. (1990). *Used numbers: Real data in the classroom.* Palo Alto, CA: Dale Seymore.

Samway, K. D., & Whang, G. (1996). *Literature study circles in a multicultural classroom.* York, ME: Stenhouse.

Santiago Santiago, I. (1978). A community's struggle for equal educational opportunity: Aspira v. Bd. of Ed. *Office for Minority Education Monograph* (No. 2). Princeton, NJ: Educational Testing Service.

Santiago Santiago, I. (1983). Political and legal issues in maintaining vernacular in the curriculum: The U.S. experience. In L. V. D. Berg-Eldering, F. J. M. DeRycke, & L. V. Zuck (Eds.), *Multicultural education: A challenge for teachers* (pp. 53–76). Dordrecht, Holland: Foris Publications.

Santiago Santiago, I. (1986). Aspira v. Board of Education: Revisited. *American Journal of Education, 95*(1), 149–199.

Schmitt, E. (1996, July 26). English as the official language wins backing of House panel. *The New York Times,* p. 11.

Shulman, L. S. (1986). Paradigms and research programs in the study of contemporary teaching: A contemporary perspective. In M. C. Wittrock (Ed.), *Third handbook of research on teaching* (pp. 3–36). New York: Macmillan.

Silverstein, S. (1964). *The giving tree.* New York: HarperCollins.

Stein, C. B. (1986). *Sink or swim: The politics of bilingual education.* New York: Praeger.

Stenmark, J., Thompson, V., & Cossey, R. (1986). *Family Math.* Berkeley, CA: University of California Regents.

Teitelbaum, H., & Hiller, R. J. (1979). Bilingual education: The legal mandate. In H. T. Trueba and C. Barnett-Mizrahi (Eds.), *Bilingual multicultural education and the professional: From theory to practice* (pp. 20–53). Rowley, MA: Newbury House.

Terrell, T. D. (1981). The natural approach in bilingual education. In *Schooling and language minority students: A theoretical framework* (1st ed., pp. 117–146). Los Angeles, CA: California State University.

Thomas, W. P., & Collier, V. P. (1996). Language-minority student achievement and program effectiveness. *NABE News, 19*(6), 33–35.

Torres, J. (1996). Dole support may escalate official English as an issue in presidential race. *Hispanic Link Weekly, 14*(18), 1–2.

U.S. Department of Education. (1990). *Staffing the multilingually impacted schools of the 1990s.* Washington, DC: Author.

U.S. Department of Education. (1996). A back to school report: The baby boom echo puts K–12 enrollments at all time high. *Update Education Initiatives, Ed. Info. Listserve.* Available online.

Valdés, G., & Figueroa, R. A. (1994). *Bilingualism and testing: A special case of bias.* Norwood, NJ: Ablex.

Waggoner, D. (1993). Numbers of school-agers with spoken English difficulty increases by 83%. *Numbers and Needs, 3*(2), 2.

Waggoner, D. (1994). Language minority school-age population numbers 9.9 million. *Numbers and Needs, 4*(4), 1–3.

Walton, P. H. (1992). CABE serves on panel to update licensing for teachers for language diverse students. *CABE Newsletter, 14*(3), 9, 30.

White, E. B. (1990). *Las Telarañas de Carlota–Charlotte's Web.* New York: Lectorum Publishers.

Williams, J. D., & Snipper, G. C. (1990). *Literacy and bilingualism.* New York: Longman.

Wink, J. (1992). Immersion confusion. *TESOL Matters, 1*(6), 14.

Wong Fillmore, L., & Valadez, C. (1986). Teaching bilingual learners. In M. C. Wittrock (Ed.), *Third handbook of research on teaching* (pp. 648–684). New York: Macmillan.

Author Index

A

Ada, A. F., 2, 7, 187
Ambert, A. N., 12, 17, 187
Asher, J. J., 179, 187

B

Baker, C., 157, 177, 187
Ballard, W., 74, 87, 114, 131, 161, 165, 187
Baratta-Lorton, M., 18, 64, 111, 162, 187
Barringer, F., 159, 187
Bell, M., 91, 162, 187
Berman, P., 158, 187
Boehm, A. E., 166, 187
Brookes, M., 63, 162, 187
Brummet, M. R., 64, 163, 187
Bullock, J., 75, 85, 162, 187
Burk, D., 64, 114, 131, 162, 187
Burt, M. K., 64, 166, 187

C

Carter, K., 7, 187
Castellanos, D., 12, 13, 187
Charles, L. H., 64, 163, 187
Chávez, E. H., 64, 114, 131, 166, 187
Clandinin, D. J., 5, 6, 7, 188
Cohen, E. G., 173, 187
Collier, V. P., 12, 15, 16, 172, 176, 177, 190
Conklin, N. F., 158, 187
Connolly, F. M., 5, 6, 7, 188
Corchran-Smith, M., 6, 188
Cossey, R., 88, 115, 165, 190
Crawford, J., 10, 11, 12, 13, 14, 15, 17, 18, 157, 173, 174, 177, 179, 188
Cummins, J., 15, 146, 169, 172, 174, 175, 188

Curtain, H., 105, 175, 177, 188

D

Dalton, E., 114, 131, 165, 187
DeAvila, E., 76, 89, 111, 115, 118, 163, 167, 188
Dobbert, M. L., 4, 188
Dolson, D. P., 4, 171, 188
Dulay, H. C., 64, 114, 131, 166, 187
Duncan, S. E., 76, 89, 111, 115, 118, 163, 167, 188

F

Figueroa, R. A., 175, 191
Fitzgerald, J., 14, 188
Freire, P., 173, 188

G

Goldstein, B. L., 7, 188
Goodman, K., 180, 188
Grosjean, F., 9, 158, 188

H

Hargreaves, A., 6, 7, 188
Headden, S., 19, 189
Hiller, R. J., 17, 190

I–J

Ivens, S. H., 48, 51, 167, 189
Jackson, P. W., 5, 189

K

Koslin, B. L., 48, 51, 167, 189

Koslin, S., 48, 51, 167, 189
Krashen, S., 177, 189

L

Labov, W., 179, 189
Lambert, W. E., 12, 16, 189
Lazear, D., 178, 189
Legarreta-Marcaida, D., 16, 146, 173, 189
Lemberger, N., 2, 16, 189
L'Engle, M., 130, 168, 189
Lessow-Hurley, J., 156, 157, 172, 174, 189
López, R., 14, 189
Louie, A., 90, 168, 189
Lourie, M. A., 158, 187
Lytle, S. L., 6, 188

M

Mayer, J., 171, 188
McCracken, M. J., 163, 189
McCracken, R. A., 163, 189
Meléndez, S. E., 12, 17, 187
Met, M., 104, 173, 189
Mishler, E. G., 4, 189
Molesky, J., 19, 189
Montero-Sieburth, M., 7, 189

N

Natale, J. A., 177, 189
Navarette, C., 111, 115, 118, 162, 188
Noone, P., 115, 164, 189

O

O'Dell, S., 127, 168, 189
O'Malley, M. J., 178, 189
Ovando, C. J., 12, 16, 176, 190

P

Pérez, B., 172, 180, 190
Perez, M., 7, 189
Pesola, C. A. B., 105, 175, 177, 188

Powell, K., 17, 171, 190

R

Ramey, D. R., 15, 176, 190
Ramírez, J. D., 15, 176, 190
Richardson, K., 111, 164, 190
Romaine, S., 173, 190
Russell, S. J., 111, 165, 190

S

Samway, K. D., 176, 190
Santiago Santiago, I., 13, 17, 18, 180, 190
Sayers, D., 170, 188
Schmitt, E., 15, 190
Shulman, L. S., 6, 190
Silverstein, S., 63, 168, 190
Snider, A., 64, 162, 187
Snipper, G. C., 173, 191
Stein, C. B., 10, 13, 158, 190
Stenmark, J., 88, 115, 164, 190
Stone, A., 111, 165, 190
Symonds, P., 64, 162, 187

T

Teitelbaum, H., 17, 190
Terrell, T. D., 177, 178, 190
Thomas, W. P., 15, 172, 177, 190
Thompson, V., 88, 115, 164, 190
Tighe, P., 74, 87, 114, 131, 161, 165, 187
Torres, J., 14, 190
Torres-Guzmán, M. E., 172, 180, 190
Tucker, R. G., 16, 189

V

Valadez, C., 146, 191
Valdés, G., 175, 191
Valdez Pierce, L., 178, 189

W

Waggoner, D., 13, 160, 191
Wainer, H., 48, 51, 189
Walton, P. H., 19, 172, 175, 191

Whang, G., 176, 190
White, E. B., 130, 168, 191
Williams, J. D., 173, 191
Wink, J., 175, 191
Wong Fillmore, L., 146, 191

Y–Z

Yuen, S. D., 15, 176, 190
Zeno, S., 48, 51, 167, 189

Subject Index

A

Administrative relations, *see also* Collegial relations; Parent–teacher relations
  district, 36, 42, 45, 85, 107–108, 123, 131
  nonsupportive, 36, 45, 67, 85, 87–88, 95, 107–108, 117–118, 123, 131, 134–135, 141–142
  overview of teachers, 36, 42, 45, 66–67, 79, 80–81, 85, 87–88, 95, 107–108, 117–118, 123, 131, 134–136, 141–142
  principals, 36, 42, 45, 66–67, 79, 95, 107, 117–118, 134–135, 141–142
  study questions for, 22
  supportive, 36, 42, 45, 66, 79, 80–81, 88, 95, 107, 123, 134–135, 141–142
  worksheet grid for, 25, 27
A Host of Tongues: Language Communities in the United States (Conklin & Lourie), 158
Alternate assessment, 132, 145, 148, 172
Aspira v. The Board of Education, 18, 180
Assembly Bill 507, 17, 107, 114, 171
Assembly Bill 1329, 17, 107, 171
Assessment, *see also* Tests
  alternate, 132, 145, 148, 172
  overview of teachers, 39–40, 64–65, 76, 102–105, 115–116, 130–133, 148
  performance-based, 59, 178
  portfolio, 64, 76, 114, 132, 148, 178

Attitudes, 8–9, 10, 14–15, 16, 152, *see also* Cultural factors
  of parents toward bilingualism, 37, 41, 52, 58–59, 77–78, 91–93, 100, 102, 116–117, 122–123
Authentic assessment, *see* Alternate assessment

B

Basal readers, 62–63, 74, 87, 90, 97, 112, 130, 172
Basic Interpersonal Communication Skills (BICS), 73, 110, 116, 172
Bay Area Math, Science, and Writing Projects, 161
Bilingual Certificate of Competence (BCC), 56, 83, 107, 139, 172
Bilingual Cross–cultural Language and Academic Development (BCLAD), 19, 172
Bilingual Education: History, Politics, Theory, and Practice (Crawford), 158
Bilingual Education Act (BEA) (1968), 12, *see also* Title VII
Bilingual education programs, *see also* Dual language programs; English as a Second Language (ESL); Immersion programs; Maintenance programs; Transitional Bilingual Education (TBE) programs
  compensatory/remedial, 99, 173
  educational resources for, 157
  enrichment, 174
  funding, 3, 12, 13, 14–15, 16, 17, 44, 135, 179
  mainstreaming, 36–37, 39, 43, 44, 57–58, 69, 71, 89, 144
  newcomer model, 69, 177

overview of teachers, 29, 36–37,
44–45, 57–60, 71–72, 89,
91, 95, 97, 99–105,
107–110, 115–116, 117,
118–119, 124–125, 146
pull-out instruction, 12, 44, 107,
109, 178
sink-or-swim, 10, 179
Spanish as a Second Language
(SSL), 86, 93, 125, 141, 178
study questions for, 22
worksheet grid for, 24, 26
Bilingual education resources, 157–169,
see also Teacher education
curricula, 161–165
demographic information,
159–160
electronic networking, 170
general foundation texts, 157
historical perspective, 158
literature, 168
political perspective, 158
professional organizations,
168–170
program models, 158
tests, 165–167
Bilingual Syntax Measure (BSM), 64, 114,
131, 166
Biliteracy, 172
Boehm Test of Basic Concepts–Revised,
114, 166
*Brave New Schools: Challenging Cultural
Literacy Through Global Learning
Networks* (Cummins & Sayers),
170

C

California
Assembly Bill 507, 17, 107, 114,
171
Assembly Bill 1329, 17, 107, 171
Bilingual Certificate of
Competence (BCC), 56,
83, 107, 139, 172
Bilingual Cross-cultural Language
and Academic Develop-
ment (BCLAD), 19, 172

Cross-cultural Language and
Academic Development
(CLAD), 19, 175
Language Development Specialist
(LDS), 57, 72, 79–80, 124,
175
limited English proficient (LEP)
in, 3–4
and project evolution, 3–4
Proposition 187, 14, 135, 152
California Basic Educational Skills Test
(C-BEST), 69–70, 83, 139
California Test of Basic Skills (CTBS), 64,
114, 130, 166
*California Test of Basic Skills Español
(CTBS Español)*, 131, 166
Canadian Immersion program, 15–16,
108–109, 174–175
Certification, see Teacher education
Chapter I, see Title I
Chinese/English language, see Diana
(personal narrative)
Civil Rights Act (1964), 12, 16, see also
specific titles
Classroom, 8–9, 10t, see also Teaching
styles
composition of, 72, 110, 125–126,
144–145
Classroom ecology, 6
Code switch, 60, 86, 146, 173
Cognitive Academic Language Proficiency (CALP), 72–73, 116, 172
Collegial relations, see also Administrative relations; Parent–teacher relations
overview of teachers, 42, 50–51,
65–66, 79–81, 84–85,
93–95, 118–119, 124,
134–135, 140–141
worksheet grid for, 25, 27
Community, 8–9, 10t, 22, see also Demographics; Parent–teacher relations
overview of teachers, 35, 71,
88–89, 92–93, 98–99, 108,
123–124, 144–145
Compensatory/remedial programs, 99,
173
Concurrent translations, 73, 127, 146,
173

Connections (Charles & Brummet), 64, 163
Content-obligatory vocabulary, 104, 173
Cooperative learning, 75, 91, 94, 113, 118, 129, 145, 173
Coral Way Elementary School (Florida), 11–12, 15
Core literature, 173
Critical pedagogy, 173
Cross-cultural Language and Academic Development (CLAD), 19, 175
Cubans, 11–12
Cultural factors, 8, 11, 12, 15, *see also* Attitudes; School culture
identification, 38, 47–48, 55, 57–59, 73, 78, 86–87, 99, 112–113, 118, 128–129, 134, 144, 146–147
in tests, 76
Culture shock, 174
Curriculum/materials, *see also specific subjects*
educational resources for, 161–165
overview of teachers, 38–39, 49–50, 59–60, 77, 87, 90, 91, 101, 103–104, 105, 115, 129–130, 142, 147–148
study questions for, 22
worksheet grid for, 25, 27

D

Degrees of Reading Power (DRP), 48, 51, 167
Demographics, 8, 9f, 13, 18–19, 56, 71, 159t, *see also* Community
educational resources for, 160–161
on language diversity, 158
on language minority population, 159–160
Developing Number Concepts Using Unifix Cubes (Richardson), 87, 111, 164
Developmental Bilingual Education, *see* Dual-language programs
Diana (personal narrative)
administrative relations, 66–67, 141–142
bilingual program, 57–60, 146
collegial relations, 65–66, 140–141

cultural identification, 55, 57–59, 144, 146–147
curriculum/material, 59–60, 142, 147–148
language diversity of, 137–139
mainstreaming, 57–58
overview of teachers chart, 28–29
parent–teacher relations, 57–59, 65, 142, 143–144
school culture, 56–57, 144–145
teacher education, 56, 57, 66, 139–140
teaching experience, 54–56, 151
teaching style, 60–64, 145
testing, 59, 64–65, 148
District, *see* Administrative relations
Drawing with Children (Brookes), 162
Dual-language programs
defined, 15, 174
origination, 11–12
overview of teachers, 59–60, 91, 95, 97, 99–105, 146

E

Early-Exit Bilingual Education (TBE) programs, *see* Transitional Bilingual Education (TBE) programs
Economics, 8, 9f, 12, *see also* Funding
Electronic networking, 170
Elementary and Secondary Education Act (ESEA) (1965), 12, 179
English as a Second Language (ESL) programs
defined, 174
origination, 12
overview of teachers, 36, 38, 43, 44, 50, 69, 72, 83, 84, 86, 87, 90, 93, 94, 96, 107, 109–110, 111, 125, 134, 150
English/Spanish language, *see* Jean (personal narrative)
Enrichment programs, 174
Equal Educational Opportunity Act (1974), 17
Everyday Mathematics (Bell), 91
Exit-criterion, 174

F

Family Math (Stenmark, Thompson, &
    Cossey), 88, 115, 165
Family Science (Noone), 115, 164
Federal policy, 3, 12–16, 17, 135, 179,
    see also specific acts; specific titles;
    State policy
Finding Out/Descubrimento (FO/D)
    (DeAvila, Duncan, & Navarette),
    111, 115, 118, 163
*Foundations of Bilingual Education and Bil-
    ingualism* (Baker), 157
*The Foundations of Dual Language Instruc-
    tion* (Lessow–Hurley), 157, 158
Funding
    for federal policy, 3, 12–16, 17,
        135, 179
    for Immersion programs, 14
Title VII, 13, 14, 17, 135, 179

G

Great Expectations in Math and Science
    (GEMS), 115, 163
Group work, *see* Cooperative learning

H

Haitian–Creole/English language, *see*
    Manouchka (personal narrative)
Heather (personal narrative)
    administrative relations, 79,
        80–81, 141–142
    assessment, 76, 148
    bilingual program, 71–72, 146
    classroom composition, 72,
        144–145
    collegial relations, 79–81, 140–141
    community demographics, 71,
        144–145
    cultural identification, 73, 78,
        146–147
    curriculum/materials, 77, 142,
        147–148
    language diversity of, 137–139
    mainstreaming, 69, 71
    overview of teachers chart, 28–29
    parent–teacher relations, 77–79,
        142, 143–144
    student language diversity, 72–73
    teacher education, 69–70, 72,
        79–81, 139–140
    teaching experience, 68–71,
        151–152
    teaching style, 73–75, 145
    testing, 71, 76, 148
Historical influences, 8, 9–12
    educational resources on, 158
History, 128

I

Immersion programs
    Canadian, 15–16, 108–109
    defined, 174–175
    funding, 14
    partial, 99, 177
    personal experience of, 68, 121
    Spanish, 108–110, 115–116, 117,
        118–119, 146, 152, 174–175
Immigrants
    assimilation, 9, 10–12, 70–71
    demographics, 18–19
    dual-language programs, 11–12
    military assimilation, 10–11
    missionary assimilation, 10–11
    program funding for, 14
*Individualized Developmental English Ac-
    tivities Kit* (IDEA), 74, 87,
        161–162
Integrated curriculum, 84, 91, 101, 128,
        145, 164, 175
Inventive spelling, 62, 75, 175
IPT—Oral Language Proficiency Test,
        114, 131, 165

J

Jean (personal narrative)
    administrative relations, 107–108,
        117–118, 141–142
    assessment, 115–116, 148
    bilingual program, 107–110,
        115–116, 117, 118–119, 146
    classroom composition, 110,
        144–145
    collegial relations, 118–119,
        140–141

community composition, 108,
144–145
cultural identification, 112–113,
118, 146–147
curriculum/materials, 115, 142,
147–148
language diversity of, 137–139
overview of teachers chart, 28–29
parent–teacher relations, 109,
116–117, 142, 143–144
school culture, 117, 118, 144–145
teacher education, 106–107, 118,
139–140
teaching experience, 106–108, 152
teaching style, 110–113, 120, 145
testing, 114–115, 148

L

Language Assessment Battery (LAB), 18,
39, 44, 48, 167
Language Assessment Scales (LAS), 76,
89, 167
Language Development Specialist
(LDS), 57, 72, 79–80, 124, 175
Language diversity
demographics, 159–160
overview of teachers, 137–139
student, 72–73
Language Diversity: Problem or Resource?
(McKay & Wong), 158
Language experience, 93, 112, 175
Language minority students, 56, 64, 79,
80, 106–108, 109, 114, 116, 117,
120
defined, 175
demographics on, 159–160
Language proficiency, 175–176
Language proficiency tests, 76, 114–115,
148, 176
Language restoration/recovery/mainte-
nance, 73, 176
Late-Exit Maintenance programs, *see*
Maintenance programs
Lau v. Nichols, 12, 16–17
Learning styles, 113, 118, 132, 176
*Life in Two Languages: An Introduction to
Bilingualism* (Grosjean), 158
Limited English Proficient (LEP)
California, 3–4

defined, 176
demographics, 19, 56, 159t
overview of teachers, 43, 64, 110,
123, 125, 131
and Title VII, 13–14
Linguistic summary, 37, 176
Literature
core, 173
educational resources, 166–167
and research methodology, 5–7, 21
Literature study circles, 63, 67, 176
Luz (personal narrative)
administrative relations, 123, 131,
134–136, 141–142
assessment, 130–133, 148
bilingual program, 124–125, 146
classroom composition, 125–126,
144–145
collegial relations, 124, 134–135,
140–141
community composition,
123–124, 144–145
cultural identification, 128–129,
134, 146–147
curriculum/materials, 129–130,
142, 147–148
language diversity of, 137–139
overview of teachers chart, 28–29
parent–teacher relations,
122–123, 129, 134, 142,
143–144
teacher education, 122, 135,
139–140
teaching experience, 121–122, 153
teaching style, 126–129, 145
testing, 130–132, 148

M

Mainstreaming, 36–37, 39, 43, 44,
57–58, 69, 71, 89, 144
Maintenance programs
defined, 15, 176–177
overview of teachers, 37, 58,
107–108, 109, 122, 125
Manouchka (personal narrative)
administrative relations, 45,
141–142

bilingual program, 44–45, 146
collegial relations, 50–51, 140–141
cultural identification, 47–48,
    146–147
curriculum/materials, 49–50, 142,
    147–148
language diversity of, 137–139
mainstreaming, 43, 44
overview of teachers chart, 28–29
parent–teacher relations, 44,
    51–53, 142, 143–144
school culture, 44–45, 144–145
teacher education, 43–44,
    139–140
teaching experience, 43–44, 150
teaching style, 45–48, 145
testing, 44, 48, 148
Marginalization, 7
Mariana (personal narrative)
    administrative relations, 141–142
    assessment, 102–105, 148
    bilingual program, 97, 99–105, 146
    collegial relations, 140–141
    community composition, 98–99,
        144–145
    cultural identification, 99,
        146–147
    curriculum/materials, 101,
        103–104, 105, 142, 147–148
    language diversity of, 137–139
    overview of teachers chart, 28–29
    parent–teacher relations, 99, 100,
        102, 142, 143–144
    teacher education, 96–97, 105,
        139–140
    teaching experience, 96–98, 152
    teaching style, 100–101, 145
Marilyn Burns Education Associates,
    101, 164
Math
    educational resources for, 64, 75,
        84, 85, 87, 88, 91, 94, 101,
        111, 115, 160–164
    Marilyn Burns Education
        Associates, 101, 164
    teaching styles for, 60, 64, 75, 84,
        87, 91, 111, 128

Math Excursions K: Project-Based Mathe-
    matics for Kindergartners (Burk,
    Snider, & Symonds), 64, 162
Math Their Way (Baratta-Lorton), 64,
    111, 162
Military style assimilation, 10–11
Missionary style assimilation, 10–11
Monolingualism
    historically, 9
    vs. bilingualism, 9, 50, 51, 66,
        79–80, 84, 93–95, 137, 141
Multifunctional Resource Center
    (MRC), 3, 55, 177
"Multiple I's" research method, 5

N

Narratives, 3–5, 6–7, see also Diana;
    Heather; Jean; Luz; Manouchka;
    Mariana; Sandra; Sofya
National Association of Bilingual Educa-
    tion (NABE), 14, 168
National Teacher Examination (NTE),
    36, 69–70, 83
Natural approach, 93, 177
Newcomer model program, 69, 177
New York
    Aspira Consent Decree, 18, 180
    and project evolution, 3–4
Nonstandard varieties of English, 177
Notional–functional, 110, 177

P

Parent–teacher relations, see also Admin-
    istrative relations; Collegial rela-
    tions
    cultural factors, 35, 37, 40–42, 44,
        53, 57–59, 78–79, 99,
        122–123, 129, 143–144
    overview of teachers, 35, 37,
        40–42, 44, 51–53, 57–59,
        65, 77–79, 88, 91–93, 99,
        100, 102, 109, 116–117,
        122–123, 129, 134, 142,
        143–144
    parent attitudes toward
        bilingualism, 37, 41, 52,
        58–59, 77–78, 91–93, 100,
        102, 116–117, 122–123

study questions for, 22
worksheet grid for, 25, 27
Partial Immersion programs, 99, 177
Performance-based assessment, 59, 178
Policy, *see* Federal policy; State policy
Political influences, 8, 9f, 12, 14–15,
   17–18
   educational resources on, 157
Portfolio assessment, 64, 76, 114, 132,
   148, 178
Pottinger Memo, 16–17
*Pre-Language Assessment Scales (Pre-
   LAS)*, 76, 167
Preproduction stage, 74, 80, 178
Principals, *see* Administrative relations
Professional organizations, 14, 168–170
Project AIMS, 84, 87, 91, 94, 164
Proposition 187 (California), 14, 135,
   152
Pull-out instruction, 12, 44, 107, 109,
   178

R

Reading, 38, 61–63, 73–75, 126–127
   basal readers, 62–63, 74, 87, 90,
      97, 112, 130, 172
   language experience, 93, 112, 175
   study questions for, 183
   whole language, 46, 61–62, 74,
      85, 91, 97, 110, 130, 145,
      180
Reagan, Ronald, 14, 18
Research methodology, 7
   and classroom ecology, 6
   interview questions for, 4, 181
   and literature, 5–7, 21
   and marginalization, 7
   "Multiple I's," 5
   observation, 4
   overview of teachers chart, 28–29
   and project evolution, 1–3
   and project value, 6
   qualitative, 4, 6
   study questions for, 21–22
   and teacher research, 6
   and teachers' narratives, 3–5, 6–7
   and teachers' voices, 6, 21

and teaching experience, 1–3, 4,
   6–7
worksheet grids, 23–27
Russia/English language, *see* Sofya (personal narrative)

S

Sandra (personal narrative)
   administrative relations, 85,
      87–88, 95, 141–142
   bilingual program, 89, 91, 95, 146
   collegial relations, 84–85, 93–95,
      140–141
   community composition, 88–89,
      92–93, 144–145
   cultural identification, 86–87,
      146–147
   curriculum/materials, 87, 90, 91,
      142, 147–148
   language diversity of, 137–139
   mainstreaming, 89
   overview of teachers chart, 28–29
   parent–teacher relations, 88,
      91–93, 142, 143–144
   school culture, 89, 144–145
   teacher education, 82–83, 85,
      139–140
   teaching experience, 82–84, 152
   teaching style, 85–87, 90–91,
      94–95, 145
   testing, 89, 148
School culture
   defined, 178
   overview of teachers, 44–45,
      56–57, 89, 117, 118,
      144–145
*Schooling and Language Minority Students:
   A Theoretical Framework*, 157
Science
   educational resources for, 84, 91,
      94, 115, 160, 162, 163
   teaching styles for, 38, 48, 75, 84,
      91, 111–112
Seven intelligences, 132–133, 178
Sheltered English programs, 57, 71, 72,
   93, 126, 134, 178
Silent period, *see* Preproduction stage

Sink or Swim: The Politics of Bilingual Education (Stein), 158
Sink-or-swim programs, 10, 179
Social studies, 38, 47, 75
Socioeconomics, 8, 9f, 44, 56–57, 65, 123–124
Sofya (personal narrative)
    administrative relations, 36, 42, 141–142
    assessment, 39–40, 148
    bilingual program, 36–37, 146
    collegial relations, 42, 140–141
    community composition, 35, 144–145
    cultural identification, 146–147
    curriculum/materials, 38–39, 142, 147–148
    language diversity of, 137–139
    mainstreaming, 36–37, 39
    overview of teachers chart, 28–29
    parent–teacher relations, 35, 37, 40–42, 142, 143–144
    teacher education, 35–36, 139–140
    teaching experience, 33–34, 150
    teaching style, 37–38, 145
    testing, 39, 148
Spanish as a Second Language (SSL), 86, 93, 125, 141, 179
Spanish Assessment of Basic Education (SABE), 114, 131, 166
Spanish/English language, *see* Luz; Mariana; Sandra (personal narratives)
Spanish Immersion programs, 108–110, 115–116, 117, 118–119, 146, 152, 174–175
Spelling Through Phonics (McCracken & McCracken), 163–164
Standard English, 179
Standardized tests, 59, 64, 71, 76, 114, 130–131, 148, 179
State policy, *see also* Federal policy
    Assembly Bill 507 (California), 17, 107, 114, 171
    Assembly Bill 1329 (California), 17, 107, 171
    Proposition 187 (California), 14, 135, 152
State professional organizations, 169–170

Submersion programs, 10, 179
Supreme Court cases
    Lau v. Nichols, 12, 16–17

T

Teacher education, *see also* Bilingual education resources
    Bilingual Certificate of Competence (BCC), 56, 83, 107, 139, 172
    Bilingual Cross-cultural Language and Academic Development (BCLAD), 19, 172
    California Basic Educational Skills Test (C-BEST), 69-70, 83, 139
    Cross-cultural Language and Academic Development (CLAD), 19, 175
    Language Development Specialist (LDS), 57, 72, 79–80, 124, 175
    National Teacher Examination (NTE), 36, 69–70, 83
    need for, 19
    overview of teachers, 29, 35–36, 43–44, 69–70, 79–81, 82–83, 85, 96–97, 105, 106–107, 118, 122, 135, 139–140
    study questions for, 22
    worksheet grid for, 24, 26
Teachers of English to Speakers of Other Languages (TESOL), 169, 170
Teaching experience, 8–9, 11f, *see also* Administrative relations; Collegial relations; Parent–teacher relations
    overview of teachers, 28–29, 33–34, 43–44, 54–56, 68–71, 82–84, 96–98, 106–108, 121–122, 137–139, 150–153
    and research methodology, 1–3, 4, 6–7, 22
    study questions for, 22
    worksheet grid for, 24, 26

Teaching styles, *see also* Cultural factors;
    Math; Reading; Science; Writing
    development
  basal readers, 62–63, 74, 87, 90,
      97, 112, 130, 172
  code switch, 60, 86, 146, 173
  concurrent translations, 73, 127,
      146, 173
  cooperative learning, 75, 91, 94,
      113, 118, 129, 145, 173
  for history, 128
  integrated curriculum, 84, 91,
      101, 128, 145, 175
  inventive spelling, 62, 75, 175
  language experience, 93, 112, 175
  linguistic summary, 37, 176
  natural approach, 93, 177
  overview of teachers, 37–38,
      45–48, 60–64, 73–75,
      85–87, 90–91, 94–95,
      100–101, 110–113, 120,
      126–129, 145
  for social studies, 38, 47, 75
  study questions for, 22
  Total Physical Response (TPR),
      60, 74, 86, 93, 110, 179
  Venn diagram, 47, 90, 180
  webbing, 75, 127, 180
  whole language, 46, 61–62, 74,
      85, 91, 97, 110, 130, 145,
      180
  worksheet grid for, 24, 26

Tests, *see also* Assessment
  Bilingual Syntax Measure (BSM),
      64, 114, 131, 166
  Boehm Test of Basic
      Concepts–Revised, 114, 166
  California Test of Basic Skills
      (CTBS), 64, 114, 130, 166
  California Test of Basic Skills
      Español (CTBS Español),
      131, 166
  cultural factors in, 76
  Degrees of Reading Power (DRP),
      48, 51, 167
  IPT–Oral Language Proficiency
      Test, 114, 131, 165

Language Assessment Battery
    (LAB), 18, 39, 44, 48, 167
Language Assessment Scales (LAS),
    76, 89, 167
language proficiency, 76,
    114–115, 148
overview of teachers, 39, 44, 48,
    59, 64–65, 71, 76, 89,
    114–115, 130–132, 148
Pre-Language Assessment Scales
    (Pre-LAS), 76, 167
Spanish Assessment of Basic
    Education (SABE), 114,
    131, 166
standardized, 59, 64, 71, 76, 114,
    130–131, 148, 178
Thematic instruction, *see* Integrated cur-
    riculum
Title I, 44, 71, 83, 172–173
Title VI, 12, 16
Title VII, 12, 16
  defined, 179
  funding, 13, 14, 17, 135, 179
  and limited English proficient
      (LEP), 13–14
  and Multifunctional Resource
      Center (MRC), 3, 55, 177
  program development in, 12–13,
      14, 16
  purpose of, 12–13
Title IX, 14
Total Physical Response (TPR), 60, 74,
    86, 93, 110, 179
Touch Math (Bullock), 75, 85, 162
Transitional Bilingual Education (TBE)
    programs
  and Aspira Consent Decree, 18
  defined, 15–16, 174, 179–180
  overview of teachers, 17, 37, 44,
      57, 71, 73, 84, 89, 122, 125,
      146
Two-way programs, *see* Dual language
    programs

U

U.S. ENGLISH, INC., 15
Used Numbers: Real Data in the Class-
    room (Russell & Stone), 111, 165

V

Venn diagram, 47, 90, 180
Vietnamese/English language, *see*
    Heather (personal narrative)

W

Webbing, 75, 127, 180

Whole language, 46, 61–62, 74, 85, 91,
    97, 110, 130, 145, 180
Wright Group, 165
Writing development
    educational resources for, 160
    overview of teachers, 46–47,
        61–62, 75, 90, 97, 127–128
    webbing, 75, 127, 180
Writing process, 97, 127–128, 180